SNAP

SNAP

SEIZING YOUR
AHA! MOMENTS

KATHERINE RAMSLAND

FOREWORD BY
DEBORAH BLUM
PULITZER PRIZE WINNER

Prometheus Books

59 John Glenn Drive
Amherst, New York 14228–2119

Published 2012 by Prometheus Books

Jacket design by Grace M. Conti-Zilsberger

Inquiries should be addressed to
Prometheus Books
59 John Glenn Drive
Amherst, New York 14228–2119
VOICE: 716–691–0133
FAX: 716–691–0137
WWW.PROMETHEUSBOOKS.COM

16 15 14 13 12   5 4 3 2 1

Library of Congress Cataloging-in-Publication Data

Ramsland, Katherine M., 1953–
    SNAP : seizing your aha! moments / by Katherine Ramsland.
        p. cm.
    Includes bibliographical references and index.
    ISBN 978–1–61614–464–7 (cloth : alk. paper)
    ISBN 978–1–61614–465–4 (ebook)
    1. Inspiration. 2. Creative thinking. I. Title.

BF410.R36 2012
153.3—dc23

                                                          2011041552

Printed in the United States of America on acid-free paper

This book is for Mike Malone,
whose invitation to learn philosophy at NAU inspired
the most transformative aha! experience
of my life

CONTENTS

SOLVE

FOREWORD

Some years ago, when I was working as a newspaper science reporter in California, my editor assigned me to do a story on Nobel Prize–winning scientists at the University of California. Frankly, I hated the idea and thought it was little more than an extension of the university's own excellent public relations. But, in fact, after I spent several days visiting with Nobel laureates—researchers who had advanced the science of lasers, discovered new elements, deciphered the intricate chemistry by which living cells make and store energy—I changed my mind.

Spending time with these scientists made me appreciate that they were not super humans. They did not radiate genius as they moved across the room. They were just people—very smart people, true—with a strong sense of purpose and a great deal of curiosity about the world around them. And they had all achieved this moment—a flash of insight, a moment of pure clarity—that had enabled them to solve a problem and make a discovery that others had missed.

I came to think of genius not as life on a higher plane but as a kind of lightning strike, that instant when the night is brighter, the air sizzles and glows, and the surrounding territory is illuminated. So it was with real pleasure that I read Katherine Ramsland's wonderful book *Snap!* More than that, I recognized it. I'd been waiting for someone to really explore and explain my sense of aha! moments. And I'd been waiting for someone to do it well.

9

Candidly, I've been a fan of Katherine's work for a number of years now. I met her when I was working on *The Poisoner's Handbook*, which is about two pioneering forensic scientists working during the wild and dangerous days of Prohibition-era New York. My story focuses on poison killers—to me the coldest and most dangerous of all murderers because they are plotters and planners. Katherine's books on serial killers and other murderers helped me figure out how to describe and explain some of the genuinely deranged characters in my story.

When I received *Snap!* I thought, *Of course!* Of course someone who had so much insight into the human mind—who had worked as a therapist, who had a graduate degree in clinical psychology— would not only be able to explain the troubled mind but also to explore what's best and smartest about the way we think.

Most of us have encountered the idea of an aha! moment before. Many of us have heard the story of the great Greek mathematician Archimedes leaping out of his bath and shouting "Eureka!" as he realized the solution to a stubborn problem. And this book does credit to the history of such ideas, from the insights of the ancients to the sudden dazzle of recognition by James Watson and Francis Crick regarding the helical structure of DNA in the mid-twentieth century, and on to discoveries of our own century.

But what really makes these moments of brilliance so interesting—and so important—is that they aren't the exclusive property of the Nobel laureates I interviewed those years ago, nor do they occur only in the famous cases I just cited. They are, rather, an entirely human attribute—all of us, in fact, have these snap moments, and for every person they open up different possibilities.

All very encouraging, you might say. But Ramsland asks another question: Is it possible to improve this potential? What if we sharpen up our memory? What if we concentrate on staying in the moment, practice the art of mindfulness? Will we become more adept at recognizing those flashes of insight? And not only does she ask those questions; she researches the answers, sifts through the science, and offers some very practical ideas about how we might make this work.

And here's why I particularly like her approach in this case. You may very well reach the end of her story and think to yourself: *Aha! I feel smarter than I did before I read this book!*

Deborah Blum
Madison, Wisconsin

ACKNOWLEDGMENTS

The person to whom I'm most indebted for this book and my writing career is my agent, John Silbersack, because he urged me to do something unique, and he fully supported this project. He also gave me several terrific ideas for it.

Second, I thank my editor, Linda Greenspan Regan, for being so enthused about it.

I'm grateful to several people who assisted me in getting certain facts right, including Karen Walton, Rodger Berg, Zack Lysek, Lisa Getzler-Linn, Kevin Sullivan, Sir Alec Jeffreys, Alice Flaherty, and Ruth Osborne. Joel Katz, Dean Koontz, Rick Arlow, Zach Bloom, George Keeler, John Knific, Tom Carhart, Tim Marks, Patrick Clasen, and Josh Berman supplied some great personal stories, and I want to thank Deborah Blum for writing a terrific foreword. I also appreciate those who read the manuscript: Dean Koontz, John Timpane, and Shelley Carson.

CHAPTER 1

PASTEUR'S PROPOSAL

It is not easy to convey, unless one has experienced it, the dramatic feeling of sudden enlightenment that floods the mind when the right idea finally clicks into place. One immediately sees how many previously puzzling facts are neatly explained by the new hypothesis. One could kick oneself for not having the idea earlier, it now seems so obvious. Yet before, everything was in a fog.

—Francis Crick, *What Mad Pursuit*

A BRAIN ITCH

The quote above refers to one of the world's most groundbreaking flash revelations: the structure of the DNA molecule. In 1953, Francis Crick, a British scientist, was working with James Watson, an American, at the University of Cambridge in England. Although biologists knew by the 1940s what comprised DNA, they did not yet know much about its appearance. As Watson and Crick tried to envision it, Watson read chemist Linus Pauling's unpublished paper about DNA. He believed that Linus was incorrect about its structure but that Watson failed to figure out a feasible alternative. A few days later, he saw an X-ray of the DNA crystal.

"The instant I saw the picture, my mouth fell open and my pulse raced," he later wrote.[1] The paired helix structure seemed eminently clear. Watson told Crick, and they commenced work on a model. Although they stalled a few times, they talked with colleagues who offered suggestions that helped spark several more revelatory insights. Things fell into place until they had a six-foot model that resembled a twisting ladder. This, they knew, was the appearance of that elusive molecule, DNA. In 1962, they received the Nobel Prize.

Their work demonstrates several important facets of the startling flash of full-bodied enlightenment that "floods the mind." First, from years of immersion in that area of study, they were prepared for it. Second, they persisted. Third, they blended intimate isolation in a lab with collegial cross-fertilization. The dramatic pop of instant, fully formed knowledge that Crick described is a latent function of our brain's processing system. It needs preparation, but it's available to anyone. Although hard work is not required for "snapping," experiencing "snaps" regularly and channeling them for specific purposes does involve training your brain.

Snaps or aha! moments often occur when, faced with ambiguity or a challenge, the brain clicks on something that instantly feels right. To try this process, read the following riddle and see if you can figure it out:

> Gerald arrives at his local railway station to catch the Waterloo train, which departs hourly at exactly five minutes past the hour. Thinking he might have just missed it, he looks up at the station clock and sees that the hour and minute hands are both between 1 and 2. He's relieved that he hasn't missed his train. If the clock is correct, how does he know?

If you saw the solution right away, great! But it's often maddeningly elusive. The problem looks so simple that it should be obvious, and yet like other brain twisters, it can thwart your most determined efforts. When you do see it, whether quickly or after considerable effort, the solution will occur as a flash—you just "see" it. *The clock's hands are both between the 1 and 2* of the 12, *so it's exactly 12:00.*

This is commonly called the "aha! moment," the eureka experience, a brainstorm, a flash of genius, or an epiphany. It's a type of perceptual shift that some experience as an incandescent moment. The solution *is* obvious, even though you might not have found it. Trying to figure out such riddles is like looking for a specific book among many titles on a bookshelf. You know it's there, but you can't see it. Finally, you give up. Later, you go looking for another book, and the first one you originally wanted pops right out. It was there all the time. You just couldn't process it. That's how the brain often works with creative insight. It has resources that seem quite mysterious but are actually the result of how we prepare our minds.

A eureka moment can occur while working alone or during brainstorming sessions in groups. It could burst forth during isolated efforts or after seeing what someone else has done. There are so many applications for this magical link between impasse and enlightenment, whether in sports, business, art, science, industry, design, law enforcement, and even the military. We'll look at quite a few different applications in this book. In fact, the Nobel Prize itself came from a snap.

Alfred Nobel, the discoverer of the formula for dynamite, read a news article in 1888 that had confused him with his recently deceased brother. The reporter referred to Alfred as the "Merchant of Death." This disturbed him. He did not wish to leave such a negative legacy. Pondering a way to be remembered for something good, the solution hit him. He could use the very thing that had inspired that dark moniker; he could apply the fortune that dynamite had given him to offer monetary prizes to people who had made a contribution to benefit the world. He made a will that bequeathed the money and died just a year later. On the third anniversary of his death, the first prizes were distributed in Stockholm, Sweden. The medal features a profile of Nobel.[2]

There are many such stories. It was the remark by William Marston's wife about her blood pressure rising when she got angry or excited that inspired the precursor to the polygraph. The way Italians stood at a bar to drink their espressos, lattes, and cappuccinos inspired the creation of Starbucks. It was an Internet search that Jeff Bezos undertook for his hedge fund employer that inspired him to recognize the Internet itself as a solid investment opportunity. His boss wasn't interested, so he left his job and launched into the sale of books online. Thus, the hugely successful Amazon.com was born. A sudden insight—a feeling of the right idea—triggered each of these ventures.

But let's be clear. This book is about more than just insight. It's about a specific type of aha! that I call a *snap*, because what I describe is closer to a spark that ignites action than to the mere recognition of the solution to a problem. A snap is insight *plus* momentum. Once the enlightenment occurs, it begs for action. It launches us forth, as it reportedly did for the renowned mathematician Archimedes.

THE FIRST AHA!

As the fable goes, in ancient Syracuse, Archimedes exemplified the "eureka" insight. For him, it was utter euphoria, an explosion of excitement that made him oblivious to the fact that he'd forgotten to dress before running through the streets proclaiming, "Eureka!" It was quite pressing—a matter of life and death. Although it's difficult to know if the details of this tale are actually true (and some experts have disputed it), we do know enough about Archimedes to believe that it *could* be true.

The earliest known account appeared two centuries after his death in 212 BCE, in a work about architecture. The author, Vitruvius, admired Greek geometers, and Archimedes towered above all others. He was a "master of thought," a mathematician, scientist, and inventor. For example, he crystallized the principles of buoyancy, which affected travel by sea or air, and he refined the mechanics of irrigation. The Roman senator Cicero hailed him as a genius beyond what any mere mortal could achieve, and even today Archimedes is considered one of the world's greatest mathematicians. He studied physics, optics, astronomy, geometry, engineering, and the art of warfare. Even the Syracusan king Hieron II reportedly proclaimed that Archimedes "is to be believed in everything he may say."[3]

So, back to the story: The king suspected that his royal crown maker had cheated him. He tasked Archimedes with determining whether a recently crafted gold crown, made to adorn a deity's statue, had been clandestinely mixed with inferior silver (thereby enriching the metal-working con man). However, there was a catch: Archimedes was not allowed to melt the crown or deface it in any manner. Although he was brilliant and knew as much as anyone back then about mathematical calculations and precious metals, he stalled. His very life was on the line, but try as he might to examine the problem from all angles, he failed to find the answer. The metal had been crafted into a series of leaves, and it wasn't clear to Archimedes, the genius, quite how to measure its exact volume.

Reportedly, he worked through every possible solution he could think of. But none was adequate. Then he took a break. Stepping into a full tub one day to take a bath, he caused the water to spill over the edge. He froze. In that moment, he *snapped* the solution: the volume of water displaced from the tub was equal to the space his body took up. "Eureka!" he shouted. (That's why it's called the eureka moment—meaning, "I found it!") He realized that silver is lighter than gold, so a block of silver equal in weight to a block of gold would be larger and would thus displace more water. Therefore, a mix of silver and gold would displace more water than the same item made of pure gold.

"That one fact," Isaac Asimov wrote, "added to all the chains of reasoning his brain had been working on during the period of relaxation when it was unhampered by the comparative stupidities of voluntary thought, gave Archimedes his answer in one blinding flash of insight."[4]

Using his calculation, Archimedes proved what King Hieron suspected: the goldsmith had cheated him. Thus, Archimedes's brilliant flash has become the touchstone for the blinding sublimity of creative genius: the mind so caught in the illuminated moment it forgets all else in an effort to capture and apply the insight. Look again at the quote by Francis Crick that opens this chapter. He described it perfectly.

THREE STEPS TO MAGIC

Most people believe that aha! moments are whimsical and unpredictable. They have launched some amazing discoveries, the tales of which are entertaining, but they strictly concern people of great achievement or of genius. The great news is this: snaps can happen for anyone, and some people get these incandescent experiences quite often. The reason is simple. They've recognized the enormous potential of a eureka experience and have learned exactly how to *prepare* for it. That is, we can set up the conditions to spark an Archimedean flash of genius when we need it. And it is not exclusive to geniuses or the highly skilled. You'll meet several people throughout this book who not only experienced a snap and exploited it for great gain but who also articulated the experience well enough to benefit others. Some of these descriptions have assisted neuroscientists, and, thanks to some clever research, we now know a lot about the brain's mechanisms during sudden insight, which helps us to understand both how and why it occurs. Let me put it in simple terms: Approaching a problem that begs for insight most benefits from a type of immersion that forms three distinct processes:

1. scanning the environment
2. sifting through information
3. solving the problem

Scan, sift, solve. Each step has specific nuances, but we'll keep them in mind as we move along. Here's an example of an insight inspired by a problem that produced an intriguing action-based solution. You can see here exactly how "scan, sift, solve" plays out.

At Harvard University's School of Medicine, thanks to the initial brainstorm of Drs. Joel Katz and Shahram Khoshbin, students engage in something that defies a long tradition of teaching. They go not just to a typical classroom for lectures about medical topics; they also go to Boston's Museum of Fine Arts. This activity seems far afield from what they're in school to study, so why does Katz have them do it? He had an idea that led to an experiment, which opened up a new approach: visual literacy for doctors.

Medical schools are aware that, according to studies, observational skills among new doctors have declined. A physical exam is essential to making an accurate clinical diagnosis, but medical students seem less equipped these days to make visual assessments with critical thinking. While this sounds alarming, we can blame improved technology. New doctors use more laboratory tests and radiological exams, which can replace the need for clinical observation—but at a great financial cost and some unnecessary risk to patients. Thus, without regular practice, observational skills required to be a proficient doctor remain unpolished. However, visual acumen is still necessary for medical personnel who diagnose and treat patients, so its reported decline is certainly a concern. Doctors must not just look but also *see*; not just hear but also *listen*. These two skills are in great decline, as judged by patient surveys. Yet it's one thing to emphasize the importance of such a skill, and quite another to help students to acquire and improve it.

Katz, an associate professor of medicine at the Harvard Medical School, was interested in curriculum innovations, so he pondered the challenge. This is the "scan" part. He attuned himself to the issue and wanted to address it. Something from his background assisted: before he'd become an internist at the Harvard-affiliated Brigham and Women's Hospital, he had been a graphic designer, so he exploited this experience to "sift" through what he knew. He understood that, like medical conditions, art appreciation is inherently ambiguous, forcing the observer to rely on an uncertain and incomplete data set to make judgments. Once Katz spotted these similarities, he set to work to develop a unique new curriculum (still sifting). He invited colleagues, including Alexa Miller, curator of education at the Davis Museum and Cultural Center at Wellesley College, to help him. The objective was to see if the structured observation of artworks improved apparently unrelated skills in patient care. To test his hunch, Katz and his colleagues devised an experiment that paired *Visual Thinking Strategies* with diagnostic instruction.

Visual Thinking Strategies are based on a theory by Cambridge researcher Abigail Housen, who worked with Philip Yenawine, director of education at New York's Museum of Modern Art, to assist viewers to better appreciate the meaning of art.[5] They soon realized that the Visual Thinking Strategies helped art viewers to develop critical thinking and cognitive abilities, so this approach was implemented in many more museums. They also introduced it into public school systems and many colleges.

As a curator, Miller was familiar with Visual Thinking Strategies, so it made sense to her to include them as part of Katz's experimental course. Both activities involved cognitive development. So with his medical colleague, Drs. Khoshbin and Sheila Naghshineh, and researchers from Harvard and Brigham and Women's Hospital, Katz developed "Training the Eye: Improving the Art of Diagnosis." It was a ten-week course in which students would meet for two and a half hours every week. The researchers invited students who were in their first or second year of preclinical training to participate, and fifty-six expressed interest. This was enough for an experimental group and a control group, since only two dozen could be accommodated in the class. Twenty-four students (59 percent female, with a mean age of twenty-four) were assigned to the experimental group, and thirty-two similar students acted as controls. Each took a precourse visual skill examination that measured the frequency of accurate observations.

While the controls continued with their education in the typical manner, students in the experimental group went to Boston's Museum of Fine Arts each week to participate in seventy-five-minute exercises of observation, coupled with a lecture about how each exercise related to physical diagnosis. They also kept a journal. During two sessions, they examined volunteer patients who had undiagnosed disorders. The students walked around the museum observing paintings by such artists as Gauguin, Picasso, Pollock, Monet, and Manet. As they stood before Norwegian artist Edvard Munch's *The Scream*, for example, they considered diverse interpretations of that bald, wide-eyed, shrieking figure on a bridge against its hallucinatory yellow, blue, and orange background. While looking at ancient aboriginal artists, they hypothesized on the role form played in the impact of the art; they then applied this same method to their observation of patients with various breathing disorders. How was the stomach moving? How is the voice generated and projected? What was happening to posture and muscles related to breathing? They also considered how such findings as color, balance, light, symmetry, and texture related to medical topics like dermatology, neurology, and radiology.

No matter which piece of art they observed, they were to offer several possible ideas about it. This exercise helped them to think beyond well-known interpretations, forcing them toward less obvious angles. In addition, the students participated in reading and visual training exercises. In an optional session, they had the opportunity to learn from a professional art teacher how to draw a live human model.

At the end of the course, the participants retook the visual skill exam, which was scored by a scientist who had no way of knowing if the test was the pretest or posttest, or if the test taker had taken the course or was in the control group. The results were impressive: the "active looking" approach had improved the students' visual skills. Compared to the control group, students who had completed the course made more frequent observations. There was an average increase of 5.41 observations per image, or a 38 percent improvement in focus, as well as a higher level of sophistication when students described what they were seeing. They were more accurate than students in the control group and better than they had been prior to the course.[6]

"Our findings suggest," Katz said, "that through the structured study of works of art and medical imagery, visual inspection skills, including those directly relevant to clinical medicine, can be improved."[7]

He recognized that the study had not achieved true randomization and that the groups had been too small to make a definitive statement. In addition, the follow-up had also been short-term, so long-term results remain unknown. However, Katz and his colleagues continue to run this popular course at Harvard. "The results hold consistent," Katz observed. "The original study was about teaching early medical students core physical exam skills. The next clue that we are investigating is a textural analysis of the types of responses of class participants, before and after, and how the exercise enriches not just the number of observations, which is what we reported on before, but on the quality and depth of the observations."[8]

These researchers demonstrate that an expanded curriculum that transcends traditional notions of medical training can effectively address the problem of declining quality in a profession on which people's lives depend. Rather than sitting around bemoaning the sorry state of medical diagnostic skills, an innovator considered this problem from a unique angle, devised a way to address it, and then tried it. Because Katz had trained in a different profession before he entered medicine—a cross-fertilization factor that will pop up throughout this book—he brought to medical training a different perspective to effectively dissolve the impasse. In addition, taking the students to a museum that is well outside their usual surroundings may have allowed them to access and improve parts of their own minds that were inaccessible based on years of highly focused and competitive schooling. The course yielded an additional side benefit for the students—greater art appreciation. We'll see another aspect of this research later.

THE PREPARED MIND

French chemist and microbiologist Louis Pasteur once said in a lecture he gave in 1854, "Chance favors only the prepared mind."[9] Current brain studies reveal that he was correct. Creative entrepreneurs take time to prepare themselves; they develop habits that yield knowledge about many aspects of their work arena and focus on those conditions in their lives that best incubate insight. They're ready to be enraptured by as many things as possible. Then they exploit the process as often as possible to prime themselves for the flash of insight. They possess no better memory or cognitive skills than anyone else, it turns out, but they nurture an attitude that keeps them sharp. They are always *looking*. They *scan*. They *want* that moment.

Because they reap a continuous sense of reward from applying themselves to disciplined study, they gain more opportunities for flashes of insight—"snaps"—that can turn into a goldmine or improve lives. It's not *what* they think about that counts but *how* they think. Actually, it's how they allow themselves to *stop* thinking in a particular way so that their brains can go to work. The trick is to achieve the right balance.

A snap is a flash of inspirational brilliance. As noted, snaps contain a sense of purpose and direction so compelling that you *snap* into action. You might jump out of bed or stop your car in the middle of the road to write the thought down. You might charge straight into seemingly impossible odds or interrupt your lecture. Snaps are not mere insight—"Aha! So that's it." Rather, they're so bursting with fullness that they push us forward. In a snap, we see a new method, a solution, or an inspiration that propels us to get right to work (or play). For example, in 1816 Dr. René Laennec had a female patient who appeared to be suffering from heart problems. He felt stymied. Moral protocol at that time prohibited him from putting his ear to her bosom to listen to her heart, but it seemed the only way to help her. He looked around, grabbed some paper, and rolled it into a tube. He carefully placed it into position and could hear the heartbeat. Afterward, he fashioned a hollow wooden cylinder for his practice and thereby created the first stethoscope.[10]

The aha! feeling is so highly charged it can prompt dramatic decisions: you *know* what you must do next to activate the insight and see how it works. It's fully formed in its mental presentation; so exquisitely *right* that the person to whom it occurs feels compelled to capture it in some act or permanent medium. A scene in the 2010 movie *Social Network*, about the creation of Facebook®, provides a good visual. Whether or not it actually happened this way, the scene nicely illustrates a snap. Inventor Mark Zuckerberg has already set up the Facebook software and is preparing to launch it, but he's not yet ready. An acquaintance comes up to him in a computer lab and asks him about a girl in his art history class, whether she has a boyfriend or ever talks about a guy. The Zuckerberg character freezes. He suddenly knows what he *must* add to the homepages of Facebook participants. He drops everything and zips across campus, knocking into things and people in his haste to get to his computer. The other student's queries had triggered his awareness of what people *really* wanted to know about each other—the thing about college life that had initially inspired the Facebook design: their relationship status. The flash of inspiration for this added refinement is so compelling, as the film shows it, that Zuckerberg *must* get it into place at once. The codes are mentally clear, and he knows what he must do; he just needs to type them into the computer.

This is the perfect representation of the way a snap works. It's a dramatic brilliance that floods the mind and clicks into place. Sometimes a snap is so powerful it can wake you from sleep. You can't wait to respond to it, so you go right to work. In some instances described later, the snap insight even occurs in a dream. At times, it happens just before going to sleep.

Physicist Stephen Hawking is renowned for his work on the basic laws that govern the universe. He was getting into bed one night in 1970 when he "saw" how to apply his work on causal structure to the concept of black holes. He compares the snap experience to sex—not as intense, perhaps, but "it lasts longer." In a speech for his sixtieth birthday, Hawking stated, "There is nothing like the 'Eureka' moment, of discovering something that no one knew before."[11] Although some theorists claim there's no such thing as a flash of insight, because true innovation emerges only after a long incubation process, brain research tells us otherwise. There is indeed a spark before it happens. No matter how long it has been incubating, a snap insight truly pops. It's a thought climax.

INSIGHT VERSUS AHA!

Just to differentiate insight from a snap, here is an example of an "ah!" versus an "aha!" An ah! moment can alter perception without an impetus to an immediate act. In 1989, Harvard psychologist Jerome Kagan was studying temperament in babies. He placed them in unfamiliar (but safe) circumstances and watched their reactions. He predicted that "high-reactors" would continue to be sensitive, growing up to become shy and anxious teenagers and adults. Baby number 19 was a prime example. In a new surrounding, she incessantly cried and flailed her arms. As she grew up, she was so disturbed by her environment so much of the time that she became a reclusive, fidgety musician who reported being highly anxious. From his studies, Kagan realized that temperament is essentially hardwired rather than learned. As a result of this insight, he looked at people differently.[12] This was a cognitive shift that many have labeled an aha! moment. However, the insight, while changing

Kagan's awareness, did not press him into action or invention. Thus, it is not what I'd refer to as a snap.

The snap is exciting and full; it feels like something has suddenly been given birth to. It's a peak experience, a payoff, a mental sweet spot. It doesn't just change our ideas; it offers a course of action. We see this in the account of danger and survival involving a firefighter named Wagner "Wag" Dodge.[13] On August 5, 1949, he led sixteen men into Montana's rugged Mann Gulch. Conditions had been unusually dry that season, with record high temperatures in the high 90s— the perfect condition for a storm front. On this day, a fire had burned through many acres in Mann Gulch, and a thunderstorm had formed that could ignite others. Dodge instructed his crew to get ready.

With nine years of experience at this job, Dodge was aware of the dangers, but every man on his team had battled blazes that summer and knew the ropes. The youngest was seventeen, and a few were World War II veterans. They rode in a C-47 plane until the pilot located a safe landing spot. One man felt anxious and opted to return with the plane, while the others parachuted out to the ravine below.

On the ground, they discovered that they had no map. In addition, the radio had been destroyed when its parachute had malfunctioned. These were important items, but not mandatory. Dodge believed that a firefighter already on the ground nearby would have a map.

It was late afternoon, and they expected to work through the night. To a man, they were confident they could deal as successfully with this fire as they had with others before. They walked single-file into the woods, meeting up with the other firefighter, but he told them some bad news: he had no map. Dodge knew they would have to make it work without one.

He approached the fire line and instructed the others to wait until he could check the area. He walked toward it on his own, and it wasn't long before he realized that this fire was moving faster than he'd expected. *Much* faster. A gusty ground wind gushed oxygen that pushed the flames directly toward him. Turning back toward the men, Dodge retreated. He found them and told them to go farther down the gulch, toward the river. On his own, he went to retrieve food that he'd left at the landing zone. When Dodge rejoined the others, he found them scattered. As he tried to pull them together, he discovered an abundance of burning embers that blocked his proposed escape route. He reversed course again, urging everyone to run. When he realized that their equipment was slowing them down, he ordered everyone to drop whatever they were carrying and *move*. As the fire raced toward them, they knew their lives were now on the line. Suffocating heat surrounded them, and flames in every tree and bush cut them off from the river. They moved into an area of tall, dry grass just as Dodge saw a grass fire sweeping toward them. Wind-swept grass fires burn faster than any man can run. He knew that unless he could think of something, they were doomed. He estimated he had a minute or less.

The wall of fire, sucking up the grass, roared louder, popping tree sap and sending out a swirl of hot embers and choking smoke. It looked as if there were no options. But Dodge had an idea. He knelt down, retrieved a book of matches, and ignited a small circle of grass. He intended to burn away the grass—the fire's fuel—from an area that could contain his whole crew. The fire would then jump over them. In short order, Dodge burned out this tight safety zone. He moved into its center, urging the others to join him. Placing a wet cloth over his face, he pressed himself against the smoldering ground. He felt the blazing heat surround and move over him, but he remained unburned. Holding the cloth, he took shallow breaths, waiting and trying to endure the scorching heat. Finally, it passed. When Dodge thought it was safe, he raised himself and looked around. No one was close. He stood up, expecting to find his men. But he was alone.

Apparently, the others had panicked and run, or had misunderstood his intent. Two had made it to a stretch of rock that offered the same type of safety zone, but the fire had overtaken thirteen men. Just an hour after they had confidently set forth to contain the fire, they had burned to death.

Later, Dodge's surviving companions said that when they saw what he was doing, they figured he'd lost his mind. Instead, he'd had a lifesaving snap based on years of training and an abundance of knowledge about the behavior of fire. When asked to explain it, Dodge said, "It just seemed the logical thing to do."[14] It was not guesswork. Dodge had had experience with fires, as well as years of disciplined study. He had read about how others before him had saved themselves from similar grass fires. When he'd needed it, the right knowledge had been there. In a snap. His aha! moment was the instantaneous flash of insight delivered from his store of knowledge and experience.

BRAIN SNAPS

Sudden insight involves a complex series of brain states that require more neural resources than methodical thinking does. The formula is simple: one must have specific knowledge and experience, a challenge within one's field of expertise, an effort to meet the challenge, and a period of mental surrender. Both the left and right hemispheres of the brain must be activated to work together. While many people believe that such insight is completely random, those who apply themselves know better. Snaps can't be forced, but they can be prompted—even in desperate life-threatening situations.

In many endeavors, deliberate practice outpaces innate talent. Researcher Anders Ericsson interviewed seventy-eight musicians and found that, by age twenty, the most accomplished had spent an average of five thousand more hours of practice than their counterparts. But the key was this: their practice involved rewarding engagement in the pursuit of achievement, not hours of mechanical drudgery. That's why they had logged so much more practice time. They loved it![15] Attitude matters: the desire to take on a challenge, to pay attention, and to improve is paramount.

Psychologist Mihaly Csikszentmihalyi, who has studied innovation in many different disciplines, has found that people who learn to control their inner experience can influence the quality of their lives. This involves being engaged with activities with an eye toward the future. "The best moments," he says, "usually occur when a person's body is stretched to its limit in a voluntary effort to accomplish something difficult and worthwhile."[16]

He tells the story of a man named Joe who worked in a factory that assembled railroad cars. Although factory labor might seem the antithesis of creativity and purpose, Joe did find a way to make his work meaningful. While his coworkers could not wait to leave at the end of each day, viewing their job as merely a means to support themselves and their families, Joe adopted a different attitude. He perceived his workplace as a series of challenges. He wanted to learn the nature and function of each and every piece of equipment in the building. Eventually, he was called on to fix some of these pieces, and he found this work quite satisfying. He looked forward to going in each day and did not watch the clock as the others did. Moment by moment, he reaped rewards. Every hour of his day felt to him like quality time. He felt stimulated and useful. Rather than give in to the boredom of routine, he took control and found a way to create.[17]

We focus our psychic energy toward achievable but challenging goals, Csikszentmihalyi found, and as we get closer we expand them. This inspires vigilance for opportunities. As each step rewards us, we're motivated to keep striving.

Parents can instill this edge-of-the-seat attitude in their children from a young age. Teaching children to move toward challenge via self-reward and a sense of adventure can yield early and regular snap dividends. Still, any of us can also cultivate this sense of adventure later in life by adopting certain habits. Training the brain for the type of neural activity that incubates problem solving has no age limit. In fact, the brain's neuroplasticity means we can create new neural circuits to support new directions at almost any age.

Among the initial steps is to experience a perceptual shift. Not all perceptual shifts are snaps, but all snaps involve a perceptual shift. In simple terms, a perceptual shift can arise from learning a new fact that changes the meaning of something you thought you understood. Here's an amusing example: Groucho Marx once said, "I shot an elephant in my pajamas." You might imagine him in his pajamas shooting an elephant until he adds, "How he got into my pajamas I'll never know." With this added information, you see the first remark differently (making the joke work). You've just had a perceptual shift. Thirteen-year-old Hart Main was watching his sister sell candles for a school fundraiser. He didn't care for the feminine scents, so he joked that someone should sell candles that males would enjoy. It was an inspired moment. With his mother's encouragement, he created candles for men—the ManCan. They smell like pizza, bacon, smoking pipes, and baseball gloves. Now he's an entrepreneur with a successful business. Making a joke about an existing product had given Main a perceptual shift that offered an idea no one had yet fully exploited.[18]

The reason this experience is important is because it signals mental flexibility. Remember the Harvard med students. Their success in improving their diagnostic skills relied on their ability to have perceptual shifts. Seeing things from more than one angle enabled them to consider alternate diagnoses.

Perceptual shifts can be developed with exercises that guide them. For example, you might look at a fork, which you would typically view as a utensil for eating. Now, try to think of other uses to which you could put that fork. Do the same with other common objects, like a pencil or a tin can. A fork could hold up a sagging plant. A pencil could dig a hole in dirt. A tin can, used for food, could become a pencil holder or a primitive telephone for kids.

Cognitive psychologists often use ambiguous pictures to provoke a perceptual shift. Recall the picture that features the side view of two identical faces looking at each other. Initially, you notice the faces, but when you learn that the space between them forms a vase, you now see the vase clearly, and the face details recede. The vase was always there, but you may not have noticed it until after you learned about it. A famous personality assessment, the Thematic Apperception Test, was designed from this concept to assist with insight during treatment. This "projective" test uses a series of ambiguous pictures about which a person being tested must offer a dramatic story. (One card is blank.) It should include what led up to the event, what the picture shows happening, what the characters are feeling, and the story's outcome. The subject's tale is not the only possible one, so it helps to reveal facets of the individual's personality. A variety of such exercises will pop up in this book because snapping relies on mental flexibility.

Taking delight in disciplined study is the key to successful snaps because it thrusts us right into the process. Each accomplishment strengthens motivation so that success breeds success. Quick apprehension comes from knowledge and awareness that has been ingrained during education and training. Thus, our preparatory state influences whether and how often we will snap. Once the skill is developed, quick decisions become second nature and eureka moments more likely. Hans Lippershey, a seventeenth-century optician, is a good example. There are several different stories about his flash of insight, but one holds that he observed two children who were using a pair of lenses from eyeglasses to better see a weather vane in the distance. He watched them hold the lenses in line with each other to magnify the effect, and because of what he knew about the function of lenses, Lippershey recognized the possibilities. He placed a similar set of lenses into a tube, inventing the refracting telescope.[19]

Here's another one: Elisha Otis worked as a mechanic in a bed factory. The owner required a cargo hoist for heavy equipment, so Otis applied himself to devising a way to ensure that the mechanism would be safe. He realized that a spring would cushion the platform in the event the rope broke, so he created the first elevator brake. His invention gave builders the assurance they needed to create taller buildings.[20]

Prior training or experience in an area incubates "prepotent candidates" (clusters of knowledge that could offer solutions for specific problems) for epiphanies, increasing our control and decreasing the impact of chance. To generate the spark that ignites flash strategy, trust in our judgment is crucial, and this comes from the excitement of achievement. It turns focused effort into an engaging process with rich dividends.

Let me elaborate now on the three steps. Once we've made the proper preparation, there are three key parts to this process:

1. vigilantly *scanning* the information that pours into our consciousness every day,
2. *sifting* it for what will work best for our goals, and
3. letting our inner lives digest and *solve* the problems.

Then, *snap!* We might receive the eureka insight, image, solution, or formula that could start a new business, provoke a world-shattering discovery, save lives, or even save the world. In the following chapters are inspiring stories in many different areas. Interspersed with them are the psychological and neurological dynamics that clarify how snaps occur, and also how you can trigger them in your own life or work. We'll look at the role of memory, the dynamics of right- and left-brain coordination, the quirks of human attention, and the importance of exposure to diverse subject areas.

KEY POINTS

- Snaps involve insight *plus* momentum.
- Our attitude matters.
- The ability to innovate starts with mental flexibility and the boldness to experiment.
- A cognitive impasse is often on the threshold of insight.
- Practice and discipline develop the database from which the brain can collect what it needs to snap at the right moment.
- We can set up conditions for snaps on demand.

SCAN

CHAPTER 2

PRIME MOVERS

BEING PROACTIVE

Anthony Zuiker is quick-witted and persuasive. He can also bounce back from seeming defeat. If not for these qualities, the *CSI* fad might never have arrived. Zuiker is a good example of the person who continually scans for the right opportunities.

Zuiker was born in Illinois, but he didn't stay there long. When he was six months old, his mother moved the family to Las Vegas. As he grew up, he hung out with friends at the casinos that lined the famous strip. Little did he know that he would one day grow rich from this very setting.

It wasn't until he went to college, attending Arizona State and the University of Nevada, that Zuiker realized he had a talent for writing. "I got my writing start by writing people's essays for money in college and high school," he told Eric Estrin in an interview for *The Wrap*.[1] "I would charge $300 to write ten pages in one night, and I was booked solid for years." He also invented board games and wrote tournament-winning debate monologues for himself and his friends. One such acquaintance used Zuiker's monologues to help him to get acting parts in Hollywood, while Zuiker remained in Vegas.

There, despite his talent, he worked as an $8-per-hour tram host for the Mirage casino. Every night he rode with tourists on the forty-second ride to Treasure Island, just down the strip, an occupation that got old fast. Zuiker had degrees in philosophy and communications, yet he knew he was going nowhere. Occasionally he made a few bucks selling an ad for a billboard. But then his Hollywood connection paid off.

An agent from the prestigious William Morris Agency called Zuiker because she'd heard about his writing talent and wondered if he wanted to try his hand at a screenplay. Zuiker was intrigued. The agent offered representation if he could come up with something good, so he went right out to a bookstore to find a how-to guide. He'd never tried anything like this before, but, undaunted, he sat down and wrote a screenplay.

To frame a story, Zuiker called on what he knew: his mother was a casino pit boss, and he was aware of "runners" who took bets to the casinos and sports bookies. In a place like Vegas, he was well acquainted with gambling addiction. He pulled this together into a story about organized crime and sent it to the agent. He felt pretty good, but to his disappointment, the agency passed on it.

What's notable here is that Zuiker did not just give up and dump his work in the trash. He seemed to know that the opinion of one agency was not necessarily the final word. He liked what he'd written, so he used another connection to try to get his screenplay read. The producer initially brushed him off but apparently decided to have a look, because he soon called Zuiker about making it into a film. He purchased it for $30,000.

Zuiker was pleased until Creative Artists Agency (CAA), where he'd also sent it, told him they wanted to represent it. They were ready to make a deal for this screenplay for $970,000, but in the eager blunder of a naive beginner, Zuiker had already signed the original deal. He tried and failed to get the rights back, so he couldn't collect on the bigger prize. Although his screenplay was turned into a film (which doesn't always happen after the purchase of rights) and he was involved in production from start to finish, he did not like the end result. *The Runner* went straight to video.

Zuiker looks back on that experience with mixed feelings, but he's aware that this small success spurred his interest in trying again. In fact, CAA had signed him as a client, which was itself an accomplishment. However, as he would soon discover, it was no guarantee.

Around this time, in the spring of 1999, heads of the major television networks were engaged in their annual battle to find series that would blow all others out of the water. They were aware that the Internet had claimed the attention of younger viewers, and that cable networks were gaining a fair share of the audience as well. Each network jockeyed for the top of the heap, but that meant finding talented writers who could offer an idea "with legs." ABC had *Lost* and *Desperate Housewives*, both surprise hits, while the Fox network had imported *American Idol* from the United Kingdom and turned it into an audience grabber. CBS had *Survivor*, with its seemingly endless renditions, and NBC ran a strong block on Thursday nights with *ER*, which had made George Clooney a star. No one foresaw the newcomer who was about change the playing field.

Zuiker was growing frustrated. He had tried a few scripts, but while some sold, nothing really gelled in a way that gave him confidence. He was still in Las Vegas rather than Hollywood, but now he was married. Jerry Bruckheimer's office called to see if he had any interest in writing for television, and while he said he did, he actually watched little television and did not know how to pitch or write a series. Although he had a future meeting set up to talk with Bruckheimer, Zuiker had nothing concrete to say. In other words, he was stalled.

To this point, Zuiker had been scanning and sifting. He'd worked his brain with the appropriate exercises in thinking and writing. He had learned a lot about Hollywood and the kind of thing an executive like Bruckheimer would expect. He also wanted to succeed. He was primed and ready, but he had no workable idea—the perfect position for a snap.

One evening in 1999, Zuiker had plans to attend a basketball game in Las Vegas with several buddies. He'd been mulling ideas about series, but nothing had really struck him. His wife asked him to stay home with her rather than go to the game. He did, and they watched a Discovery Channel cable show about crime scene responders, *The New Detectives*. Zuiker was fascinated. As he watched how these teams used science to process crime scenes, an idea hit him: *this* could be the basis for a fictional series. *Snap!* He could pitch a show to Bruckheimer about forensics. Faced with an impasse, Zuiker had taken his mind off the problem, which ironically had given his brain the chance to go to work. Now *it* was sifting, but without the clenched desperation of someone overly focused on a problem.

He set his fictional crime scene unit in Las Vegas—what city offered a better venue for a wide variety of crimes?—and started writing a proposal for *Crime Scene Investigation*. Zuiker interviewed cops, visited the crime lab, and was invited along to crime scenes. He was unsure whether the idea offered a constant sense of excitement, but everything he saw looked promising. He even got to participate in some trace evidence collection. After he had experienced a dramatic moment when a suspect who was hiding at the scene nearly scratched him before cops swarmed in to place her in handcuffs, he was convinced this was a *great* idea for a television series. As Zuiker outlined a treatment, he added a fresh angle—a snap-zoom lens effect to show the gory evidence in startling detail. The more he thought about how unique this show could be, the more excited he grew. It felt like a sure thing. Now he just needed the right people to open doors—a bit of luck and synchronicity.

That fall of 1999, Zuiker pitched the idea to Bruckheimer, using the full force of his enthusiasm to persuade. Bruckheimer was entranced. He agreed that the project had real potential. He took it to ABC because he already had an agreement there to work with them, but the executives from the drama department did not share the vision. They passed on it (to their later regret). Zuiker was disappointed but still certain his show would find a home.

Jonathan Littman, a top executive for Bruckheimer, put in a call to a friend at CBS. He knew that as they neared November, the pitching sessions would have concluded and the networks would have made their decisions about the pilots for which they had commissioned scripts. Most of the executives were exhausted and awaited their brief break before the pilot scripts arrived. Nevertheless, Littman knew how to ask for favors, and he called Nina Tassler, a CBS programming executive. Despite her protests over hearing another pitch at this late hour, Littmann assured her that, whether or not she bought the series, she would find the session worthwhile. Since Littman was a friend, and since he'd told her the show was about forensics, she agreed to give Zuiker a hearing. Although she enjoyed forensics shows on other networks, she had purchased none among the recent slate of candidates.

Littmann accompanied Zuiker to the appointment. Zuiker was ready. He had already broken many script-writing rules, and now, rather than sitting down across from Tassler, he perched himself on the arm of the couch where she sat. Then he removed his glasses and closed his eyes, as if he needed to see inside his own head to pull out the magic. He began to describe to her the arena of forensic medicine. He had created a squad of crime scene responders, a Vegas-based crime scene investigation unit supervised during the night shift by Gil Grissom. The lead character was an odd guy devoid of people skills who nonetheless inspired loyalty among his crew, due to his Sherlock Holmes–style knowledge and approach. The show would be about the use of forensic science, Zuiker told Tassler, to solve crimes. The viewers would see intricate details of a crime lab that had never before been part of a TV series, and would in fact see the scene as the responders saw it, with blood spatter, wounds, decomposition, and bugs. It would be fascinatingly icky but also educational. Viewers would learn about DNA analysis, glass fragments, bullet comparisons, explosives analysis, and the processing of trace evidence.

Zuiker described his snap-zoom effects that followed a bullet trajectory from the initial penetration and throughout a body, for example, or showed how a blow to the head produced a specific type of blood pattern on the wall. Grissom might deduce from the slightest evidence that a suicidal jumper was not a suicide after all. He might decompose a pig right there at the crime lab or reconstruct an apparent drowning with an artificial water chamber. As Zuiker described all this, he gestured with excitement and bounced on his perch. Sometimes he got up to act something out. Tassler was hooked. She'd already emptied her budget, her slate was full, but right there in the room—the dream of every writer making a pitch—she bought it. She wanted to make this show. She hired Zuiker to write a script as fast as he could, and by December he produced the pilot. At the same time, actor William Petersen was in a deal that asked of him only that he listen to Tassler's pitches. She sent Zuiker on his way, and Zuiker worked the same magic on Petersen for the role of Grissom. Despite his reluctance to act in a television series, Petersen wanted the lead in this series.

CSI: Crime Scene Investigation was the last show to be picked up for development for the fall 2000 season. It was slated for a Friday night, and there were plenty of doubters. Zuiker was an unknown writer, and it was a unique type of show with an unproven track record.

However, the ratings started out strong and remained there, especially among the coveted young adult audience. The show would go on to launch an entire industry worldwide and become one of the most successful shows in television history.[2]

But Zuiker wasn't done. During a writers' strike in 2007 and 2008 that stalled TV shows for three months, he considered how the typical attention span for young audiences had shrunk, so he devised an innovative way to keep them engaged with reading a novel: the "digi-novel." Starting with a typical novel as the foundation, the story features a retired FBI agent, Steve Dark, who returns to hunt down Sqweegel, a unique serial killer who dresses in white latex and uses contortions and butter to squeeze out of tight situations. About every twenty pages, the reader could go to a website to see a video-based cyber-bridge from one narrative scene to the next. There was also a social community experience to assist readers to talk about the characters and events, as well as to access film stills, to watch behind-the-scenes production, and even to discuss ideas with the creators. The idea was to make a novel into a multidimensional experience. Zuiker released this unique "cross-platform" project in September 2009, calling it *Level 26: Dark Origins*. He embedded special codes at specific intervals in the text to prompt readers to go to a website to see one of the twenty film clips. "The future of business," Zuiker foresees, "is the convergence of different mediums."[3]

He wanted to tell a story that was "too hot" for television and that would give readers of mystery and crime a richer overall experience than novels typically yielded. He thought it would attract more readers from the generation that enjoys video games and engaging visual experiences. Zuiker, with plans for two more such books, believes that within the decade, every television series will have an interactive component to let viewers or readers continue the experience from within their own imaginations. (Apple immediately created a touchscreen application to make digi-novel access simpler for readers, and in 2010 *CSI* devoted an episode to the digi-novel's villain.)

Zuiker moved into opportunity, always thinking, always scanning. Despite a routine dead-end job, he had pondered ways to do something more. Thus, when doors opened, he was ready. Each new venture gave him the experience and confidence to believe he could take on the next one, and rather than accept the status quo, he moved into opportunities—or created the conditions for them. He also gained experience and knowledge that fed his mental database for this arena. It gave him the means to efficiently and effectively sift through ideas to identify those that would work. His brain absorbed it all and packaged the snap.

THE HAPPINESS QUOTIENT

It takes a bold person to put ideas into action. World-renowned psychologist Nathaniel Branden declared his clients to be healthy once they had accepted that nobody was coming to direct their lives; *they* were their own director.[4] That is, when we embrace responsibility for our decisions, we realize what's at stake and can become proactive, absorbing the demands of discipline and commitment as second nature. We recognize discipline not as drudgery or penalty but as an essential ally in our striving to become more. It is the frame for the life we're building, and we can move toward the future with a sense of purpose—even of destiny and adventure.

The idea of destiny is interesting. Many people think it means that a path is already laid out and they need only step on it; the right people will come and take their hand to bring them toward fulfilling their purpose. However, it is much more complex than this romantic (and passive) notion. The philosopher Aristotle proposed that humans are born with an inner purpose, like an acorn is meant to become an oak tree. He called it *entelecheia* or *entelechy*, which means "having its end within itself."[5] That is, the thing is *real* in its fullest sense. It has the qualities of persistence and completion.

Although this has been interpreted in many different ways, Aristotle addressed the concept to the human psyche, or soul. The potential is within us, so anything of which we are capable is our potential. Some possibilities will became realities, some will not, as determined by factors such as our culture, our physical traits, our economic means, and so on. Not all possibilities are equal in how likely it is that they will be realized in our lives. Aristotle specifically associates entelechy with pleasure and happiness. That is, you find the thing that brings out your fullest nature or expression. He also added another dimension: something is actual when it is done *well*. It exhibits stability, endurance, and excellence. In sum, we all have the potential to resonate to a particular manner of existence, but it will develop for us less by chance than through our effort.

Some people have interpreted entelechy to mean that the completion of any person is what they do at work. It is their calling. The late folklorist Joseph Campbell gave this an elegant label: he called it our *bliss*. By this, he meant our sense of purpose. On *The Power of Myth*, a televised interview with Bill Moyers, Campbell urged viewers to direct their lives toward the special track that was waiting for us. Once found, the life we should be living "is the one you *are* living."[6]

Each of us has skills and talents that collectively move us toward authentic self-expression. Some people know the first time they put pen to page that they were born to write. "I knew from my early childhood that I wanted to be a writer," said British mystery writer P. D. James, "and began, as many must, by telling stories to my younger sister and brother in the nursery. . . . Then at seven I produced and edited a family magazine."[7] Others feel most at home with law or plants or children. Mary L., a marketing director, came into her own after years of trying other occupations. She was delighted that she had finally found something that utilized her creative energy. As soon as she entered the field, she felt at home. To anyone who asked, she explained that in the process of reaching into herself, she had created something that others enjoy.

Entrepreneur and inventor Dean Kamen is the embodiment of bliss discovered early. He was always trying things out and tinkering with tools. He was eight when he heard the tale of David and Goliath. He liked the way a small guy would boldly challenge someone of Goliath's stature. "Here's a little guy with a really big problem, a Goliath of a problem, and he realized he could take a stone and a slingshot and solve that problem."[8] In fact, the biblical hero's weapon of choice—a slingshot—impressed him so much he later named one of his inventions after it. Overcoming dyslexia and attention deficit disorder, he often felt like David against staggering odds, especially when he presented ideas to corporate executives who dismissed him. But Kamen, it turns out, is a visionary. He is responsible for numerous devices, such as a portable dialysis machine, a stair-climbing wheelchair, a thought-controlled prosthetic arm, and a unique water filtration system. Most renowned is the Segway PT, a self-balancing motorized scooter on two wheels. His bliss, which calls on his technological expertise and humanitarian streak, is to use technology to improve the world. It all began with a simple device.

One day when Kamen was in high school, his older brother came home from med school. He appreciated Dean's skill with machines and offhandedly suggested that he try devising an automated method for delivering drugs to patients. Inspired, Kamen set up a shop in his parents' basement and created a prototype for the AutoSyringe, a wearable infusion pump. Years later, when he was thirty, Kamen sold the patent for $30 million. With the money, Kamen created DEKA Research and Development Corporation, staffing it with three hundred engineers dedicated to research and development—that is, playing with ideas for new products. In other words, Kamen has funded a brainstorming arena, meant to create even more innovation. In 2005, he was inducted into the National Inventors Hall of Fame, just one of his many awards and recognitions. Despite receiving no college degree, he has several honorary doctorates.

In a way, Kamen had simply re-created his childhood home, where his father, Jack Kamen, had worked day and night to illustrate comic books like *Weird Science* and *Tales from the Crypt*. His mother taught accounting, his brilliant brother achieved his MD and PhD on the same day, and his younger siblings were also tinkerers. So, Kamen emerged from this inventive atmosphere with a sense of business, an appreciation for hard work and persistence, and a relentless focus on his own ideas. In junior high, his hero and role model was Sir Isaac Newton. In the early years of college, he declined to waste time in classes; instead, he believed that his tuition had paid for access to the faculty as business consultants.

In addition to his succession of machines that earned him enough to purchase his own private island, he started a robotics competition for high school students. Called FIRST (For Inspiration and Recognition of Science and Technology), its intent was to show kids how cool engineering could be. "We've got to create a generation of kids that are as passionate about innovation as they are about football."[9] Even so, he insists that it's not about science and technology per se, nor invention for invention's sake. It's about people and their stories, especially their needs. For example, he'd like to perfect a human launching device that would assist SWAT units to get to the tops of buildings.

FIRST sounded to some critics like an offbeat idea that would have difficulty catching on, but in twenty years, it has grown from a local to an international competition that attracts large corporations to look for future employees. "Science and technology and engineering and innovating," Kamen stated on a morning news program, "it's for everybody. It's critically important, it's accessible, it's fun."[10]

On DEKA's website, Kamen is credited with holding 440 patents, many for medical devices. On his two-acre island in Long Island Sound, he has worked to make it "carbon-negative," that is, off the grid. This is where he uses the Slingshot, a no-emission water purifier and source of power. Kamen lives by a moral imperative of improving the quality of life for as many people as he can and hates the idea that anything is impossible. He thinks we must live as if we believe we can succeed. This means working hard, thwarting the demoralizing effect of failure, and keeping your vision alive—even if no one else can see it.

BLISS ALONG LIFE'S WAY

We can think of bliss as both the stimulus and the goal that gets us through an obstacle course—life! It's the idea that our style, background, and personality best match a particular vocation or avocation, and when they cross the right path, we recognize it. The more we work within our bliss, the more satisfying and *right* it feels.

Although we might hinder our ability to reach our bliss because of fear and bad habits, we can also use discipline and self-awareness to achieve it.

So, first things first: we must learn a few things about ourselves. We must discover what depletes our courage and our energy. Is it fear or self-criticism? Is it insecurity about our abilities or capitulation to someone who discourages us from trying? Are you worried, bored, lazy, or disorganized? Perhaps rigid, intolerant, or too much of a perfectionist? On the flip side, we must also learn about our personal strengths. Are we open-minded, energetic, alert, and eager to try new things? Can we boldly take risks and ignore what others might say about us? Are we self-starters with an internal reward system? Can we reframe setbacks? Self-correct? Allow ourselves to be challenged? We must learn how we hinder ourselves on the path to success as well as how we facilitate it. Our self-evaluation must be honest and realistic. But even within that frame, limitations can be stretched and remarkable things can occur.

When Liu Wei was a ten-year-old in China, he was playing hide-and-seek. He came into contact with a high-voltage wire and received a severe electric shock. To save him, his arms were amputated. After such a traumatic loss, some people would give up, but Liu quickly learned to use his feet to accomplish basic skills. "For people like me," he later said, "there were only two options. One was to abandon all dreams, which would lead to a quick, hopeless death. The other was to struggle without arms to live an outstanding life." His dream was to become an accomplished pianist, so when he was eighteen, he took on this daunting challenge. Not only did he master this skill with his toes but he also became a prodigy. He was twenty-three when he entered the televised show *China's Got Talent*, inspired by similar shows in the United Kingdom and the United States. He impressed the judges and won the contest. In interviews afterward, Liu said that he didn't think too hard about how others regarded him, whether they thought he couldn't achieve much or felt sorry for him. "It is enough for me to do the things I like," he stated.

Finding himself faced with a challenge that many might view as insurmountable, he worked his way around it so he could do what he loved.[11]

Because bliss is inner-driven, we know when we've reached it, and it feels as if we've slipped into the most comfortable clothes we've ever owned; it's a pair of well-worn walking shoes. Once we pull them on, we want nothing more than to get going. Bliss becomes our driving force. We are complete in our purpose. We have discovered the activity that most fully expresses and satisfies us. It gives us that Aristotelian *telos*: when something exists "actually," it is in the form it is meant to have.

Successful people like Zuiker, Kamen, and Liu sensed the seeds of their purpose within themselves and moved eagerly toward goals that developed it. Whether this meant practice, practice, practice, immersion in research, or taking a road trip to introduce themselves to the right person, they didn't hesitate or second-guess: they moved. Why? Because they foresaw the great joy they could derive from a specific activity. They were persistently attracted toward their future selves. Such people become the "prime mover" of their lives as they respond to an inner imperative that feels increasingly more real as they draw close. Whatever training or experience may be required, they devote themselves without a second thought, and even this commitment *sizzles* with energy. In the process, their brains develop neural circuits and pathways that support their activities. When the spirit becomes willing, so does the flesh, and it starts with an attitude about discipline and goals that can be taught and nurtured.

Innovators stay alert for improving their chosen field, as Zuiker did with the digi-novel. This helps to maintain excitement in their daily endeavors. Historian Natalie Davis uses curiosity as her ultimate guide. "It just hooks in very deeply . . . I may not know what is personally invested in it, other than my curiosity and my delight."[12] Their entelechy is, to them, a sacred journey. Some will sacrifice anything to it.

So, entelechy or bliss means that we feel something within us that drives us forth. We coordinate our inner experience with our external situation to develop what is our unique function. Positive feelings + continuous opportunities + inner momentum = progress toward bliss. Back to the acorn metaphor: given the right conditions, an acorn will become an oak tree, not a maple tree or a zebra. Its function or purpose is to be an oak tree. It contains an internal order that evolves according to a genetic design. It will reach its purpose only when it *is* an oak.

We move toward balance and fulfillment. For example, someone whose bliss urges artistic expression may respond strongly to color and texture. One man who stumbled across poetry as a boy and developed his talent said, "I was enveloped by it. It seemed the most complex, rich, full-of-possibilities sound I'd ever heard. It put images right into my brain, and I wanted to do that, too." A mathematician knew that working with numbers just felt right. "Numbers came easily to me and it seemed right to see the universe in terms of the regularity of math. I'm not sure I *could* do something else."

The actor Ving Rhames, who has appeared in *Pulp Fiction*, *Con Air*, and other films, tells the story of how he defied odds that would have put him in the streets among drug dealers. His *dream* had been to play football in the NFL—a common dream for many boys. However, he soon learned that his *bliss* was something else.[13]

Rhames grew up in Harlem surrounded by violence, crime, and drugs. By the time he was eleven, he sensed something in him greater than his situation suggested. He was determined to make more of his life than what he saw among others around him. He appreciated all that his mother had sacrificed for him. Still, he was not quite sure in what direction he would be going.

One day, he and a friend followed a couple of girls, trying to talk to them. They went into a youth center, so the boys entered, too. They found themselves in the midst of a poetry class. This was not what they had in mind, but Rhames began to listen. The professor talked about the great black poets, such as Paul Lawrence Dunbar, James Baldwin, and Langston Hughes. Rhames was impressed. He began to attend readings for the Dance Theater of Harlem, and one of his teachers told him he was gifted. Feeling confident, he auditioned for the High School of the Performing Arts. To his great joy, he was accepted. This introduced him to a world he had not even known existed.

When he performed a scene during his junior year from *A Raisin in the Sun*, he sensed he was in the right place, doing the right thing. According to him, it felt as if God had intervened to lead him straight to the thing he was meant to be. Rhames continued to receive scholarships, which only confirmed his sense of direction. By the time he was physically large enough to think about being a professional football player, he no longer cared. He knew what he wanted to be, what he was *meant* to be. "I look at my life," he says, "and I know that some presence or power has had a hand in it. If you just allow that hand to guide you, you'll be fine."[14]

THE RIGHT MOMENT

Rhames found his way to acting because he crossed paths with girls who led him to a poetry class. This illustrates one more concept in the "bliss" category: synchronicity. This occurs when events synch in such a manner that they seem magically to work out in just the right way at just the time we need them. Whether some metaphysical element is involved, who knows, but that's often the feeling that people report when they see how a single connection, just when they were ready, seemed to transform their lives. Synchronicity is *meaningful* coincidence, and it's not something we can predict or control, but it frames many eureka moments.

There's an amazing story about a man in need of money who brought a barrel full of books to Abraham Lincoln when he was a young man. Lincoln himself tells it: "One day a man who was migrating to the West drove up in front of my store with a wagon which contained his family and household plunder. He asked me if

I would buy an old barrel for which he had no room in his wagon, and which he said contained nothing of special value. I did not want it, but to oblige him I bought it, and paid him, I think, half a dollar for it." Lincoln put it away and forgot it until he was going through his storehouse later. He emptied the barrel and found Blackstone's *Commentaries*. He picked them up and started to read. "The more I read, the more intensely interested I became. Never in my whole life was my mind so thoroughly absorbed. I read until I devoured them."[15]

Lincoln went on to become a lawyer and then president of the United States. Such things occur often. It can be as simple as someone just saying the right thing to make us think of some new direction, or leaving a book open at a page that makes an idea pop. When we're working toward our inner potential, we may discover that our efforts fit into a larger dynamic. Famed Swiss psychoanalyst Carl Jung crystallized the concept of synchronicity in 1951, and it has been absorbed into many philosophies since.[16]

We cross many paths in our lives, some of which mean nothing, while others offer entirely new directions. It's often a matter of one of these chance encounters occurring at a specific point of our development. Had Lincoln been engaged in another profession when he emptied the barrel, the law books might have meant nothing. Had Rhames come into the youth center at a different time, or with a different teacher or subject, that particular incident might have had no impact. No one knows when an event in our lives will actually *be* synchronistic. However, as Pasteur said, chances like these favor those who are prepared.

When people begin to sense their bliss, they often work harder, watching for opportunities to deepen it. Thus, they create better conditions for snaps to occur. As an undergraduate at Princeton University, Josh Berman had focused on public policy, winning a Fulbright scholarship to Australia to study the educational system there. He loved politics, urban planning, and educational planning. He also went to both law and business school at Stanford. Still, his true love was writing. As the urge beckoned, he looked for opportunities to fulfill it. Then, synchronicity occurred. For a story for the Stanford Business School newspaper, Berman interviewed former NBC entertainment president Warren Littlefield. When Littlefield saw the final article, he was impressed. He asked Berman to consider working at the network. Berman said yes.

He gave up his other career directions and moved closer to his bliss, based on how right his direction felt. When this opportunity was offered, because he was prepared and eager to succeed, he accepted it. "I started in Hollywood at the age of twenty-four as a summer associate at NBC," he recalls.[17] He then became a development executive for NBC Studios. When NBC ran a contest, Berman spotted another step up in his plan. He penned a spec episode for *Seinfeld* and won the contest. He knew this could help him move into a solid writing position, so toward this end he wrote and produced a clever spoof of *Ally McBeal*, a popular show on the Fox network. NBC soon made him a writer.

"At that point in my life," he says, "despite having a fourteen-hour work day, I couldn't fall asleep unless I wrote. I could've written anything—it could have been a letter, it could have been a script—but that was my way of relaxing and clearing my head. I loved it so much that I thought if I could make a living writing, there would be nothing better."

In 2000, Berman read the pilot script for *CSI*. He appreciated its element of mystery. "I love being able to craft a story where you don't see the whole picture until the very last piece is put into it." His agent submitted samples of his material, and when show runner Carol Mendelsohn read it, she invited Berman for an interview. She then hired him as an executive story editor. He soon became a coexecutive producer, and then executive producer. After several successful seasons, Berman left CBS and signed a deal with Fox to write new pilots. He had reached the "snapping" point.

"For years and years," says Berman,

I worked on procedural shows, like *CSI* and *Bones*, and shows that I created called *Vanished* and *Killer Instincts*. A lot of these shows are heavily researched and you might have an inspiration for a plotline, but you don't really have an "aha! moment" with those shows because they're structured almost like a legal brief. Everything has to be meticulously thought-out.

But when I was trying to come up with a new TV show to write, I was literally at my desk and my eyes fell on a photograph of my grandmother, who had helped to raise me. She was the most inspirational person in my life. And I thought, "Oh my God, I have to write a show about my grandmother"—I didn't mean literally my grandmother, but the *spirit* of my grandmother. For me, what was so amazing about her was that she was a Holocaust survivor, she was under five feet tall, and she was overweight, but she carried herself like a supermodel: She'd survived the Holocaust and had her entire family murdered by the Nazis, so after that, other problems in life paled in comparison. She carried herself like she owned every room she entered, and she made me believe I could do anything I wanted.

In that moment, I wanted to write a show about my grandmother, a supermodel in a plus-size woman's body. So I thought, why don't I just take the risk? Networks' jaws might drop, because that's not what they're expecting from me, but I *had* to write it. I knew that was going to be my next project.[18]

As he sat there pondering, the perfect title, *Drop Dead Diva*, popped into his head. He wrote up an outline and created characters and a pilot episode. He later sold it to Lifetime.

There's a beating heart within our creative development with a life of its own. It's a radiating hot spot that warms us as we approach. Then it inflames us.

As each example in this chapter shows, one of the most important qualities is mental flexibility. We must be able to shift when opportunity beckons. This brings us to the idea that there are many types of attunements to bliss.

Developmental psychologist Howard Gardner presented the concept of multiple intelligence during the 1980s. He disliked the assumption that intelligence was a unitary, cognitively based capacity measureable by standardized instruments that produce an Intelligence Quotient (IQ). The IQ tests, he thought, placed too much stock in language and logic. Gardner believed that there were other types of intelligences, all of which are worthy of recognition. There were artists, musicians, athletes, shamans, craftspeople, and others who demonstrated competence that relied on some sort of intelligence. "I wanted to broaden conceptions of intelligence to include not only the results of paper-and-pencil tests but also knowledge of the human brain and sensitivity to the diversity of human cultures."[19] The competences he had in mind did not lend themselves to methods that measured ordinary forms of logic or language. They might not be measurable at all—at least not by means we've developed thus far. Gardner devised his own definition: "An intelligence is the ability to solve problems, or to create products that are valued within one or more cultural settings."[20]

Gardner lists eight criteria for counting an ability as intelligence, including the presence of core components and its place in evolutionary history. It should also have a distinct developmental progression and a susceptibility to encoding within some symbolic system (language, art, music, or gestures, for example). He offers nine different types of intelligence, from linguistic to spatial to musical. He even includes intrapersonal and interpersonal intelligences, which are now regarded as part of "emotional intelligence," as well as "existential intelligence" for the abstractly inclined. Although his theory is controversial in that empirical support is lacking for some areas, his work, for our purposes, reminds us to remain open about snap abilities.

For example, naturalistic intelligence involves an attunement to our natural environment. Poet Annie Dillard demonstrates this in a poetic narrative, *Pilgrim at Tinker Creek*.[21] She describes how she walked through the woods for long stretches and sat observing the intricate manifestations of nature. She had no agenda for what she wanted to see but just relaxed and remained alert to whatever was surrounding her, overhead, or at her feet. Dillard allowed nature to spontaneously appear as it was, even if nothing at all happened. Thus, she developed a keen sense of vigilance and witnessed remarkable events among insects, wildlife, and plant life that most people fail to see—even if they had been in the same area with her.

Dillard developed a deep focus that transcends ordinary day-to-day awareness. It fully involved her so that she was able to feel the flow of natural life. And her learning, while engaged and alert, was also relaxed and satisfying. As with Dillard, the reward for developing our own particular form of intelligence in accord with our bliss is this: We feel in harmony with our life process. We know why we were born. We know where we want to go, and we have momentum into a future. As we absorb and *become* our bliss, the conditions for snaps improve. But there is one more important element.

Although entelechy moves us toward our potential, achieving it is not inevitable. It is not synonymous with fate, though the possibilities are ever before us. Sometimes, however, a lack of faith in ourselves or some adverse circumstance can thwart us. An acorn will become an oak tree if the right amount of sun, water, nutritional soil, and space are available. Likewise, our bliss needs careful tending. It's an ongoing process in which attention must be paid at each step.

Each person, we've noted, experienced an awakening that snapped him or her into action. Sometimes it occurred early, sometimes only after trying other occupations. However, all had the right attitude about wanting to grow, and they were able to recognize the road to opportunity, as well as to move at the right moment. Changing their lives, their locales, their self-beliefs meant nothing. Surrendering to their muse was their priority.

The ability to act on opportunities that lead you to your bliss involves effort and enterprise. Opportunities are there as part of the meaningful arrangement of events that respond to your talents. As they say, when the student is ready, the teacher will come, but the student must then take advantage, as Zuiker, Kamen, Berman, Lincoln, and Rhames all did.

KEY POINTS

- Realize your life direction is not fate but the result of becoming your own prime mover; don't wait, initiate.
- Your bliss relies on developing your specific form of intelligence.
- Be alert, proactive, and flexible, so you recognize synchronicity when it happens.
- Snaps arise best in activities with meaningful goals, in which you can experience full absorption and from which you can gain an enriching sense of reward.

CHAPTER 3

THE MASTER'S ZONE

EARLY TRAINING

F emale chess players represent less than 1 percent of world-class champions, yet Hungarian education specialist László Polgár turned all three of his daughters—literally, all his children—into champions. He'd devised a method for raising geniuses before he was even married, confident that he could follow the path of other parents who had accomplished it. Even as a young man, the principle of cause and effect was clear; talent was but a minor part of the equation.

Polgár grew up in a humble home in Budapest, Hungary, under the domination of the Soviet Union. While it was tough for his father to make ends meet, Polgár did not let this get in the way of his dreams, even that of finding the right partner. Polgár's future wife, Klara, lived just across the border in a Hungarian-speaking enclave of the Ukraine. Their families were acquainted, and one day Polgár's mother mentioned that she would bring him with her for a visit. Klara sent a formal invitation on her family's behalf, to which Polgár responded, although he didn't end up traveling there. Klara was delighted to discover that they were both educators. They began an avid correspondence, and in 1965 Klara went to Budapest to meet Polgár. Apparently not shy about revealing his dreams, he told Klara that he hoped to have six children, whom he would train to be highly successful individuals. Klara listened politely but felt no romantic interest. Still, because they shared a passion for education, she continued to correspond. It took a year and a half before Klara decided that Polgár was a man with real vision and devotion. He seemed to sense that she was yielding to him, so he wrote a love letter, punctuating it with a marriage proposal. Then he went to see Klara, and she accepted. The day before their second wedding anniversary in 1969, they had their first child, Susan.

To identify factors in the lives of successful people, the Polgárs have together analyzed hundreds of biographies of great intellectuals. It was clear to them that the most compelling common denominator among great people was early and intense training. Mozart's father, Leopold, set the example. Leopold Mozart was himself an accomplished musician—a composer, violinist, conductor, and teacher. Noticing signs of musical ability in his children, he started training his oldest child, Nannerl, when she was seven. Wolfgang, just three, watched them and began to imitate Nannerl on the piano. This drew Leopold's attention. Under his daily lessons, the child excelled. Three days before his fifth birthday, Wolfgang required just half an hour to learn his first musical composition. Soon, he was composing bits of music himself. Leopold let his own career slide in order to prepare his two talented children to tour the courts of Europe. This included daily lessons and an ambitious concert schedule. As he had hoped, they became quite famous. The making of young Wolfgang into a musical "miracle" became Polgár's model.

Polgár believed that training had more influence on Mozart's gift than had innate genius. Of course, many of us would not dismiss Mozart's genes, since his father was an accomplished musician. Be that as it may, Polgár believed strongly in training and discipline, so he set a course similar to Mozart's for his own children. Still, Susan was a girl. All the biographies had been about great *men*. The Polgárs were not certain the same approach would work with girls. Polgár decided to give it a try, but this proved easier said than done.

Susan was a hyperactive child, unable to focus for more than a few minutes. This was hardly conducive to a rigorous training regimen based in discipline, but Polgár was patient. He wanted Susan to find the thing that would engage her. He let *her* lead the way. She didn't settle on anything until she was four years old, but when she did, she was hooked. One day, she went looking for a new toy and discovered a chess set in a cupboard. The small pieces were strange and intriguing, so she begged her mother to show her how to play with them. Klara told her to ask her father. When Polgár came home that evening, Susan ran to him. She wanted to know *right now* what to do with the chess pieces.

Polgár enjoyed chess as an occasional hobby. He sat down with Susan and picked up some pieces, explaining that they were part of a game. Then, despite its complexity, he decided to teach her the game. He thought it might be the perfect medium for his method. Susan was at the right age. If it held her attention, the game was sufficiently challenging for her to be able to develop real skill. He would also be able to quickly see the results of his training and to track them as she progressed. In addition, there were competitions in their own city that could test her abilities and afford opportunities to play with opponents who could challenge her.

For a while, Susan recalls, they played a game called "pawn wars."[1] In this way, Polgár introduced each chess piece, one at a time. Susan became absorbed in learning; it helped to calm her and direct her powers of concentration. Polgár created checkmate puzzles, setting up the chessboard for the end of a game and asking her to figure out how the players had reached this point. He then taught Susan about checkmate traps.

Klara agreed that chess could be a terrific platform for their experiment in early education. It did not deter the Polgárs that few females—as noted above, less than 1 percent—had ever achieved top status in chess championships. Their enterprise was about the use of discipline and goals, not about developing latent talent. They realized that they had not started as early as Leopold Mozart with young Wolfgang, but they still envisioned great things.

Polgár purchased as many books on chess as he could afford and set up a card file, as well as an index of competitors' tournament results. His file soon filled the shelves of one wall of their home. He gradually worked Susan up to six hours a day of intense play, including having her play speed games while blindfolded. Although Klara was concerned about the intensity of these sessions, Susan thrived. In just six months, she seemed ready to take on adult players.

"Some time after my fourth birthday," Susan wrote, "I entered my first chess tournament. I remember everybody being shocked that such a tiny little girl wanted to enter the competition."[2]

It was a regional tournament at a local club, Varos Meteor. Susan found a partner who agreed to humor her and let her play him, and she won. This didn't sit well with the members, who'd been certain the whole thing was just a joke. They didn't like being humiliated by a little girl not even five years old. However, Polgár was pleased. The experiment that he'd long plotted and planned had come to fruition.

Next was the Budapest championship tournament. Susan was the youngest player to enter. She wasn't daunted by any of this; she was having fun. As she played one game after another, she handily won them all. Her finishing score for the championship was 10–0.

The media quickly learned about her and labeled her a wunderkind, which placed her in the spotlight. The Polgárs described their parenting method and took some sharp criticism over it. However, they knew that Susan had chosen this game, and she enjoyed it. No one had forced her to do it, and no one was forcing her into these competitions.

The Polgárs added one more cerebral exercise by enrolling her in a Russian-speaking nursery program. She quickly became bilingual, and added German. Then, at a time when home schooling was rare, the Polgárs applied to the government to be allowed to teach Susan at home. She was already adept in reading, math, and writing—advanced beyond other kids her age. The Polgárs received begrudging permission (and even public ridicule that verged on threats). Every year, Susan easily passed all the required tests that home-schooled children had to take to prove they were keeping up.

To further improve, Susan worked on her visual and motor skills with daily table tennis games. She also studied the great games of past and present chess grandmasters, talked with other coaches, memorized game patterns, and played with a wide variety of opponents. Her father also included sessions for play, even for telling jokes. He believed that laughter, exercise, and fun were important for training a child. When she was ten, Susan became a national female master. The following year, she traveled abroad for her first international tournament. As she met (and beat) chess players from other countries, she was more motivated than ever to improve her game. By this time, Susan could complete a game in less than a minute, play without seeing the board, and play five different games simultaneously in her head. However, the question remained whether this was all due to training or to genius. Susan could very well have had an innate gift. Training another child would help solve the mystery.

Next came Susan's sisters, Sofia and Judit. (In fact, Susan was immersed in a chess game when she first learned that she had a sister). Although it was probably tempting to push one or both toward the same training medium, the Polgárs waited until each one developed an interest and asked to play. Susan continued to spend a lot of time behind closed doors in the "chess" room, but there was a small window through which the other two could peek. They became intrigued. They wanted to play this game, too.

However, the Polgárs wisely withheld the privilege. They believed that the appropriate age for learning chess was five, and they did not want to risk exposing their other two daughters to this rigorous training before they were ready to pursue it seriously. This only whet their appetites. In fact, Klara was now playing, too, so the game created a family bond. The two youngest witnessed the special aura that surrounded the game for some of the family. Once introduced, Sofia and Judit became expert players as well. Susan recalls that even as a very young girl, Judit had started to look for challenges. She had a firm sense of commitment.

In 1984, Susan was proclaimed the number one female chess player in the world, and the following year she beat a grandmaster, becoming the first female grandmaster. Still just a teenager, Susan was featured on the front page of the *New York Times*.[3] At times she qualified to play in male championship tournaments, but the rules of her country prohibited this. One Hungarian leader tried to get her removed from the world rankings, and each time she accomplished one more feat, she faced resistance, both nationally and internationally. "I did not give up the fight," she says.[4] Her bravery and persistence helped to create inroads for her sisters, but some people were angry that three girls from the same family were getting so much glory. None of this deterred them. They just got better and better at what they loved.

Susan did once learn a tough lesson: outside interests could undermine focus. In a match in Monaco, she had included her boyfriend on her team. At first, she played to her usual level, winning her games and maintaining the lead. But she sensed something amiss with her boyfriend and could not shake the feeling that something bad was about to happen. She thought he was acting strangely, but when Susan questioned him he refused to tell her anything. The suspense divided her attention. Unable to sleep, her concentration failed. "The anticipation and mystery took a huge toll on me physically, mentally, and emotionally," she later wrote, "my head was a complete mess."[5] She lost her aggressive edge, just hanging on during each game while she tried to repair the relationship during rest periods. Her opponent drew even with her score. In a best-of-eight match, they were 4–4. Allowed two play-off games, Susan won the first one but lost the second. They had two more play-off games, and Susan again won the first one. She had but to win one more to become the world champion. But her feelings got the better of her. Despairing over her emotional problems, Susan once again allowed her opponent to draw even.

This now put them into a situation, according to the rules, where luck rather than skill would decide: the judges would draw lots. Susan lost. She never forgot this difficult lesson. She believed she could have maintained her advantage if she hadn't allowed her personal problems to interfere. It was a hard lesson, but it offers an important insight about snapping: the more intense and attuned the focus, the better the momentum. Divided attention is a poor medium for seizing an aha! moment and taking quick action.

Susan competed against some of the world's most skilled male players—Garry Kasparov and Bobby Fischer among them—proving wrong the popular notion floating around the chess world that the female brain is not equipped for high-level play. Susan's sisters accomplished many of the same things. Twelve-year-old Judit won eight competitions in a row, while Sofia beat four grandmasters.

Of the three, Judit, with her intense spirit of competition, was deemed the strongest female player in the history of the game. This is due to a number of factors, all of which are relevant for the best conditions for innovative snaps. From birth, Judit was exposed to a chess-playing household, exemplifying the principle that whatever surrounds us educates our emotions. Although she did not start to play until she was five, she watched her sisters and traveled with the family to their tournaments. Her older sisters enjoyed mentoring her. By age seven, she could play with a blindfold, and when she was nine, she played five tournament-level players simultaneously—blindfolded—and beat them all! By fifteen, she became the youngest grandmaster ever, beating Bobby Fischer's 1958 record. She also beat Garry Kasparov, who was considered at this time to be the strongest player of all time, and she was the first female to be among the chess world's Top Ten. In 1988, the three sisters together won the Women's Olympiad for Hungary.

The Polgárs believed that Sofia possessed the most innate talent. One night, when Polgár had found her playing chess, he told her to leave the pieces alone. "They won't leave *me* alone," she'd insisted. When she was fourteen, Sofia shocked the chess world in 1989 when she defeated a string of Soviet grandmasters and achieved the highest performance rating of any chess player, male or female, in any open tournament in chess history.

However, talent or not, Sofia proved to be the least enticed. For her, the daily discipline became rote. Although she won her first national title when she was just five years old, as Susan watched Sofia develop, she thought that her sister did not have the same focus. "She liked playing chess, but the analytical part was a burden to her. . . . She was striving too much to find beauty."[6]

Sofia developed other interests, especially art, which diminished her commitment to the game. "I could give up easier than Judit," she said. "I never worked as hard as she did."[7]

Thus, Sofia's story offers insight to the mysteries of snapping. She could apply herself when she wanted to, and did pile up a number of titles and records, but apparently she did not have a driving desire. Mastery, it seems, is not necessarily about talent, just as Polgár had suspected. Mastery can be taught. It could easily be argued that all three girls were innately gifted with high spatial intelligence. Still, even if this is true, Polgár guided them to the pinnacle in their area, something that likely would not have happened without his vision and dedication, as well as the girls' own sense of motivation. In fact, after Polgár published a book on his method, the number of child chess prodigies increased. Leopold Mozart had also made his method public, and in his day the youthful development of musical mastery increased across Europe. It seems to be the case that exceptional performance is strongly associated with training and with attitude.

Discipline, motivation, and immersion improve the activities of scanning and sifting. They facilitate tapping the brain's other side.

MEMORY MUSCLES

Chess requires its players to think critically along several levels: know the rules, anticipate potential moves, focus on visual-spatial angles, and decide which move in several scenarios is best. Once the knowledge base is established (with many thousands of configurations), reasoning becomes second nature. Just a glance at the board can provide information about numerous moves. As Susan Polgár said, "Once you have a winning position, play with your hands not your head. Trust your intuition."[8]

Deliberate practice, such as the Polgár girls undertook, means more than just rote activity: it involves critical feedback, trying new things to feed momentum, and stretching oneself to meet ever greater challenges. Being fully attentive is an important factor. The brain engages with meaningful stimuli and embraces novelty. Deep and focused concentration develops its neural circuits for increased speed and fluidity. Focus, challenge, engaged practice: these items are essential preparation for snapping.

Research on the brain activity of master chess players reveals that people who can develop this degree of expertise have developed a unique relationship with their memory system. Essentially, we have three types of memory: sensory memory lasts just a few seconds, short-term (or working memory), a little longer, and long-term, indefinitely.

Typically, working memory is transient and limited to a few items at any given time, which allows it to stay fluid so we can react to new situations without information overload. Whatever we remember within this frame can be easily displaced by new information. (A common sitcom joke plays off this: while one person tries to remember a phone or license number, another mentions a date, which dissolves the first person's efforts.) To get along in life, we need a memory source that allows us to recall things on a short-term basis, such as when we read a menu, find our way in a new building, or drive to a destination. Psychologist George Miller published a seminal paper in 1956 regarding the "magical number seven, plus or minus two" in which he identified the capacity of short-term memory retention as approximately five to nine items, or "chunks."[9] However, we're not quite as mentally limited as this sounds.

Miller thought it should be possible to increase our capacity for this type of memory by recoding groups of what he called "low-information" content items into a smaller number of "high-information" content items. "A man just beginning to learn radio-telegraph codes," he wrote, "hears each dit and dah as a separate chunk. Soon he is able to organize these sounds into letters and then he can deal with the letters as chunks. Then the letters organize themselves into words, which are still larger chunks, and he begins to hear whole phrases."[10] The telegraph operator goes from an inexperienced trainee who can recall only a few symbols to an experienced technician who can remember dozens of coded phrases.

To illustrate, Miller described an experiment that had been undertaken in 1954, in which subjects were trained to listen to a string of binary digits and mentally organize them into groups of five. They were then to recode each group with a name, and work on remembering the names. In this manner, some subjects were able to recall up to forty binary digits. In other words, they created meaningful groups that assisted their memory retention. "Recoding is an extremely powerful weapon," Miller concluded, "for increasing the amount of information that we can deal with."[11]

One such strategy is called "chunking," because it organizes pieces of information into chunks that the brain can easily digest and retain. It recodes them into manageable units of perception and meaning. For example, color codes can quickly convey threat level. In fact, Joshua Foer describes in *Moonwalking with Einstein* his experience at the US Memory Championship, where he learned how to remember with ease typically difficult items of information. Following the model of Cicero, a famous statesman in ancient Rome, Foer discovered that relying on weird or colorful image associations made storing and recalling information easier. His example illustrates that almost anyone can improve their memory.[12]

Expert knowledge is generally organized for a specific purpose, with relevant patterns: "Chess masters have been shown to recall the layout of boards not as separate pieces but as functional clusters . . .

expert readers see whole words and even phrases, not the letters in a word; expert musicians recall passages, not notes; expert waiters recall patterned combinations of meal components, not separate menu items."[13] This means that as we gain experience in some activity, we organize a knowledge base that becomes second nature.

We're assisted in recoding by a neurological device that structures chunks into hierarchical sequences. During the 1980s, psychologists studying motor control demonstrated that each seemingly linear sequence contained subsequences, each of which contained yet more subsequences. In other words, the brain organizes information in priority levels. This helps to store the information in an overall structure for later retrieval.[14] The greater the expertise in some activity, the more spontaneous the organization. That is, in new situations, we can snap right into a familiar pattern, making our abilities in this situation faster and more fluid. Sometimes it can be so fast and automatic that we fail to feel the rush of insight: "I *know* this!"

A "chunk," then, is an organization of elements that have a strong neural association with one another. Anyone can pack a lot into his or her own chunks. To experience this, look at the fourteen letters printed below for about ten seconds:

XIBMSATMTVPHDX

Now cover these letters and try replicating them in the space below:

You may have discovered that it's difficult to remember them all in the right order. This occurs because they don't mean anything. But if you *chunk* them into recognizable groups, it's easier:

X IBM SAT MTV PHD X

Via six "meaning units," you can better recall the fourteen letters. But there's more to chunking than this. Instead of just seven distinct items, we can make each item stand in for a more detailed grouping of information. It's like using a series of computer icons to represent a set of instructions. They're visual shortcuts that relieve the pressure from our memory systems. We look at a picture of a folder with a specific label, for example, and we can recall its contents without having to sort through them all. Mobile devices rely on representing whole systems with a single brief graphic, an icon. The diagnostic manual for mental health experts uses specific codes to represent a long list of symptoms. When items are categorized, they're easier to remember.

Imagine playing a memory game like this: A number of items are presented on a tray. One is removed outside your view, and you must decide what's missing. If the items were all jumbled on the tray, the task would be difficult, but if they were grouped according to color, size, category, or shape, the task would be comparatively easier.

So, chunking involves reorganizing or representing large amounts of information in manageable ways: we pack each of the five to nine items with much more than its surface value. To chunk successfully, the chosen system must be perceptually simple or meaningful. Chess grandmasters, for example, can recall roughly fifty thousand to one hundred thousand chunks of information about the game, derived from their experience with the layout of a chessboard and the function of each piece. They chunk a given position with numerous possible strategies.

A study of chess masters that was undertaken in the 1990s found that a "template" theory better explained chess expertise. The researchers concluded that chess masters had developed large retrieval structures in long-term memory. A template, or recognizable pattern, would allow for the development of greater memory capacity than chunking and would frame selective search strategies.[15] It seems that, as people devote themselves to a skill, they develop knowledge-based schemas that become long-term templates that influence their brain's encoding system. Information gets chunked, and chunks evolve into complex data structures that enhance perceptual speed. One thing that sets chess experts apart from amateurs is their eye movements. They search more deeply for strategies because their templates more effectively reduce the possible number of move sequences: they more rapidly recognize patterns and explore moves and consequences. Their mental templates augment short-term memory with "slots that can be filled rapidly with information about the current position."[16]

Christopher Chabris and Daniel Simons are cognitive psychologists. They experiment with cognitive illusions to study some elusive aspects of memory. Aware of experiments that had demonstrated the prodigious memory of chess masters, they tested an acquaintance who was a grandmaster. They allowed him to see a chess position from an obscure master game for just five seconds. Then they asked him to re-create it on a board. Despite his brief exposure to the game setting, he was able to do this task from memory with a near 100 percent accuracy. This feat, they stated, went well beyond the typical seven-item limit. At their request, he repeated it several times and then explained how he combined the pieces into groups based on their relationships to the others. "In essence, by recognizing familiar patterns, he stuffed not one but several pieces into each of his memory slots."[17] Chabris and Simons add that by honing his skill with this game, he also had developed more vivid mental imagery, more accurate spatial reasoning, and greater visual memory.

Still, only when the chess pieces were meaningfully arranged into patterns that chess players used could the subject accomplish this feat. When the pieces were arranged randomly, the player's memory proved to be no better than anyone else's. He no longer had a practiced database on which to call. Like other chess grandmasters, he could perform well within his specialized arena, but this did not make him a savant for other memory tasks.[18]

In an analysis of four hundred games that compared grandmasters playing regular chess to the same experts playing blind chess, the rate of errors made was nearly equal. "The Grandmasters had trained so well they could perform their art without even looking at its elements."[19] Although they had to work hard at gathering a powerful mental database, once they had it, they could let themselves flow into their skill. The same thing applies to any other activity, because the brain has created neuro-pathways to support the focused activity, and practice has reinforced them.

Masters of a discipline or skill can tap faster and more fluidly into their stored information than most other people. Because they're aware of the range of strategies for any given situation, they can calculate ahead for swift decision making. Their memory skills and capacity may be no better than those of the average person, but they can exploit a well-organized system of neurological connections without the restrictive impediment of conscious analysis.

All experts chunk what they know into manageable categories. This gives them quicker access to information when they need it, and thus a greater ability to snap. Intense study in a specific enterprise provides the framework for this type of recoding. Learning music, chess, medicine, or any similar activity combines the flexibility of working memory with the durability of memory storage. Built around neurological templates that encode information about familiar patterns (moves and positions), accomplished people develop the ability to simultaneously store and evaluate.

WAYS OF KNOWING

Earlier, I mentioned Howard Gardner's concept of multiple intelligences. While developing it, he studied prodigies. He describes a scenario in his book *Art, Mind, and Brain* that features three four-year-olds, each of whom could play some exquisite musical piece. They were considered prodigies because they could perform well beyond the skill level of their peers and had developed these skills at an accelerated rate. However, studies of the minds of such "genius" children,

Gardner points out, have long failed to identify the spark of creativity. Too often, traditional researchers on intelligence have equated ability with a high score on a cognitive IQ test. They err by viewing intellect as a seamless entity and creative skill as a fixed trait.

Gardner found that prodigies like these children move through a specific domain at a rapid rate. Heredity plays a part, as do role models and cultural support. In addition, some domains are self-contained, with little interaction with the outside world. Individuals can progress quickly, without much hindrance, because they rely on only themselves and their own tenacity. However, some domains require years of exposure before mastery can be achieved, as well as interaction with a professional world. In addition, in any given culture, some domains are unavailable or undeveloped. "Even the most gifted mathematician cannot make genuine innovations if he lives in a culture where mathematics has been little developed."[20] Gardner adds that while Mozart was gifted, his renown may have been due to a certain amount of serendipity: a "special fit" between his flair and the style of music preferred during his era.

He's a good example of what Gardner conveys about prodigy. Mozart's own descriptions of his process also correspond well with what we've discovered about accomplished chess players like the Polgárs. In addition, he assists in our understanding of the development of snaps as a benefit of expertise.

Wolfgang Amadeus Mozart thought he could compose more readily when he was in a positive frame of mind, which for him meant being active. He liked to travel or to take a walk after a good meal. When he was alone, of "good cheer," the ideas that most pleased him arrived unpredictably, and no matter what he was doing, he could always retain them to write down later. If he was in a good mood, feeling creative, he could feel his music grow and change until it reached the stage that, for him, felt final. All this took place in his mind, much like a Zen master, before he wrote anything down. He had no idea how they came to him. He could never force them. Often, they were so natural he would hum them without realizing it until someone told him. "Provided I am not disturbed," he wrote to a friend, "my subject enlarges itself, becomes methodized and defined, and the whole, though it be long, stands almost complete and finished in my mind. . . . Nor do I hear in my imagination the parts successively, but I hear them as it were all at once. What a delight this is I cannot tell."[21] To him it resembled a "lively dream."[22]

The fluent ease with which Mozart composed music displays the way constant rehearsal made the process and product a natural part of him. While the early stages can be difficult, since he began as a child to inculcate the process and rules of his era, his malleable brain was able to accommodate the musical impetus quite readily. One biographer stated that witnesses had reported how Mozart would write a complex piece of music as rapidly as one might write a letter—as if he were just reading it out as his mind's eye saw it. Nothing seemed to disturb his dedicated focus. However, Mozart also played with many different combinations of music, humming fragments, pondering them, or playing something on the piano. In other words, he would immerse. He *became* the music. While this is not necessarily the only way a prodigy might approach the creative process, for Mozart it was effective. It was the rhythm into which he fell and the one on which he continued to rely. He recognized rules but tried out many other possibilities until he was able to produce exquisite deviations that made listeners shiver with delight.

For Mozart, it was musical composition. For someone else, it might be the preparation of a great feast, the direction of a film, or the ultimate challenge in chess. It requires the constant exercise of memory, a solid knowledge of one's subject area, the ability to stay on track, a certain amount of energy, and the courage to try things out; that is, to place your own signature on them. Creative aha! moments occur so regularly along the way that they seem enmeshed with all the rest.

George Keeler, an avid outdoorsman, wanted to design a better backpack. He had worked at REI, in the camping and hiking department, and one of his responsibilities was to sell backpacks. "I was basically shopping all day," he said. "When you work with products you love it is easy to pick up on every little nuance and feature. I consider myself to be very detail-oriented. I pay close attention to the final finish of a product or prototype. I'll put on five extra coats of paint when I don't need to, just to get it that much smoother. I'm very picky about every stitch placement and consistency at our factory. Having this mindset is part of the reason I am able to easily visualize a new design rather than [needing] to sketch it out on paper."[23]

During his junior year at Lehigh University in Pennsylvania, Keeler won the Thalheimer entrepreneurship contest. From his inspiration for a backpack design, he formed a company, George Guest, with one of his friends.

> I had to teach myself how to sew on a borrowed neighbor's sewing machine in order to construct a crude prototype to test my design. I took inspiration from the shape of a drawstring bag, but I incorporated my roll-top closure system. The unique thing about this patented design is that it's similar to a roll-top you would see on a waterproof dry bag for kayaking or canoeing, instead of a zipper— you roll it as if you were rolling a paper bag shut. This system keeps water out and is much stronger and more weatherproof than a zipper. It gave my bag a very different feel aesthetically and functionally.
>
> The goal of this system was to gain the weatherproof benefits of a roll-top that was as quick as a zipper. I wanted to design something where you could just roll the top of the bag shut and then use the gravity of the bag to lock it closed. I came up with a system that is closed by pulling a top handle that engages a string system, pulling the ends of the bag shut.

Keeler understands the concept of experience and immersion merging with mental states to produce the aha! moment.

> I'd say that 30 to 40 percent of the ideas I had for this particular product came to me when my mind was clear, my eyes were closed,

and there were no other distractions around me. Many times I'd have trouble falling asleep in my college dorm—you know those nights when you can't sleep because your mind's on something else? This was often the case for me when I was first designing the bag. When I should have been sleeping, all I could think about was . . . how can I solve this, redesign that, or change this? Many of the initial breakthroughs that I had were when I was visualizing a particular detail or problem I was facing with the bag design, while I was lying in bed. When I figured something out, I would hop out of bed and immediately record my ideas. Sometimes when I came up with a solution or a new idea it energized me to the point where falling asleep would be impossible. I had no choice but to get out of bed and continue to flesh out my new idea.

I also had a few breakthroughs in the shower or while driving. I think this had to do with the fact that both of these daily tasks are very habitual and require little to no thought. They are such a normal part of my routine that I don't have to think about what I am doing. Instead I created a 3-D image in my mind of the aspect of the bag I was working on. If you could project these mental prototypes they would look very similar to an Autocad model, except in color. I have never been a huge fan of computer-aided design programs like Autocad because they have too many restrictions. It's a lot easier for me to test a new concept mentally than it is to figure out how to modify something on a computer.

I'm decent at sketching and drawing, but 50 percent of the design process occurs mentally for me. I can picture how I want to construct it, and I'll write down a few notes, and maybe a crude sketch, but the real breakthroughs don't start happening until I'm physically working with my hands. This is when I test my mental prototypes on the materials I plan on using. A lot of the time, an idea may seem like it will work when I first come up with it, but in reality the characteristics of the leather, canvas, etc. are different than how I pictured them. The prototyping process reveals these issues and forces me to rethink, reinvent, and sometimes to start over. This is why only 50 percent of the design process occurs mentally for me. Every other aspect of a new product comes to life during the trial and error process of construction.

When I design new products, like leather belts, bracelets, and other bags, I am not always enthused by the new idea. When I'm thinking about a new way to buckle a belt or a new look for a leather camera strap, I'll mull it over, not overly interested, but the second I get that *snap*, and the solution becomes clear, I'm instantly energized. I then get to my studio as fast as possible, where I can start prototyping. Sometime I'll be in the zone for hours. I'll be up until three in the morning and not even know how long I've been there. Once I get that initial spark, it locks me in and I can't stop.

Helping the process along is, of course, the brain—the seat of emotions, of passion and pleasure. So, let's examine the elements. We all have cells—neurons—that form our nervous system, and they rely on chemicals called neurotransmitters that help the entire physiological system to function properly . . . or not. I want to focus on the neurotransmitter called dopamine. So much happens as a result of this chemical that plays a significant role not just in snapping but also in much of the preparation leading up to these electric aha! moments.

So, how does it work? Dopamine, along with other neurotransmitters like serotonin and melatonin, helps neurons convey information around the brain and from it to other parts of our bodies. In essence, they choreograph the information-processing system. Scientists identified dopamine a century ago, back in 1910, but they've significantly updated their theories about how it works. At first, biologists believed that dopamine played a small role in our feelings or behaviors, that it was merely a helper to more important chemicals. They actually didn't pay much attention to it until the 1950s, when they discovered high levels of dopamine all by itself in areas of the brain where they didn't expect it, particularly in the *nucleus accumbens* in the forebrain. This region fires up whenever people anticipate a reward.

After a few experiments, researchers realized that dopamine played *several* roles in the nervous system, and all of them were pretty significant. For one thing, dopamine affects our memories. It is also involved in how we move around. The more scientists have studied it, the more they have discovered. About thirty years ago, they learned that dopamine influences the quality and intensity of the pleasure we feel, whether falling in love, for example, or anticipating something we really want to do. In other words, dopamine helps make our positive experiences even better. At first, we thought it *caused* pleasure, but recently scientists found that it has a more complex process and is intimately involved whenever we're considering our options.

When we're confronted by novelty, dopamine levels surge, along with those of another neurotransmitter, norepinephrine, triggering the brain's reward system. Thus, we approach with anticipation those behaviors and situations that may feel good, and dopamine in particular provides an edgy high that spurs us to seek that experience again. It also helps us to notice particular stimuli. Thanks to this neurotransmitter, we make a biological investment in life's twists by developing a keen appetite for what's around the bend. Our evolutionary apparatus supports such curiosity.[24]

Dopamine appears to be heavily involved in helping us to focus. That is, when something important happens, the release of dopamine assists us in being alert to new material so we can make sense of it. Thus, novelty stimulates the brain, which then stimulates us into action. Because dopamine is so involved in the thrill of being alive, it is likely implicated in the sense of engagement with something beyond ourselves that accompanies activities that make us learn and grow.

Yet, to keep a certain balance, the brain also adapts. Dopamine keeps track of whether we actually get what we anticipate getting, and its levels increase or decrease accordingly. It's a gauge. It records how we feel when we anticipate something and later compares what we expected against what we got.

Think about an outing or a trip you'd really like to take. When you feel the sensation of pleasure, that's the dopamine. Some people call it the "dopamine rush." It jumps right in—to focus you on what you're hoping for. It measures the pleasure you *expect* to have at your destination. If the actual experience feels as great as you had anticipated, your dopamine levels remain stable: the pleasure is what you'd expected, so your brain thinks that all is well. But if the experience is *not* as great, your dopamine levels drop, leaving you disappointed. Yet on the other hand, if your trip was even *better* than you'd hoped, dopamine levels rise and heighten your mood. *This was so much better than I could have imagined!* So, the quality of your pleasure depends on how well your dopamine gauge functions. It can even inspire you to repeat your experience.

You might also be inspired to act when dopamine levels diminish because you want to avoid the feeling of disappointment and find some way to recoup the pleasure. In addition, research indicates that those people with fewer dopamine receptors in the brain do seek greater levels of stimulation and may thus be vulnerable to addiction or compulsive pleasure seeking.[25]

Recently we've seen experimental evidence that supports what I just described. Here was the setup: We know we can mentally simulate a possible future event. You just did it, right? And you could probably tell me on a scale from one to five how it felt when you imagined your pleasure trip. It's exactly this ability that allows researchers to set up imagination exercises in which they can manipulate the research subjects' dopamine levels. If we're right, higher levels should increase the pleasure when we think about doing something fun-filled.

Some British researchers tested this in four steps: a rating scale, an imagination exercise, a choice between options, and a final rating scale.[26] First, the researchers flashed depictions of eighty vacation spots on a screen, from Hawaii to Greece, and asked subjects to rate on a scale from one to five their expectation of being happy at each place were they to plan a holiday there. Second, the researchers gave the control group a placebo and the experimental group a dopamine enhancer, L-dopa, and asked them all to now *imagine* being at each spot and then rate their level of pleasure.

The following day, the researchers showed each person sets of destinations that were paired according to their own ratings during phase one. In other words, if someone rated Greece the same as Brazil the day before, they now had to *choose* between them. The researchers discovered that those who'd anticipated more pleasure while imagining Greece under L-dopa's influence consistently chose Greece, even though they'd initially viewed this destination without L-dopa as equal with Brazil. But the control group showed no such bias. So dopamine appears to have enhanced the anticipation of pleasure sufficiently to have influenced the final choice.

"We had reason to believe that dopamine would enhance expectations of pleasure in humans," said Dr. Tali Sharot, from the Wellcome Trust Center for Neuroimaging at the University College London Institute, "but were surprised at the strength of the effect. The enhancement lasted at least twenty-four hours and was evident in almost 80 percent of the subjects."[27]

Dr. Shelley Carson, a psychologist affiliated with Harvard University, teaches a course called Creativity: Madmen, Geniuses, and Harvard Students. She has served as a subject matter expert and consultant for the Department of Defense to provide innovative assistance to returning service members. Having studied hundreds of creative individuals, she published *Your Creative Brain*, in which she outlines the CREATES model of brain activation states, or "brainsets," for innovation. CREATES, her shorthand for these brainsets, translates to connect, reason, envision, absorb, transform, evaluate, and stream.[28] Among her findings is that creativity correlates with eccentricity, and that both might be the result of genetic conditions that increase cognitive disinhibition. In other words, they can process a lot of unfiltered information without being overwhelmed, which gives them a greater range for seeing and combining unique associations. "Cognitive disinhibition," she surmises, "is also likely at the heart of what we think of as the aha! experience. During moments of insight, cognitive filters relax momentarily and allow ideas that are on the brain's back burners to leap forward into conscious awareness."[29]

Carson also describes dopamine's role in this process. Citing a Swedish study that used a PET scan to examine the density of dopamine D2 receptors in the subcortical region of the thalamus in fourteen "divergent thinking" subjects, Carson says that they appeared to have a diminished amount of dopamine bindings compared to what is normally found.[30] This condition, Carson believes, might be involved with the decreased cognitive filtering. So, while dopamine plays a role in anticipation and excitement, its part in the information-filtering process might also support a certain type of openness to innovative thinking. Although divergent thinking and focused attention might seem contradictory, having just the right balance between focus that blocks information and focus that allows it might be exactly how an aha! moment is possible. We achieve momentum but also remain open to new connections.

So, what has this to do with snapping? If we look again at the Polgár sisters, we notice how much pleasure they derived from their practice sessions, and in particular from their most engaging challenges. They anticipated with great excitement the idea of participating in tournaments. When they won, they surely felt the dopamine rush. Quite often, the achievement was greater than they had anticipated. Thus, they kept on track, winning honors and titles and taking on even more challenges—except for Sofia, who was not quite as enthralled. But their father emphasized the process of learning over particular accomplishments, which is a good way to trigger dopamine.

People who stay focused on their process grow quite intimate with it over time. They know how it works. They're used to it and can read all the signals. They can sense when they're getting offtrack the way a bloodhound loses a scent. They fully embrace their work, sometimes experiencing more from it than from their relationships with people. Even when engaged in mundane pursuits of daily life, they remain mentally attuned to their projects or goals. Some feel as if they cannot thrive without it. To others, they might seem lonely and solitary, but to them, life feels rich and full of possibility. Thus, at almost any time, they can flash to a strategy that will serve some unexpected purpose.

In the next chapter, we'll return to the subject of memory to more clearly describe how encoding and recoding can assist with snaps. Some of these aha! moments have changed the lives not just of those who had them but of the rest of us as well.

KEY POINTS

- Mastery is not just about innate talent; it can be learned.
- Short-term memory can be exercised via practice for greater utility and endurance.
- People who acquire the skill to snap learn to merge the respective strengths of short- and long-term memory to produce a more muscular working memory.
- As we develop habits, the brain programs itself to support them, which makes these habits easier to maintain.
- Dopamine reinforces the excitement of these moments.

CHAPTER 4

MENTAL HYPERLINKS

JUST DO IT

Tim Berners-Lee built his first computer while he was a student in physics at Oxford. The son of two mathematicians who had worked during the 1950s on the first commercial stored-program computer, he became a software engineer. In 1980, he landed a temporary consulting contract at CERN, the renowned particle physics laboratory in Geneva, Switzerland, that is dedicated to nuclear research. The company had a central control room for its computers, so most employees did not have access to individual terminals. In addition, many of the scientists came there from, or worked in, other countries. Berners-Lee had to work with slow and complicated access to projects and people. Frustrated, he found this to be an unnecessary waste of time, not to mention a hindrance to focused production. So, he flashed on an idea.

He wrote a program, Enquire, to help him remember the connections among all the people, projects, and systems at CERN and its international associates. The name was a brief version of the title of a British book of common sense that Berners-Lee had enjoyed as a boy: *Enquire within upon Everything.*[1] It nicely captured his personal philosophy about information access, and it worked with a simple structure. The program had an internal link among its pages and an external link that allowed him to move between organized files.

Berners-Lee left CERN, giving away his program on an old floppy disc, but in 1984 he returned for a fellowship. He remembered Enquire and sort of wished he had kept it, but now he thought he could devise something better. He started to write a program that he called Tangle. It worked via pattern recognition, but it failed to operate as he'd hoped. Still, he could imagine creating space on his personal computer to digitally connect all CERN computers and allow everyone access to information that others had. He then envisioned making it even bigger than just the CERN environment: he wanted to connect everything to everything else. For him, this was the key to growth and freedom, a way to make society itself mirror the human mind. "There would be a single, global information space."[2] He started re-creating Enquire.

Berners-Lee was aware of ideas from four decades earlier that had described information storage based on associations, and by now other computer programmers had created and used hypertext, which allowed documents to be published in a nonlinear way; users could delve deeper into various areas in an electronic document without having to leave it altogether. For example, "CERN," hypertexted, could open into a full report of its history. In fact, hypertext had allowed Berners-Lee to create Enquire. In addition to this cyberfunction, the Internet linked computers via standard protocols for communication and the transmission of documents, even if people were using different software.

Berners-Lee considered all this. He wanted to bypass the necessity to format documents for compatibility with CERN's main system—especially since so many CERN employees in and from other countries worked on incompatible systems. The challenge for him was not to make everyone correspond to a single system but to create a program that would be flexible enough to work with whatever system other users already had. Berners-Lee wanted to make his own database freely available, as well as gain faster access to the work of other employees. Hypertext seemed the right display medium.

His parents had modeled and nurtured this desire for greater connectivity, especially of making computers work like the mind, and he'd never forgotten this notion. As early as high school, Berners-Lee had been pondering how it could be done. "I wanted the act of adding a new link to be trivial; if it was, then a web of links could spread evenly across the globe."[3] Through addresses that could be easily referenced, documents would all be equivalent.

In 1989, he submitted a proposal to CERN to develop a way to create this information web. No one in authority responded. Undeterred, Berners-Lee went to work. He wrote the Hypertext Transfer Protocol (HTTP) and designed a way to give documents Internet addresses. He called this a Universal Resource Identifier (URI), which would evolve into the Universal Resource Locator (URL) in use today. He added a way for anyone to view and retrieve documents, labeling this interconnectedness the WorldWideWeb. He then formatted pages with his own invention, Hypertext Markup Language (HTML) and created software to store web-based pages (a web server), for access. He was excited. He believed he was on the right track. He presented his idea once more to CERN officials, this time more fully formed and with support from others, but they were slow to recognize its value.

Berners-Lee knew its value. Thus, he went elsewhere. He posted his server and browser on the Internet and let several newsgroups know about it. Computer enthusiasts responded in force, setting up sites to link to his—and some even tried to compete with Berners-Lee by inserting their own products. Soon a global information network began to form. Scientists recognized its usefulness for posting their data, as did university and government groups. Through these highlighted addresses, users were able to jump easily to a new page of information, on their site or on other sites that were connected—even with different operating systems. They could pull together a lot of information in a small space, and do it quickly. It was an idea that opened doors everywhere.

Berners-Lee realized that he had to move this all off his specialized personal computer to something with broader applications. Other people, including CERN colleagues, created new browsers. More information was added to the digital arena, which helped to attract more users. Because Berners-Lee saw the right way to bring two tools together, the World Wide Web was established.[4]

Thousands of people in this same field had been working with the same tools, but *only he* had snapped on the connection. He had a vision and the impetus to create something that would be practical for computer users. He also had the right personality: he shared rather than hoarded it. He wanted to see global connections, not exploit a marketable idea for private gain.

Although Berners-Lee denies in his memoir that he had a eureka experience, everything he describes is in fact consistent with one. He prepared for just such an event. He persisted over several years. He worked at it, mulled over it, played with programs, and then recognized what could be done in a way that had not been done before: "The Web resulted from many influences on my mind, half-formed thoughts, disparate conversations, and seemingly disconnected experiments. I pieced it together as I pursued my regular work and personal life."[5]

As we have seen thus far, this is the foundational formula for snaps. Berners-Lee recognized the power of a weblike organization of information. He even describes the revelation as a breakthrough: "The Web arose as an answer to an open challenge, through the swirling together of influences, ideas, realizations from many sides, until, by the wondrous offices of the human mind, a new concept jelled."[6] With a bit of synchronicity, the right person was in the right place at the right time with the right idea: "I happened to come along with time, and the right interest and inclination, after hypertext and the Internet had come of age. The task left to me was to marry them together."[7]

THE WONDROUS OFFICES OF THE HUMAN MIND

Berners-Lee's story is not just an example of a snap. One of his tools—hypertext—is also a metaphor about what happens when people specialize, focus, and develop expertise. We can build hyperlinks into our memory system by crunching or chunking data into smaller units, as we saw in chapter 3, and the quicker we can access a lot of information in an organized and contained manner, the more prepared we are to evoke epiphanies. "There are billions of neurons in our brains," Berners-Lee wrote, "but what are neurons? Just cells. The brain has no knowledge until connections are made between neurons. All that we know, all that we are, comes from the way our neurons are connected."[8] He made this statement around the time that a team of researchers from Princeton University and MIT were creating "Doogie," the smart mouse, and learning about the cluster-cell structure of human memory. This gives us our next link—hyperlink—in the process of understanding snaps, which bridges the aforementioned chess players with other experts.

First, some basics. Memory involves three recognized processes: encoding, storage, and retrieval. Our brains convert information that comes through our senses via encoding to transform it for storage. We described in chapter 3 how some data get stored for brief periods and some indefinitely. When we want to remember or recall an idea or event, we retrieve the stored information. The quality of a memory depends on the quality of the encoding, as well as on whether there were any interfering factors during either encoding or recall. It also depends on how our senses actually work. What we receive is not an exact replica.

Take the visual system. The eye takes parts of images of what we see that will help the brain make sense of them and ignores whatever seems incidental. It can then make the limited information it has extracted into a seemingly complete picture. When you look at the following message, for example, you can make sense of it:

Aoccdrnig to rscheearch, it deosn't mttaer waht oredr the ltteers in a wrod are, the olny iprmoetnt tihng is taht the frist and lsat ltteres are at the rghit pclae. The rset can be a tatol mses and you can sitll raed it wouthit a porbelm. Tihs is bcuseae we do not raed ervey lteter by itslef but the wrod as a wlohe.

You can also read messages like this when some letters are missing. The brain makes sense of patterns, helped along by what we know.

OK, back to Doogie. Let's get elemental. Neurologist Joe Tsien and his colleagues discovered that to form a memory the brain relies on a population of neurons in the hippocampus that act in concert.[9] The same is true of mice. In 1999, scientists had designed a way to create a strain of "smart mice" that would be engineered for superior memory. To accomplish this, the researchers manipulated a gene that encoded a specific receptor, NDMA, that assists us to make associations between signals from two independent sources. First, they removed the gene and found that the mutant mice failed to learn. Then they gave other mice extra copies of the gene and found that they learned faster. The latter became the "Doogie mice," named after the TV character Doogie Howser, a brainy kid who became a doctor.

When compared with their counterparts in the wild and to the mutants, these genetically engineered Doogie mice seemed able to remember things for longer periods. For example, the mice were allowed to cozy up to two unfamiliar objects for five minutes. Then, after a few trials, one of the objects was switched out and a novel one introduced. Doogies devoted effort to exploring the new object but not to the one they already knew, whereas ordinary and mutant mice devoted equal time to both. Seemingly, unaltered mice had not noticed the switch or remembered the original item.

The mice were then put into a chamber and given mild electrical shocks. They were placed back into this chamber one hour later, one day later, and ten days later. The Doogies showed more fear to the chamber across the board, which suggested that they had formed emotional memories and did not want to go back in.

In a third step, the research team similarly conditioned the mice to be frightened of a chamber and then left them inside without any jolts. When time passed and nothing happened to them, the Doogies calmed down more quickly. They seemed to get it.

But they still had a spatial test to pass. The mice were all dunked into a tank of water with a hidden ramp. After just three dips, the Doogies learned where the ramp was and remembered it. The other mice took twice as long to find it and did not remember its location as well. Even better, in experiments designed to test them as they aged, the Doogies showed greater plasticity. Their brain patterns seemed to remain fairly youthful.

In this early experiment, the scientists deduced that memories arise as the result of two neurons forming a lasting connection.[10] However, they believed that this was not the whole story. They sought the organizing principles, the fundamental neural network dynamic.

A few years later, they designed better equipment to simultaneously monitor the activity of large groups of neurons—well over two hundred at once. They then devised experiments that would cause "flashbulb" memories of dramatic events, the type of memory that seems to remain robust and vivid for a long time. Typically these occur for humans after a dramatic, even traumatic, event. The experiments had to replicate such conditions as closely as possible. There were three conditions.

The mice were placed in a container and shaken to simulate an earthquake experience. Then they had to endure a sudden blast of air on their backs, such as it might feel when an owl attacks. Finally, they had a fun ride into a vertical free fall, to feel like the sudden drop of an elevator. Each mouse, Doogie or otherwise, had to go through seven repetitions of each event, with only a few hours of rest between.

The research team analyzed the resulting data with a mathematical 3-D pattern–recognition program and found "bubbles" of activity associated with four states: the resting brain, the earthquake experience, the air puff, and the elevator drop. They realized that sets of "neural cliques" encoded different aspects of each event. In other words, the brain contained functional coding units, each designed to represent a specific type of information. "The brain relies on memory-coding cliques to record and extract different features of the same event, and it essentially arranges the information relating to a given event into a pyramid whose levels are arranged hierarchically, from the most general, abstract features to the most specific."[11] The brain records key features for here-and-now coping, while also extracting information to apply to a similar future event. Each neural clique coordinates with all the others to form and store a whole memory.

Although this may seem perhaps more fundamental to the aha! experience than we need, it will be useful to understand how the brain's memory system is organized as we get into the neurological research that focuses specifically on the way snaps occur. A robust memory system is an essential part of an equally robust ability to snap.

In addition to the quality of our cellular activity, recall is influenced by what makes sense to us. In an experiment on jury perception in 1992, run by researchers Victoria Holst and Kathy Pezdek, subjects answered questions regarding their beliefs about common scenarios, such as what occurs during a convenience store robbery. Common beliefs proved to be widely shared about how a criminal cases a store, acts inside the store, uses a gun to demand money, and drives away in a getaway vehicle. The second stage of the research was to expose the same subjects to a mock trial of such a robbery. Most of the aspects of a typical script were played out, but some key elements were missing: The robber did not case the store, use a gun, or take money. Nevertheless, when asked after the mock trial to describe what they remembered, the subjects included these very elements. The implication is that prior ideas and beliefs get mixed into actual events when a person is making sense of familiar situations for recall.[12]

Although many people believe that memory is like a video recorder, it is actually constructed from a diverse set of items. One is, obviously, the original experience. However, exposure to new information between storage and retrieval can also affect what is recalled, even if that information contains errors about the original experience.

Consider this experiment for eyewitness research. Subjects were exposed to a film. They then received written information about it, but in the narrative, half were misled about certain details: a critical blue car was described as white, for example, or an intact window was described as broken. Those subjects who were exposed to the errors directly after the screening tended to report the incorrect information rather than what they had actually seen. In fact, error rates for some subjects were as high as 40 percent. Some remembered seeing things they had not seen at all, merely because the written narrative included them.[13]

This is called the *misinformation effect*. When we're exposed to erroneous information after an event, we can make erroneous reports. Worse, this information can become part of our memory for that event. In other words, misleading or new information can supplant our original memory. This effect strengthens with time because the original memory has often eroded.

In one set of studies, subjects shown advertising about Disneyland® that included the image of Bugs Bunny® (who is *not* a Disney® character) resulted in 25–35 percent of people reporting that on their trip to Disneyland they had met Bugs Bunny. After the following was suggested to them during questioning, two-thirds of these subjects recalled shaking his hand and nearly half remembered hugging him. In another experiment, the photographs of subjects, in the company of a relative, were pasted into a prototype photograph of a hot-air balloon. Subjects were shown the faked photo and asked to describe everything they could remember about that "experience." Fifty percent supplied some details, and some embellished it quite a bit.[14]

One might object that such "memories" would feel different than actual memories, but evidence from research fails to support this. Subjects who reported erroneous information from the misinformation effect retrieved the "memory" as quickly as they did an actual memory and felt confident that they had had the experience that they "remembered." Clearly, memory is malleable. We cannot rely on our memories to be accurate, no matter how confident we may be, as research has shown that even confident people have been mistaken.

Human memory can be contaminated, distorted, and re-formed with added details. The more plausible or anticipated those details are, especially if they fill in gaps in a narrative, the more likely it is that they will be integrated into the actual memory. However, it's this very quality of flexibility that assists with the aha! moment.

TAKE CHARGE OF MEMORY

A team of scientists at NASA was working on the Hubble telescope, trying to fix a distortion in the lenses. An optics expert offered a suggestion, but they couldn't figure out how to accomplish it: tiny mirrors would have to be placed in areas that were difficult to reach. They were at an impasse. None of their tools worked. But then one of the engineers, Jim Crocker, was in the shower in a hotel in Germany. Something about the showerhead caught his attention. He paused and looked more closely. The showerhead was mounted on adjustable rods. He knew at once what he'd need to do to solve the problem with the telescope. He could mount the mirrors on adjustable folding arms, just like this showerhead. Taking this back to NASA, he applied his solution.[15]

The leap to sudden insight means a shift in our typical framework. This takes us back to neural networks. Scientists at Heidelberg University in Germany and the Brain Research Centre at the University of British Columbia in Canada were interested in discovering how neural networks function as new strategies replace old ones.[16] Did it occur gradually in the brain, they wondered, or was the transition abrupt?

Computational neuroscientists Daniel Durstewitz and Jeremy Seamans studied the encoding of clusters of neurons (neural cliques) in the medial frontal cortex in rats (no Doogie mice here) as they forced the animals during trial-and-error tasks to deduce novel rules. Within the medial frontal cortex, the visual field and motor area have been implicated in the control of voluntary action during tasks that involve rapid choices between competing demands. In rats, this area appears to be involved in decision making and adjusting to new situations.

Thirteen rats were trained on a simple visual task. They saw two levers, each of which had a light above it. When the light came on, the rat learned that it could now hit the bar below the light to get food. Once the rats could perform this task without error, the researchers introduced a new element. Only one level delivered food, even though both lights continued to come on. To most effectively get the food, the rats had to forget or suppress what they had just learned in order to grasp the new system. "Ah! It's just the one lever."

When each rat figured out the new system, the brain changed, which registered on the computers. The scientists found that unique networks formed in the same neuron population that had activated while performing the familiar task. Cells that had fired weakly before now fired with strength, whereas the strong firings weakened. Even though it took some rats more trials than others to "get" the new rule, the neurons always showed the abrupt transition that corresponded with the new behavior. It appeared that the new information built up and then switched on certain neurons. The researchers thought what they saw resembled a revelation. "In the present problem-solving context where the animal had to infer a new rule by accumulating evidence through trial and error," Durstewitz commented, "such sudden neural and behavioral transitions may correspond to moments of sudden insight."[17]

In other words, as the rats realized what they needed to do to perform this task, they had the rat equivalent of an aha! moment. This means that learning can occur in some cases faster than traditional notions attest. The standard model holds that as we learn, neural pathways are created to support learned items with repeated use while others wither away. But this takes time. Sudden insight is instantaneous. Switching neural tracks might help solve a telescope problem, yield a world-changing invention, or even save lives.

When Captain Chesley "Sully" Sullenberger faced a midair crisis while flying US Airways Flight 1549 in 2009, he had just seconds to act.[18] He had 154 people in his care. He knew he had to save them if he could, but nothing was certain. He was pilot in command of the Airbus A320, which had just left New York's bustling LaGuardia Airport. They were heading to Charlotte, North Carolina. Although it was a clear morning, just two minutes into its flight, at around three thousand feet altitude, the plane encountered a flock of geese. They slapped into the craft, pelting it with so much force it reminded Sullenberger of a Texas hailstorm. He felt the engines vibrate in an alarming way and heard disturbing noises, like a tennis shoe being thrown into a dryer—"only louder." The engines sputtered. Suddenly, both lost thrust, and the plane stopped climbing and went eerily silent. The engines had died. An odor filled the cockpit of burnt birds. Sullenberger had trained for this moment—had even trained other flight crews for such in-air emergencies—and here it was. He could hardly believe it.

He grabbed the stick and said, "My aircraft," meaning he was taking control.

First Officer Jeff Skiles affirmed, as per protocol, "Your aircraft."

Sullenberger knew this situation was his responsibility now, and his father had always taught him to take his duty seriously. Everyone onboard was depending on him. He tried to start the engines, and when this failed, he tried an auxiliary engine. He felt the shift as the plane lost altitude over one of the most densely populated areas in the world.

As Skiles worked on emergency procedures, Sullenberger called in to air traffic control, "Mayday! Mayday! Mayday! Cactus 1549."

He didn't know that the left engine had caught fire, but some of the passengers had noticed. In fact, he had less than three minutes to make the right move. He was already in emergency mode, letting his experience and training dictate his actions. He knew this was a bad situation, but he also believed there was hope. He just needed to keep the plane gliding in a way that allowed the airflow over the wings to provide lift.

In a calm voice, he reported the bird strike and requested an emergency return. The plane continued to glide. Sullenberger and Skiles worked hard to keep it level. Balancing airspeed with gravity was their best strategy against the inevitable descent.

The controller reported that runway 4, the one they'd just used to take off, was open and instructed Sullenberger to turn left. He barely avoided a collision with another plane. Sullenberger wasn't sure he'd make it, so he asked about Teterboro, a small airport in New Jersey. Even as he asked, he knew he'd need more altitude to safely land, so he stated, "We can't do it."

He'd suddenly realized, about one minute after the bird strike, the very real possibility that they might not have enough thrust to make it to *any* airport. Sullenberger felt as if he were in a box that he must escape. His mind blocked out everything except the need to focus on landing the plane. Fortunately, they were over water. He knew it was possible to bring the plane down there, if necessary. In fact, it was their only hope. "We may end up in the Hudson."

The ATC cleared the situation with Teterboro and added that a runway at Newark was available.

"Unable," said Sullenberger. He and Skiles worked to keep control as they barely cleared the George Washington Bridge.

The ATC seemed not to hear. He repeated that runway 1 at Teterboro was ready.

"We can't do it," said Sullenberger. "We're going to be in the Hudson."

He saw below that there was enough room among the boats and barges to take the plane down, as long as they could keep it level and glide over the water. From everything he knew about flying, he realized that he would have to simultaneously perform a number of tricky moves, any of which depended on things going exactly right: he had to touch down with the wings precisely level, the nose up, at a survivable descent, at just the right speed—barely above the minimum needed to fly.

He picked up the intercom and in a restrained tone alerted the passengers, who already knew they were going down, to brace themselves for impact. He heard the flight attendants giving orders to passengers to stay in their seats and keep their heads down. His stomach churned as he felt the plane angle downward, but he suppressed the adrenaline rush. He knew the water would be frigid at this time of year.

He and his copilot focused on the controls as they drew near the water. Aware of planes breaking apart while trying to land in water, they looked for a place to avoid hitting boats but to also be near an area where someone could rescue them. As seconds ticked by, Sullenberger felt confident he could make this work. The plane skimmed the surface, and he felt the impact. It was hard. Water sprayed up on both sides, blinding his view. The plane skidded across the surface for several seconds—as astonished onlookers watched from seacraft and the shore—before it slowed and finally came to a stop. The nose went down, and the plane shifted to the left.

Both pilots breathed out and looked at each other. "That wasn't as bad as I thought," Sullenberger said. They had safely landed in the Hudson River without incident. However, they knew that the plane could fill with water and sink. They still had a job to do.

Everyone went into motion. Sullenberger opened the cockpit door and ordered, "Evacuate!" Skiles and the three female flight attendants assisted the passengers to disembark in an orderly manner. Each person was helped to step out onto the wings of the plane, already under water. They stood there until first responders arrived in boats to assist. The crew was the last to board the boats.

His heart still pounding, Sullenberger walked the aisles of the passenger cabin twice to ensure that everyone was off. He waited until the last crew member was safe before he grabbed the logbook and disembarked. The passengers later lauded him for his poise and sense of control during the crisis. As the news spread, airline pilots around the world marveled at this near-miraculous feat and hailed the crew as heroes.

In numerous interviews, Sullenberger praised his crew and attributed his fast but controlled response to years of training and experience. "We train all the time for emergencies," he said. He viewed the experiences he'd had and the skills he'd honed as a lifelong preparation for this very moment. "One way of looking at this might be that for 42 years I've been making small, regular deposits in this bank of experience: education and training. And on January 15, the balance was sufficient so that I could make a very large withdrawal."[19]

He was right. Because his brain had developed strong neural pathways via discipline and constant exposure, Sullenberger's working memory was sufficiently agile and connected to what he knew to grab the stored information in a split second. This same combination operates in the incubation of a creative snap.

So, let's pull together the different elements of a snap that we can see in this incident. As a boy, Sullenberger had been keenly fascinated with planes. He'd seen military jets take off at Perrin Air Force Base near his home in Texas, which had inspired him to build model airplanes.[20] He certainly had the intelligence to pursue a career that required a good memory and a sense of detail. By the age of twelve, Sullenberger was a member of the renowned genius organization Mensa International. When he was sixteen, he learned to fly. Sullenberger had realized his "bliss" early and had eagerly pursued it. After high school, he enrolled in the United States Air Force Academy and was selected for a cadet glider program. Within a year, he was an instructor pilot and on graduation received an award as an outstanding cadet. He was also the top flier of his class. As an officer, he attended Purdue University, achieving a master's degree in industrial psychology. For five years he was a fighter pilot before becoming a training officer and accident investigator. After leaving the air force, Sullenberger became a commercial airline pilot. By the time of the incident over the Hudson, he had some forty years and 27,000 hours of flying experience. He had also run a consulting business in airline safety. As he put it, he had placed deposits into his memory bank (template) throughout his entire life. This had developed and strengthened the neural cliques and specifically prepared him for emergencies. When he faced one, he was ready, and because the necessary acts were now second nature, his mental template took over to guide him.

KEY POINTS

- To get the most from our working memory we must keep stretching it.
- A more elastic working memory provides a base from which to launch creative insights.
- Expanding ordinary memory capacity for faster access to more information, such as hyperlinks on the web, involves specific types of practice.
- Memory templates absorb deposits from our efforts and experience, preparing to assist us to snap.

CHAPTER 5

THE BRAIN'S BIG BANG

THE KIRK EFFECT

Martin Cooper sat outside on his patio, enjoying a nice day, when the phone rang inside. Annoyed, he got up to answer it. Typical of the late 1960s, the phone was attached to a wall, with the listening and speaking mechanism corded to the phone's body. As a chief engineer at Motorola and general manager of its Communication Systems Division, Cooper believed that phones should be as mobile as people were. Thus, there should be a way to carry a phone from place to place without all the cords. In other words, he shouldn't have to interrupt a pleasant time outside to get up and answer a phone. Get rid of the wires! He'd been working on it, but he just wasn't there yet.

The concept of wireless transmission got its foot through the door in the 1930s from the crude mobile radio phones used in police cars. The first public mobile phone call made from a car occurred in Saint Louis, Missouri, in 1946. However, the primitive wireless networks of that era—basically, one central tower (antenna) per city—handled only a limited volume of calls. Each mobile phone had to stay within the cell area serviced by its base station, so there was no range or continuity. In addition, the phones required powerful, clunky transmitters.

In an effort to refine the technology, AT&T Bell Labs employee

D. H. Ring (yes, really) conceived of sending phone calls through a series of grids rather than a single tower. Each would use low-power transmitters that would hand off calls from one cell to another. Thus, many calls could use the same frequency simultaneously, and each call could travel much farther. It was a great idea, but the technology for it did not yet exist. AT&T executives asked the Federal Communications Commission to allocate more radio-spectrum frequencies so they could expand their customer base and get funds for research and development. But the FCC gave little ground, so the status of mobile communication remained as it was until 1968. That year, the agency finally increased the frequency allocation.

In keeping with Ring's idea, AT&T began building cell towers with radio transceivers and base station controllers for handling a larger volume of calls. This would allow mobile phone transmissions to move through several cell areas during a single conversation. The competition heated up to invent a truly mobile phone that could exploit the technology.

At Bell Labs, Richard Frenkiel and Joel Engel ran this project, but at Motorola, Cooper was also at work. He thought that AT&T had it wrong. Those scientists and engineers were hoping to design better car phones, while he wanted a phone so portable that people could carry it on their person. He knew how it should work, but the necessary parts would require a suitcase.

There was no sense of quitting in this Chicago-born executive. Computers had gotten smaller over the past decade, and he knew that phones could as well. They could also be easier to use.

Even as a child, Cooper had been an inventor. When he was only eight, he'd envisioned "magnetic propulsion," so that trains could levitate over roadways. However, he soon realized that it's one thing to envision a neat idea; it's quite another to make it happen. Thanks to teachers who encouraged him, he read voraciously and went to college for an engineering degree. After a four-year stint during the Korean conflict as a submarine officer, Cooper went to work for Motorola. It was not long before he was directing others to help transform ideas into products. A well-designed mobile phone was among them.

One day during this period, Cooper was watching television. He enjoyed the popular science fiction series *Star Trek*, which gave its characters all manner of "impossible" items, from teleportation systems to spacecraft that zipped through the universe with ease. Cooper watched "Captain Kirk" flip open his handheld communicator and give an order to one of his crew. Suddenly, Cooper sat up. He'd seen it many times, and yet *now* he really noticed. That's what he wanted! A portable device you could carry around in a pocket or purse, flip open, and talk to whomever you wanted, no matter where they were. In particular, he wanted a voice-controlled device. Cooper knew what he needed: an antenna and a series of integrated circuits that could transform voices into readable data, all inside a very portable package.[1]

In order to work, cell phones have codes that identify the phone, the service provider, and the phone's owner. The phone makes or receives calls through a special frequency via its home system. As the caller moves toward the edge of a cell, two base stations coordinate to hand off the call to the next cell. Motorola ran a contest among five different industrial designers, and Cooper picked the simplest design from among them. It was christened the DynaTAC. However, with hundreds of parts, this device was far from Captain Kirk's handheld flip-phone. It was more like a brick with an antenna sticking out, and the caller still needed to program it by hand. But it was a good start on the world's first portable cordless cellular phone. Motorola employees tested it in-house, using the cell towers that AT&T had already prepared. Finally, it was time to go public.

On April 3, 1973, Cooper walked down the street in New York City with the DynaTAC pressed to his ear. He enjoyed how people gaped at him, and he thought he probably looked like something out of *Star Trek*. All the better. He punched in a number and made the first public cellular call, bouncing off the city's transmission towers until it rang . . . in the office of Joel Engel at Bell Labs. Cooper just had to gloat.

Then, as he crossed a busy street, he placed a call to a radio reporter to make public the fact that he and his cronies had been the first to shift the communications market: "The most important thing we did back in 1973," Cooper says, "was to prove that a telephone number should not be a location like a house or a business but rather that a telephone number should represent a person."[2] The cell phone's inventors had relied on inspiration, immersion, genius, and the persistence to achieve a vision. "It's great to let your mind run free," Cooper advises, "to think of new ideas, new ways of doing things, to daydream. But an inventor needs a foundation of science or engineering, of education to make these dreams come true. An inventor needs imagination *and* practical knowledge."[3]

It took another ten years and a considerable drop in price before cell phones became more consumer-friendly. By the late 1980s, there were more than a million US subscribers. By this time, the cell phone had lost weight, going from forty ounces to less than one-tenth of that. Today, there are over a billion in use around the world—many of which respond to a voice command, just as Cooper had envisioned—and they contain cameras, MP3 players, and tiny computers with multiple applications. Captain Kirk would have been jealous.

SWITCHING ON

The flash that explodes as a snap originates in the brain's right hemisphere, the area of the brain that picks out metaphors, nuances, and emotions. The left hemisphere gets to analyze facts and abstract language. It's not quite equipped for the excitement of a snap. That's good news for neuroscientists; because the electrical activity involved in an insight feels distinctly different from analytical A-to-Z reasoning, researchers can—and have—set up conditions to measure and compare them.

Jerome Swartz and his colleagues at New York's Swartz Foundation and California's Swartz Center for Computational Neuroscience say that relevant information might come from either the external world or from the brain.[4] What brings the snap insight from the tip of the tongue to the top of the mind is the selective triggering of well-formed stimuli. For example, you might come to an impasse while at work on a crossword puzzle. At some point prior to this, you had walked through a market that contained the correct answer. At another point, what you had observed will converge with your impasse and *bang!* You have the answer. It seems to have arrived from out of the blue, but it didn't. You've been primed, and once the brain has had time to associate the stimuli from your mental accumulation, it delivers.

Also testing this notion, Bhavin Sheth at the University of Houston, Simone Sandkuhler at the Austrian Academy of Sciences, and Joydeep Bhattacharya of London's Goldsmiths College devised a set of problems that they believed would provoke insight.[5] Such problems had to be simple but not widely known, such as one might find on a brain-teaser website. They could not lend themselves to a methodical solution. One was the following:

> You enter a two-story house. On the ground floor is a set of three light switches. Two do not work, but one illuminates an old-fashioned lightbulb on the second floor that is invisible to you from downstairs. When you enter, this light is off. Your task is to figure out which light switch turns it on. You may flip the switches as much as you want, but you may only go up to the second floor once. Under these conditions, how might you determine which switch controls the second-floor light?

Eighteen participants, connected to an electroencephalograph (EEG), had ninety seconds to solve this puzzle (after thirty seconds to read it). If they gave up, they received a hint: turn one switch on and leave it for a while. (The solution is to turn on switch A for several minutes. Then switch it off and turn on B. Then immediately go upstairs. If the light is on, switch B turned it on. If the light is not on, feel the bulb. If it is hot, then switch A turned it on. If it is cold, switch C will turn it on.)

Because the problem required both speed and concentration, the scientists reasoned that the solution for those who solved it would likely pop as a sudden insight. The EEG readings confirmed this. They showed different results between those who solved the problem and those who could not. And better yet, just a second or two before the reported insight occurred, there appeared to be consistently identifiable brainwave activity. More interesting, the EEG readings allowed researchers to predict an aha! moment up to eight seconds in advance, because increased activity in the right frontal cortex—associated with shifting mental states—announced it. These researchers also found that a positive mood assists insight.

In a related study, the researchers gave twenty-one subjects three words, such as *head*, *shade*, and *post*. They were to think of one word (*lamp*) that would make a compound word with all three, while hooked to an EEG monitor. Mental blocks correlated with high gamma activity in the parietal cortex, which is associated with selective attention. For those subjects with the highest gamma readings, even clues failed to move them toward a solution, suggesting that a mental fixation can block insight. They were mentally clenched, like a fist. Those who experienced sudden insight showed a drop in gamma activity levels just before they reported the insight, but there was no such drop during conventional problem-solving strategy. Theta waves, which assist the brain to encode new information, increased before an aha! moment. The researchers believed that the brain was forming new associations from whatever information it had.[6]

In an experiment that also relied on verbal associations, researchers Mark Jung-Beeman (Northwestern University) and John Kounios (Drexel University) monitored the brains of participants solving insight-inspiring problems. They had already learned that the brain functions differently during a flash of insight than during ordinary methodical processing. This time they were to bring together a number of different angles to try to spot just when the brain begins to generate the aha! moment.

First, prior to starting the experiment, they examined each participant's baseline neural activity. To monitor activity-related neural events, they had subjects press buttons to indicate their thought processes: one for when they started solving a problem, and the second for arriving at a solution. If they did get there, they chose from two more options: (1) normal reasoning or (2) a sudden insight. Nineteen subjects were hooked up to an EEG while working on 186 timed problems. Twenty-five received 135 timed problems while functional magnetic resonance imaging (fMRI) measured blood flow in their brains. So, two buttons were designated for the processing, two for the solution type, and two methods were applied for measuring physiological responses.

The research relied on a process called *comparative remote association*. A problem consisted of three words, and subjects had to come up with a single word that would form a common compound with all three. For example, they were shown *tank*, *hill*, and *secret*, and the answer was *top*. The EEG participants solved about 46 percent of the problems, labeling 56 percent of their solutions as sudden insight. The fMRI participants solved 47 percent of the problems correctly, with an insight 56 percent of the time.

The physiological measures revealed that about one-third of a second before an insight occurred, some left-brain areas showed decreased activity while high-frequency brainwaves increased in parts of the right temporal lobe: the anterior cingulate cortex (ACC), posterior cingulate cortex (PCC), and the anterior superior temporal gyri (STG). In these areas, new associations form or attention is reoriented. The fMRI results confirmed the EEG results, and the EEG added one more thing: about 1.5 seconds before insight, there was an increase in lower-frequency brainwaves. This disappeared just as the high-frequency waves spiked. In contrast, little activity was found in these areas during non-insight solutions.[7]

Something was definitely happening in the right temporal lobe, just before and during the experience of insight. It's possible, the scientists surmised, that the right hemisphere has access to more brain resources for insight because its dendrites are longer, denser, and more broadly connected around the brain than those in the left. Perhaps it took some time to reach the more remote areas. They thought that the lower frequency activity that showed up 1.5 seconds prior to insight acted as a "gating effect," packing energy for a spurt of momentum at the threshold of insight. "This is like closing your eyes so you can concentrate when you are trying to solve a difficult problem," said Kounios.[8]

An intriguing development was that a subject's preparatory brain state prior to tackling a problem appeared to influence whether it would be solved with insight or with analytical processing. Although no personality tests were administered to these participants, this finding might be related to the difference between a mindfully engaged person, ready for action, and one who's just following directions. It appeared that the brain controlled whether a solution would derive from methodical thinking or from sudden insight. This suggested that people who are at work on something can prepare for an insight by focusing attention inward to reduce visual input and silence irrelevant thoughts. This approach may set up conditions for the brain to do its best work. "At a certain point," Jung-Beeman remarked, "you just have to admit that your brain knows more than you do."[9]

Researchers suspect that problem solving by insight demands a great deal of cognitive energy. In that case, it might be restricted to special needs rather than those used for daily calculations. We might think of the left brain as the plodder and the right as the sprinter. When left-brain cognition reaches an intense impasse, neural mechanisms in the right hemisphere can take over. The need arises, the energy gathers, the brain redistributes its resources, and if the person is receptive, the insight flashes.

In short: for the aha! moment, the relaxed (unclenched) mind can wander into uncharted territory to spark remote associations in the creative parts. It searches beyond known databases into hidden resources. Since you're not actively calculating, it might feel as if you're no longer working on the problem. You might think you've reached the end of your rope and simply cannot come up with the solution. You might even doubt your abilities. But on its own, the brain is still working for you. People who learn to work *with* this neurological quirk can make amazing discoveries.

LIGHTNING STRIKES

When James Watson and Francis Crick outlined the double-helix structure of deoxyribonucleic acid (DNA) in 1953, Kary Mullis was just getting curious about science. Like other eight-year-old boys of this era, he'd received chemistry sets for Christmas and liked to make things explode. By his teenage years, he was trying to launch mini rockets with his own concoction of potassium nitrate and sugar. "We could buy dynamite fuses from the hardware store," he said, "with no questions asked."[10] Most of these rockets sputtered out, but "after many experiments and much thought, I came upon a nice little engine that built up enough thrust to move itself."[11] Mullis also blew a frog high into the air and got it back alive. And yet, despite his scientific bent, he said in an autobiography—penned for an esteemed committee—that he'd once seen the ghost of his deceased grandfather. By this time, the consummate surfer had won fame far beyond what might be expected of the son of a general store manager from the Blue Ridge Mountains. He'd also won a Nobel Prize, the result of blending the right ingredients for another explosion—this one in his head.

When Mullis was a precocious grad student in biochemistry at the University of California at Berkeley, he possessed a "creative nonconformity that verges on the lunatic."[12] To his mind, a science lab "is just another place to play," and an intellectual frolic is the secret source of genius. Despite his apparent penchant for chaos, he appreciated elegance. Thus, he was initially disinclined to focus on DNA. While at work on his PhD, Mullis found the structure of DNA disturbingly clumsy in the way it "spirals off without limits and only ends because it gets broken or because it spontaneously terminates out of a morbid fear of being endless."[13]

Nevertheless, after a stint with pharmaceutical chemistry in which he found DNA's cloning potential to be wondrous, Mullis sought closer encounters with the molecule when he went to work in 1979 for Cetus, a biotechnology corporation. Scientists around the world at this time were struggling to get past the molecular "junk" attached to DNA so they could analyze pure segments. To that point, no one had succeeded.

Decades earlier, Phoebus Levene had discovered that the nucleus of individual cells contains two types of acid: ribonucleic (RNA) and deoxyribonucleic (DNA). Within each cell are twenty-three pairs of chromosomes made of DNA, which transfers the unique "instructions" from our parents for how each of us will look, among other things. Each DNA molecule contains four chemicals units: adenine (A), guanine (G), cytosine (C), and thymine (T). When strung together in paired chromosomal strands (the double helix), A always aligns with T, G with C, and so on. This has the appearance of a twisted ladder, with the strands as the sides and the alternating pairs as rungs. Inside the cell, DNA coils tightly, but when unrolled a DNA molecule is approximately six feet long. Although some parts of our DNA are universally human (species-specific), certain sections contain the codes that correspond to our unique assets, and every cell of our bodies mirrors this alignment. The base pairs in these polymorphic regions are called Variable Number of Tandem Repeats, and they provide the possibility for genetic identification. To an astronomical degree of probability, experts can determine whether a particular strand of DNA from a biological sample matches the DNA of a particular person.

A polymerase is a naturally occurring enzyme that ensures the formation and repair of DNA, which in turn ensures the accurate replication of all living matter. Scientists had worked hard over past decades to understand this process and control it. "Like a FIND sequence in a computer search," Mullis explains, "a short string of nucleotides in a synthetic molecule might be able to define a position."[14] They just had to find a place to start in the midst of the tangled DNA tape.

Mullis began to experiment with oligonucleotides and DNA polymerase, but he kept bumping his head against the wall of DNA's complexity. "What I needed to make this work," he said in his Nobel speech, "was some method of raising the relative concentration of the specific site of interest."[15] In other words, he needed a way to enlarge his biological workspace. "I kept thinking about my experiment without realizing that it would never work."[16] Thus, he was at an impasse.

He pondered this problem as he drove along a highway in Mendocino County one Friday evening in the spring of 1984. Mullis and his girlfriend were heading to a cabin he was building in Northern California. She was asleep in the passenger seat, leaving him alone with his thoughts. "My hand felt the road and the turns, my mind drifted back to the lab. DNA chains coiled and floated. I see the lights on the trees, but most of me is watching something else unfolding."[17] He casually glanced at the blossoming buckeye stalks along the road, breathing in their oily aroma. Then: aha! In that instant, he knew what he had to do. Mullis stopped the car right there in the middle of the road, at marker 46,7 on Highway 128. His girlfriend awoke, confused, but he couldn't talk. "I was just driving and thinking about ideas and suddenly I saw it," he recalls. "I saw the polymerase chain reaction as clear as if it were up on a blackboard in my head, so I pulled over and started scribbling."[18] He broke the pencil lead, so he scrambled for a pen. He knew he was on the verge of something big. His snap offered an efficient method of getting at a pure DNA fragment.

He could still smell the buckeyes, but just barely, as sensory input receded in favor of his fervent mental activity. He started driving again, and again pulled over as his head exploded with the realization that he had solved the "most annoying" problem in DNA chemistry. In a series of flashes in just moments, Mullis envisioned polymerizing the junk parts of DNA and stringing them all together so they could be swept aside. He could then apply the same process to the denatured DNA. In short, he'd conceived of a way to start and stop a polymerase's action at specific points along a single strand of DNA. He could also initiate the creation of complementary new strands. By harnessing molecular-reproduction technology, the target DNA could be amplified—and many, many more copies could be made.

But he wasn't sure. He thought getting the answer had been too easy. He kept pestering his girlfriend throughout the weekend as he drew diagrams all over the cabin and kept coming back to the same thing: his vision while driving. But he wanted someone else to affirm it, or else to tell him he was crazy. He couldn't sleep. He was in the grip of the flow of his inspiration. Even when some mundane task pulled him away, he was able to pick right up with his mental process where he'd left off. He was in a state of total absorption, which felt to him like semiconsciousness. Uncharacteristically, he could hardly wait to get back to work in the lab.

But no one at Cetus was quite as excited. Disappointed, Mullis shrugged off the lack of support and examined the research. He found no evidence that someone else had tried this idea and failed. None of his colleagues could recall someone who might have done it, although every isolated step in the process had been performed in other contexts. "It was not easy in the post-cloning, pre-PCR year to accept the fact that you could have all the DNA you wanted," Mullis stated, "and that it would be easy."[19]

He continued talking to other molecular biologists, and in September, several months post-snap, he tried his first actual experiment. One evening, he put human DNA and the nerve growth factor primers into a tube. He boiled this concoction for several minutes, cooled it, and added ten units of DNA polymerase. Then he sealed the tube and left it at 37 degrees. He recalls that it was exactly midnight. He was heating the extracted DNA in a thermocycler to make it split, and each time the temperature decreased and increased, it produced a copy. The process repeated multiple times, with chemicals added to locate specific regions of the DNA.

The next day, an impatient Mullis checked his results and was gratified to see partial success. He was on the right track. Over the next three months, he refined his methods, and on December 16, he finally produced a successful batch. With this, he knew he had changed the rules in molecular biology.

Mullis showed his colleagues his results and convinced Cetus to get this technology into gear. Once the scientists had succeeded in making the polymerase chain reaction reliable, they realized they had an immensely powerful technique for providing unlimited quantities of the genetic material that molecular biologists required for their work. In a matter of hours, the target sequence could be amplified a billion-fold. It was a discovery that would reverberate in so many important ways.

Cetus eventually sold the patent for PCR to Hoffman-LaRoche for a staggering $300 million—the most money ever paid for a patent. In 1993, Mullis won the Nobel Prize in chemistry and the prestigious Japan Prize. (The next year, he waited in the wings to provide expert testimony for the defense in the O. J. Simpson double homicide trial.)

In less than a decade, PCR became simultaneously a routine component of practically every molecular biology laboratory and a versatile tool with as-yet-unknown potential. The process expanded to more than 130 US patents. PCR can sequence a disease, help identify the perpetrator of a crime, or trace a lineage. It has also become the basis of paleobiology, due to its ability to amplify DNA from fossils, and in the future it will solve other biological mysteries. On *Nightline*, Ted Koppel announced, "Take all the MVPs from professional baseball, basketball and football. Throw in your dozen favorite movie stars and a half dozen rock stars for good measure.

Add all the television anchor people now on the air, and collectively they have not affected the current good or the future welfare of mankind as much as Kary Mullis."[20]

Mullis's immersion in DNA research had paid off, but it was the soothing drive on that California highway on which he pondered his work in a relaxed mental state that had let it gel. On that evening, Mullis had been in "flow."

FULLY ABSORBED

Imagine being occupied in an activity that you fully enjoy: drumming, sailing, rock climbing, writing a song, or building a shed. You have the right equipment, and you can devote at least an hour or so to the activity. Your full attention is on the project, and you know the rules. You're there, doing it, because you enjoy it. As time passes, you become more fully engaged, concentrating deeply. You feel terrific.

A positive mood makes an insight more likely to occur, and the experience of flow is among our most vital mood-heightening experiences. Sports figures call it "the groove" or "being in the zone," while psychologists identify it as the central component of peak performance. This is better known as "flow," the experience of complete absorption in a given activity that produces a sense of effortless concentration. It could happen during a game of tennis, while performing neurosurgery, or in the midst of preparing a gourmet meal. It could arise from an intense business negotiation or from making a dress. Whatever it is, the moment is exciting and alive. Time stands still, and we're less aware of our external environment. Music might be playing, people talking, machines clicking, or motors running, but we remain attuned to the activity at hand.

The concept of flow has been closely linked to a deep state of Zen-like meditation. A central tenet is the idea of "oneness," which means being inseparable from the essence of what you are doing. Thus, you work or play without hindrance. Flow is about our best functioning as individuals—we find our niche and do it so well that we feel fully satisfied and successful. The work we do during flow feels like *quality* work, and we believe that our time is well spent. Thus, it complements discovering our bliss, Aristotle's entelechy.

Psychologist Mihaly Csikszentmihalyi is commonly called the architect of the experience of flow, because he articulated its dimensions. He initially studied flow with surgeons, artists, and mountain climbers who had reported great joy from complete immersion in what they were doing. He then expanded his work to other areas. Arriving in the United States from Fiume, Italy, at the age of twenty-two, Csikszentmihalyi attended the University of Chicago, where he acquired his undergraduate and graduate degrees. He remained there to teach and eventually became chair of the Psychology Department. Now considered one of the foremost spokespeople for Positive Psychology, his primary areas of interest center on creativity, happiness, and flow.

Csikszentmihalyi discovered that flow arises from within a single-minded purpose or motivation, which produces a joyful alignment between ourselves and our achievements. It's an organic process in which personal desire and behavior come together in a feeling of achievement. In an interview with *Wired* magazine, Csikszentmihalyi described flow as "being completely involved in an activity for its own sake. The ego falls away. Time flies. Every action, movement, and thought follows inevitably from the previous one, like playing jazz. Your whole being is involved, and you're using your skills to the utmost."[21]

People have described the experience as being in a current that carries them along—flow! They report feeling "most alive" or "at full throttle"—a sense of having been transported into a new and sharper reality. As flow sets in, the pace increases as the rhythm picks up. There's greater fluidity as perception, imagination, and manual operations function at a higher than normal level. Thought and motion seem perfectly integrated as focus narrows.

Flow may be experienced in a single time frame, or may arch

over a period of time that is also punctuated by non-flow events. A machinist described how he was able to come back to work each day and pick up with a project where he'd left off, getting back into this heightened performance almost immediately. "The experience is like day-dreaming," he said, "only my body had stopped working."[22] Kary Mullis described the same thing: it was as if the flow of his idea was still there, even if he interrupted it to drive or work on his cabin.

Flow arises as mental energy before it deepens into heightened performance and a trancelike state. Best-selling writer Dean Koontz has experienced it. He had spent the early part of his career writing just about anything to keep ahead of the bills. As he became more established and successful, he could spend more time developing plots and characters and deepening his structure. The more he wrote, the more he knew he was born to write, and the better at it he got. For him, finding his bliss paid off, and finally he was able to relax. As he did so, he developed a rhythm that offered him an unexpected bonus.

One day he was writing his novel *Watchers*, which features a dog with artificially developed human intelligence. Initially, Koontz had found this tale to be difficult to write, and he took eight months to complete the first two-thirds to his satisfaction. As he took up the last third, however, he had gained a clear sense of direction coupled with a feeling of control and spontaneity. It was then that he had an incredible experience, as the pages seemed to write themselves. "It just flew," he said. He began to write fast and did not stop, save for one break, for two days. "I got up one morning and went to work. I ate a sandwich at my desk, kept going, worked around the clock, and finally fell into bed the next evening, totally exhausted. I slept that night, and the next morning got up and worked twenty-four hours straight. In the first session, which was about thirty-six hours, I wrote something like forty pages. In the second session, I wrote around forty pages in even less time. That's about thirty thousand words in two sessions, and it needed almost no revision."[23]

When the state of flow recedes, reorientation brings an aware-ness of being hungry or cold or stiff. You're surprised at how much time has passed. It's almost as if you've been channeling some highly creative spirit. You may be delighted by all that you've accom-plished—and possibly you won't even remember much of what you did during the time of flow. You have worked with a sense of pur-pose, as well as an instinct for how to achieve that purpose. It's an organic process, beginning inside, in which personal desire and behavior come together to flow into a sense of achievement; it pro-duces a sort of pride in ownership. It's about craftsmanship—caring about what you're doing—as opposed to just working at something. Csikszentmihalyi went on to study this phenomenon with specific groups of people who had reported feelings of great joy from com-plete immersion in what they were doing. He then expanded his work to other areas, including creativity.

"Action follows upon action," he stated, "according to an internal logic that seems to need no conscious intervention by the actor. He experiences it as a unified flowing from one moment to the next, in which he is in control of his actions, and in which there is little distinction between self and environment, between stimulus and response, or between past, present, and future."[24]

To study people in flow, Csikszentmihalyi gave his assessment device, the Experience Sampling Method, to several thousand par-ticipants. All received a pager that went off at random times within a two-hour segment of their day, and all were shown how to rate their experience on a scale. Whenever the pager buzzed, they were to write down in a journal what they were doing and thinking, where they were, who they were with, and what rating they would give their present emotional state.

The results indicated that the state of flow occurred most often when people were doing their favorite activities but three times more often during work than during leisure. It also occurred while driving and talking to others, but not during passive activities. The activity that produced flow most often had clear goals, opportunities for concentration, experiential feedback, and rules of performance. People who read books reported it more often than people who watched television. People who were depressed, fatigued, or bored did not report any flow experience. "Each of the flow-producing activities," Csikszentmihalyi concluded, "requires an initial investment of attention before it begins to be enjoyable."[25]

The surprise is this: while we think that flow occurs spontaneously, it can actually be harnessed into a regular experience. People who control their inner experience, Csikszentmihalyi claims, can determine the quality of their lives. To make it happen, we should seek a challenge that stimulates our perceived level of skill, because it would keep us interested in a given task. However, the challenge must be manageable. If it's weak, it's not stimulating. If too hard, it's anxiety provoking or demoralizing. (One group of researchers found that only those employees with a high need for achievement found the combination of high skill/high challenge to be flow producing; unmotivated employees apparently did well enough with low challenge but did not report task interest or work reward.) As we see with Martin Cooper and Kary Mullis, challenges that feel reachable encourage us to develop new skills and think in fresh ways. And this is where brainstorms occur.

Achievement-oriented employees reported not only a more positive mood and greater task interest than other employees; they also showed greater organizational spontaneity. They were more creative when it counted: they looked for ways to improve the effectiveness of their work, made constructive suggestions to improve overall work environment, offered creative suggestions for company objectives, and encouraged other employees to be innovative. People who were able to turn dull jobs into something of a game or to ponder novel improvements described more experiences of flow.

Housewife-turned-entrepreneur Joy Mangano is an example. She'd been envisioning products to improve her daily experience since she was a teenager. She'd once thought up a luminescent dog collar to help owners see their dogs at night, but then watched in disappointment as a pet company put a similar idea into production. She vowed to find ways to make her ideas a reality. Yet as a divorced single mother of three, she was struggling just to pay the rent. Until she could dig out, she had to be content to keep her projects small. Still, she kept spinning ideas, reinventing daily products in her mind. Then one day in 1989, during a waitressing stint, Mangano was engaged in the nasty business of wringing dirty water from a rag mop. As she concentrated on her task, she suddenly envisioned a very different type of mop, one that would keep her hands clean: "It came to me," she says. "A self-wringing mop." She could see exactly how it should be designed and, more important, how superior it was to what was currently available—and what she was using that day. She got investment money and created the Miracle Mop® prototype, which became a hit on a home-shopping program. Inspired by her ability to snap on ideas, and with her new financial grounding, Mangano established a company, Ingenious Designs. Currently, she holds patents and trademarks for over one hundred products.[26]

Csikszentmihalyi believes that focus can become a habit—and can be improved—to better the quality of our lives. He is talking about "mindfulness," the practice of being present and attuned, even vigilant, no matter what one might be doing. He suggests keeping a diary to take stock of our day and learn about the influence on our moods of various things we encounter, so that we make awareness a habit. When we see which activities produce the high points, we can experiment by increasing the frequency of the positive encounters.

Innovators like Cooper, Mullis, and Mangano care about making their time count. They prioritize, organize, and figure out how best to achieve their goals. They protect their mental energy and let it play where it will be most effective. Developing a sense of serious playfulness, their focus is clear, and they remain alert to how life's clues appear for their advantage.

In terms of human consciousness, flow operates at the deepest level of conscious awareness, where it seems to merge with trancelike conditions. To better understand this, we need to see how each level of consciousness and focus functions in our lives.

The first level—day-to-day consciousness—provides the background for everything we do. Sit quietly for a moment and then pick something—a chair, a lamp, or a framed photograph—on which to focus. Notice how the background recedes to allow you to see the item. Now refocus on just the backdrop and notice how the item blurs. The point is, focusing helps us to get a defined perception. *Not* focusing gives us only a blur. We do need background to see a figure, but we would hope for more in our daily lives than just this monotone as a backdrop.

The second level occurs when we pay attention. Since we cannot perceive everything at once with the same level of awareness (we'd soon be overwhelmed), we tend to move to the second level only when we need to. For example, we concentrate on one specific building on a city block only when we have business there. Or we concentrate on reading a stop sign or yield sign while driving, attending to the specific lyrics of a song, or sniffing an odor before we step into a room. We notice that one manhole is different from the next one down the street, or that a counselor is saying just what we need to hear. We might also be pulled into the second level of awareness when startled, such as hearing a car run into something, awakening to a noise in the night, or having a toothache.

When we pay attention voluntarily, this is "top–down" attention. When something draws our attention, it's "bottom–up." The second level involves varying degrees of attention, on a continuum from passive interest to mildly attentive to full consciousness. We are more engaged than at the first level, although unless we exercise this focus, we may derive only short-term benefits. As we develop a defined or vigilant awareness, we notice more things. We become more attuned to the immediate world. Small details take on more meaning.

Think of it as seeing a female friend in a crowd of people. This person stands out because of what she means to you. Active, or top–down, perception means you grow more alert to *looking* for a friend in a crowd. What turns one thing rather than another from background into figure is the attention we pay—the significance we attribute to it. We become more mindful as a habit. We look *and* we see. The *habit* of focus keeps us awake and alert.

Dino Zaharakis, just eleven years old, liked to invent things. He noticed something awkward about a stand his father had rigged for a new iPad® and believed he could create a better one. After several trials, he came up with a device that he called the dzdock®. His father helped him create a prototype and set up a website to market it. They founded a company to produce them, and from Dino's alert eye, a new business was born.[27]

The third level of consciousness makes the art of focus more a part of us. We move from energy and excitement into periods of quiet joy. Flow stretches people beyond their perceived limits. It bonds them with the activity, yielding both stamina and euphoria. "Flow," wrote Csikszentmihalyi, "is the way people describe their state of mind when consciousness is harmoniously ordered, and they want to pursue whatever they are doing for its own sake."[28]

Yet flow has a paradoxical character. Although it may appear effortless, flow does evolve from discipline and skill. It's a sort of relaxed intensity, which clearly aligns the experience with the eureka moment. The best conditions for flow derive from a balance of focus, motivation, organization, vision, energy, and the ability to allow inner resources to be freely expressed. "I have to be committed to it and prepared for it," said an entrepreneur, "or I won't get the full experience."

We are all capable of achieving peak performance in the pursuit of quality and creativity. Those who make it a priority are more apt to develop the frame of mind, neurologically speaking, that snaps. Let's look at one of the first people to articulate how this process occurs.

MUTUAL IMPACTS, NEW COMBINATIONS

"Universalists" make significant contributions in many different fields because they are fully versed in each field and they allow their knowledge bases to merge. Whereas most people see only distinct subjects, universalists spot and exploit productive connections. Leonardo da Vinci was such a person. So was Jules Henri Poincaré, an engineer who was a mathematical savant, adept in astronomy, topology, and theoretical physics. His mind has been compared to a bee flying from flower to flower because he pollinated ideas in so many different areas. An initiator of relativity thinking and the father of chaos theory, Poincaré had all the right stuff for snapping. When he did, he transformed paradigms. He was also the first scientist to notice how and when an aha! insight occurred, and he delved into psychology to spell out its conditions.[29]

Born in 1854 in Nancy, France, into a prominent political and intellectual family, Poincaré was top in his class in all subjects except drawing and sports. He entered university to become an engineer but excelled in mathematics, publishing his first professional paper at the age of twenty. He had a penchant for novelty, always looking for new ways to achieve a result. Poincaré would pace while he pondered thorny problems, and he often worked out something in whole before committing it to paper. "If I have the feeling, the intuition . . . so as to perceive at a glance the reasoning as a whole," he once wrote, "I need no longer fear lest I forget one of the elements."[30] However, he tended to ignore questions about his reasoning process as well as suggestions for greater compositional elegance. He was a path*finder*: let others decorate the path he left in his wake.

While still at school, Poincaré became a mining inspector in northeastern France. Then he was invited to become a lecturer in mathematics at Caen University, although he remained chief engineer of the Corps de Mines. This activity gave him a respite from his intellectual work, while the change of venue provided fertile ground for a snap. His most famous snap occurred when he was working on his dissertation on differential equations. One day he'd reached an impasse, so he went on a "geologic excursion" for the school of mines. As he traveled to different parts of France, his mental work receded. One morning, he went to the bus stop. The bus arrived, the door opened, and he lifted his foot to step inside. Out of nowhere, he had the elusive solution, fully formed. "As I put my foot on the step, the idea came to me, without anything in my former thoughts seeming to have paved the way for it."[31] He felt complete certainty about it, so much so that he got on the bus, sat down with his companion, and continued their conversation without taking any notes. On his return, he verified the result.

Poincaré knew he had an idea that would neutralize one of the most vexing problems of modern mathematics. The equations he'd been considering were formally identical to those that characterized the non-Euclidian geometry proposed by Russian mathematician Nikolai Lobachevsky. Poincaré believed that Euclidian geometry was a tidier system because it started with obvious truths and used deductive logic to produce certain results. Lobachevsky had proposed a different set of axioms that offered bizarre results, so he'd inspired hostile resistance among intellectuals. They hoped to prove that his non-Euclidian system was self-contradictory, and many mathematicians—Poincaré among them—were looking for its internal contradictions. But his aha! moment transformed his perception of the task. He'd been looking at it all wrong. When he returned home, he created a relative consistency proof that allowed the axioms from Lobachevsky's system to be as acceptable as the axioms in the Euclidian system. That is, each system yielded valid conclusions based on the axioms of the particular system, Euclidean or non-Euclidean. Neither system was inherently true or false. Each yielded conclusions based on its own axioms. While this realization challenged classical notions of truth, it provided a new frontier for mathematics.

It was clear to people around Poincaré that he could become occupied with many things at once, seeking solutions with passion but indifferent to the finer points of the process. He had a reputation for being disorganized and forgetful, but his perception was highly intuitive and his memory acute. Thus, he earned increasing respect. He was a fairly young scientist when he impressed an international audience of his peers.

Since Isaac Newton's time, scientific societies have offered prizes to lure clever men into solving the world's most vexing mathematical problems. This practice provided a means for young scholars to make a mark, even, perhaps, to shift things in new directions. Sometimes the contests were highly political, so the solutions might be roundly disputed.

The nineteenth-century king of Sweden and of Norway was Oscar II. To honor his approaching sixtieth birthday in 1889, Professor Gösta Mittag-Leffler devised an intellectual contest in which mathematicians were to address one of four questions that featured a key issue at the frontier of current research. One question asked for proof within the frame of Newton's celestial mechanics of the solar system's stability. That is, could someone show that influences on planetary bodies in our solar system would alter their courses only slightly or temporarily, such that Earth's residents could expect things to remain status quo indefinitely?

This question was the result of a tantalizing remark from a mathematical scholar, Peter Gustav Lejeune Dirichlet. Reportedly, Dirichlet had told his top student, Leopold Kronecker, that he could prove with differential equations the solar system's stability. Differential equations express the physical laws that govern relationships among our solar system's planets. From these equations, mathematicians tried to deduce the various trajectories, past and future. Figuring out each instant, piecemeal, and putting them all together should yield the future's Big Picture—how the solar system will behave into eternity.

Yet Dirichlet had not divulged his actual work before he died, and the elusive proof had tormented mathematicians from America to Russia. Many had tried but failed to figure out the solution that

Dirichlet had taken to the grave, but they were convinced that if *he'd* done it, one of them could too. Mittag-Leffler believed that a contest that challenged the best minds would finally lift the rock beneath which this mystery was hidden. They could be on the verge of new and significant knowledge.

While on the face of it, the idea of such a contest seemed a simple matter, a problem arose when Mittag-Leffler tried to convene an international jury of renowned mathematicians who could achieve a consensus—without impaling one another. There was no shortage of self-important divas among accomplished mathematicians, so planning the event soon became a political nightmare. The situation worsened when Kronecker, who viewed himself as the foremost expert on "the Dirichlet question," announced that he had discovered it to be impossible to answer. The contest, he said, would only humiliate the scientific community and embarrass the king, and he planned to reveal this to Oscar. Mittag-Leffler thwarted a grand disaster by inviting Kronecker onto the esteemed jury.

The planning proceeded and the prize was announced: a gold medal and 2,500 crowns. Mathematicians from all over the world sent in their entries, among them Poincaré, now thirty-five. His complex paper on the use of differential equations to address the behavior of multiple bodies in free motion was over two hundred pages in length.

With his preference for topology and holistic reasoning, Poincaré had been the perfect person to approach the imposing problem. He adopted a unique geometrical perspective to address the nine simultaneous equations. He also proposed the notion of dynamical chaos; that is, order and randomness might mix together so intimately that it would be impossible to clearly distinguish them. Thus, no one could know the laws of nature so exactly as to predict accurately all successive moments of the universe. Since the laws can be known only approximately, we would need a formula that allowed us to predict the future with the same uncertainty. However, miniscule differences during early stages can increase exponentially and thus become much greater at later stages. So, the prediction of stability has a sensitive dependence both on the initial conditions and on the measuring instrument. Poincaré stated that there would always be an element of irreducible uncertainty in the calculation process.

Although he did not complete the solution to The Question, he had proposed such an important new idea that he was awarded the prize anyway, along with worldwide acclaim. One judge stated that what Poincaré had achieved would inaugurate a new era for celestial physics.

Poincaré's approach is now regarded as the birth of chaos theory. Essentially, he demonstrated that there was room in deterministic systems for the unpredictable. His indirect, qualitative approach via geometrical pictures shattered the more rigid framework of quantitative calculations. What he was mentally able to construct more than a century ago is now re-created with high-powered computers. Thus, he demonstrated the transformative nature of a eureka moment.

Poincaré asserted that the best way to work on a complex problem is to first immerse in it until you hit an impasse, and then distract yourself. He'd known success from such experiences in his own life. Apart from his eureka moment on the bus, he described several more in a lecture in 1908, given in Paris to a group of psychologists. It's among the earliest self-reflective descriptions of the creative process—and a rare illumination from Poincaré. He believed that mathematical creation should be of interest to psychologists, because "it is the activity in which the human mind seems to take least from the outside world, in which it acts or seems to act only of itself and on itself."[32]

Aside from the experience on the bus during his mining expedition, Poincaré described among his enlightened moments how he'd striven for two weeks during his doctoral research to prove that "Fuchsian functions" could not exist. (Today they're called automorphic functions.) He sat at his worktable each day for an hour, maybe two. Although he tried and tried, he reached no result. Then one evening, he changed his regular habits and drank a cup of coffee, which gave him a case of insomnia. "Ideas rose in crowds; I felt them collide until pairs interlocked, so to speak, making a stable combination."[33] By the next morning, he had established a class of Fuchsian functions. "I had only to write out the results, which took but a few hours."[34] He believed that the caffeine stimulant had no influence on his ability to mentally wrangle with his ideas; it had merely made him more present to the material his unconscious produced than if he'd been sleeping.

On another occasion, after reaching an impasse on a series of arithmetical questions, he went to the seaside to relax. He went for a walk one morning when the idea he needed struck him at once. It was brief, sudden, and "immediately certain." Upon returning, he got back to work, but there was one aspect of this problem that remained stubbornly mysterious. He worked on it systematically, day after day, to no avail. Again, he went on a trip for military training, and while walking on the street, the solution came to him. After his training stint ended, he was able to easily reproduce the insight.

Comparing unconscious ideas to atoms, Poincaré said, "During a period of apparent rest and unconscious work, certain of them come unhooked from the wall and put in motion. They flash in every direction through the space where they are enclosed. . . . Then their mutual impacts may produce new combinations."[35] Conscious work was needed to unhook them from the wall, but it could go only so far. This is the moment that divides the conscious reasoner from the innovator. "We think we have done no good because we have moved these elements in a thousand different ways in seeking to assemble them and have found no satisfactory aggregate. But after this shaking up imposed on them by our will, these atoms do not return to their primitive rest. They freely continue their dance."[36] Those who grasp the function of the work–rest interplay know when to sit back and let it occur in its own way.

For the psychologists, Poincaré listed five distinct points about creativity that involved the interplay of two distinct egos. "The conscious self is narrowly limited, and as far as the subliminal self, we know not its limitations, and this is why we are not too reluctant in supposing that it has been able in a short time to make more different combinations than the whole life of a conscious being could encompass."[37]

Creativity that produces insight begins with a period of conscious work, Poincaré explained, followed by unconscious work. Then the unconscious work must be verified, that is, put on a "firm footing." Third, one had to trust the "delicate intuition" of the unconscious, which "knows better how to divine than the conscious self, since it succeeds where that has failed."[38]

For the fourth point, he offered a conjecture: the unconscious mind could present an unfruitful direction that was nevertheless elegant, so the conscious mind had to make a decision about its usefulness. Wrapping up his lecture with his fifth point, he cautioned that whatever the unconscious mind does present is not full and complete but only a "point of departure." The rest can be worked out with the discipline of the more logical conscious mind.

Poincaré's first biographer, Édouard Toulouse, was a psychologist at the School of Higher Studies. He noted Poincaré's exceptional ability to recall verbatim passages he'd read or things he'd heard, as well as his routine work pattern: a regular schedule of short periods of concentrated intellectual work that always began with basic principles, and that added breaks. Poincaré did not waste long hours on a resistant problem because he trusted that his subconscious would continue working on it. He resisted the limiting structure of logical thought and preferred the free play of visual imagery.

> It is certain that the combinations which present themselves to the mind in a kind of sudden illumination after a somewhat prolonged period of unconscious work are generally useful and fruitful combinations . . . all the combinations are formed as a result of the automatic action of the subliminal ego, but those only which are interesting find their way into the field of consciousness. . . . A few

only are harmonious, and consequently at once useful and beautiful, and they will be capable of affecting the geometrician's special sensibility I have been speaking of; which, once aroused, will direct our attention upon them, and will thus give them the opportunity of becoming conscious. . . . In the subliminal ego, on the contrary, there reigns what I would call liberty, if one could give this name to the mere absence of discipline and to disorder born of chance.[39]

VIGILANCE AT PLAY

Putting the whole brain in play is not, of itself, sufficient to spark insight. For serendipity to be productive, we must have knowledge about the context of the problem. That is, we can be rewarded with a eureka moment only when we're prepared for it. Kary Mullis was immersed in DNA technology when he snapped on the PCR process. Martin Cooper was a long-time engineer with Motorola when he put two and two together for the mobile phone. Poincaré knew math and physics backward and forward. All three understood how important it is to stay immersed, to utilize challenges for optimum performance, and to keep the radar up at all times. All three let their minds tumble with a problem as both work and play. All three could move into flow and snap a significant solution that had long-range effects. On the other hand, Joy Mangano was just washing a floor. However, she had developed a habit of looking for ways to improve her life, so her vigilant mind was at work on even that mundane task.

Thus, the best way to inspire effective snap judgments is (1) to be diligently working within the parameters of the problem, (2) after intense effort, relax, and (3) let the brain play with what it already knows. The impasse, or "plateau moment," as frustrating as it may feel, is an important part of the process. Giving up the effort of thinking offers a way to clear the mind and make room for a breakthrough. The snap is there; it's just incubating.

KEY POINTS

- The right hemisphere is instrumental in producing the aha! moment.
- Letting the mind wander revs up its resources.
- Flow is a full engagement with a task that lets the mind play while it works.
- Flow occurs most often when we're engaged in a challenge from activities that we enjoy.
- Eureka moments are associated with people who can get "in the zone."
- Snapping comes from knowledge, mental play, memory, and the alert mind.

SIFT

CHAPTER 6

PERCEPTUAL SETS

COGNITIVE MAPPING

An accident in Paris in 1903 sparked a snap that created an industry that made the world safer. Chemist Edouard Benedictus was reading a newspaper when he came across a report about a recent rash of car accidents. Driving was an exciting new experience in Paris, but many drivers were more enthused than skilled, so accidents were almost a daily occurrence. Somewhere in the article, Benedictus came across a description of how broken glass had disfigured one accident victim and killed another. The image snapped him to an incident that had occurred in his lab just a few days before. As he recorded in his diary: "Suddenly there appeared before my eyes an image of the broken flask. I leapt up, dashed to my laboratory, and concentrated on the practical possibilities of my idea."[1]

Benedictus had knocked a beaker off a shelf. It shattered, but to his surprise, the pieces hadn't scattered. Instead, the beaker had retained its form. Benedictus had picked it up to examine it more closely and discovered that it had earlier contained nitrocellulose, or liquid plastic. Although this substance had evaporated and the beaker was now empty, a thin layer still coated the glass. This incident, juxtaposed against what he'd just read about the dangerous glass in the accident, meshed in an unexpected snap.

As with many snaps, his excitement fueled the energy he needed to sustain a long stretch of focused activity. He worked for twenty-four hours straight, and he succeeded in creating the product of his idea: a transparent celluloid adhesive that would make glass that shattered less dangerous. "By the following evening, I had produced my first piece of Triplex, full of promise for the future."[2]

He was right. Used initially in military applications, safety glass has improved many products around the world, from car windshields to windows to workplace goggles. Benedictus snapped within the frame of his knowledge and efforts—what we would call his cognitive map.

"Cognitive mapping" is a concept from psychology that describes how we become habituated to a specific perspective. It goes by other names, like a cognitive model, a mental map, a script, a frame of reference, and even a mind map, but the basic idea is the same. We encode, recall, and recognize our "situated existence" according to familiar parameters. That is, we learn things from our families and culture that influence our personal interpretation of the world. This helps us to remember things. We create maps in which we mentally "place" things. When we need them, we can find them because we know the routes we created.

Researcher E. C. Tolman believed that successful learning occurred spatially. In the 1940s, he ran rats through a maze, finding that once they became familiar with it, they could make their way through it with fewer errors during later trials—even with roadblocks placed in their way. If the maze was filled with water, he discovered, they could also swim in the correct route. They even managed this feat without any reward. He surmised that they had internalized the route; they had an inner field guide or a "map control room."[3] More research since then appears to confirm that the neurological system is set up to encode locations, distance, and directions. Humans have it, too. To understand how it works, try the following:

Think about where you are right now—presumably in some room—and look for a door. Now imagine walking toward it. Just at this moment, something interesting is happening in your brain. It's preparing for you to walk over to the door, and if you actually do, it will record your movements and create a map. Our brains appear to code how we move through space, like a satellite navigation system such as you might rely on while driving. It won't give you a traffic report, but otherwise, it's pretty sophisticated.

Although we had identified this mapping feature in rodents, for a long time we weren't sure if the human brain functioned in the same way. But we've now devised a research method that offers a better picture and strongly suggests that human brains do map the environment. This brings us to a specific type of neuron known as "grid cells." They help us to become familiar with our environment, and they're located in and around the hippocampus, the brain structure that stores memories. Grid cells "wake up" as soon as we look around with the intent to get up and go somewhere. They also remain active the whole time we're moving. They're busily creating a map by placing mental grids against a visual picture of our location.

Back to the room: You're anticipating walking to the door. Your grid cells fire up to record where you're looking. Before you take a step, they lay out a map from here to there, like a regular map that has latitude and longitude lines that run down and across (except that mental grids are shaped as triangles, not squares). So if you think of a map with a series of triangular grids, you'll understand how this network of brain cells works.

Now, envision these cells lighting up when you look toward the door. They project a path of overlapping triangles onto your mental map, like unrolling a carpet between you and the door. If you start walking in that direction, each time you step into any part of a triangle, the grid cells for that section light up—and keep lighting up all the way along the path. Each time you take a step, a new triangular grid lights up. Then another step and another triangle. If we were to transfer these triangles from your brain to paper, you would see a path of triangles that runs from your chair to the door. Thus, your brain created a map, stored it in your memory, and now this path will be familiar. You'll know how it lays out and how far it is.

No matter how fast you move from chair to door, whether you walk or sprint, the grid cells will adjust to your speed.

To figure out how grid cells worked in the human brain, researchers placed forty-two male participants inside a scanning machine that was equipped with a virtual reality environment. The participants could see—virtually—a grassy plain, a cliff, and some mountains. They were to envision themselves moving through this area. Sometimes they moved quickly—like running—and sometimes at a slower pace. As they did this, the scanner picked up signals, which indicated certain brain cells waking up and going to work. It was quite similar to what we'd seen in a rat's brain when the rat was in motion—including increased activity with greater speed. So, if we know that the rat brain relies on a network of grids to map its location, it's reasonable to surmise that we do, too.[4]

Nobel Prize winner Eric Kandel, renowned for his work on memory, considered this inner spatial map in 1992. He followed the work of other researchers, learning that the spatial map does not form in a rat instantaneously but develops over a period of about ten minutes from the time the rat enters a new environment. Once it has fully learned the map, the memory stabilizes for several weeks. Thus, Kandel says, we have a hardwired capability for forming spatial representations, and within this representational arena, we can form maps related to our specific situations. When we pay attention, we bind the components into a whole and give it more stability.[5]

In any event, this mental map influences the paths we take and the ways we think, which then tend to further confirm our maps and habits. They get more and more entrenched. The brain then links our perceptual sets with our physiological systems, so that our very habits become neurologically encoded. "The work in process," Carl Jung once said, "becomes the poet's fate and determines his psychic development. It is not Goethe who creates *Faust*, but *Faust* which creates Goethe."[6] This "embodied cognition" or "body memory" explains such things as "gut feelings," some forms of déjà vu, and anniversaries that provoke "felt" memories, even after many years have passed since the event. Our holistic physiological encoding process is fundamental to our ability to snap. It's part of the memory template that makes the construction of our inner database possible. Going beyond long-term and short-term memory, it is a full-bodied enhancement of our sense of certainty.

BODY MEMORIES

Once more: when we store memories, we create specific neural pathways by increasing the number of synapses in the brain. An interesting experiment provided evidence of how training in specific activities strengthened certain areas of the brain. Researchers at London's University College studied the size of the hippocampus in cab drivers because they surmised that these cabbies must have an enhanced working memory of locations. Their training ran for two years, and they had to prove they could locate thousands of sites all over London. Compared to a control group, their hippocampus, where memory gets consolidated, was more developed. The more years they had been on the job, the larger its size.[7] That is, they had developed strong body memories to support their skills.

Body memories are based in the way the brain sends information to the cells, whether brain, muscle, nerve, or organ cells. This is also called embodied biological intelligence or grounded cognition. We used to view intelligence as brain-generated abstractions that get filed into specific neural circuits. Different circuits were linked to different abilities and activities, and these "knowledge bases" were of a higher order than those devoted to basic life processes like perception and emotion.

However, we now believe that cognition is grounded in an interaction among *all* the brain systems, basic or otherwise. "These systems increasingly coordinate their activity as an individual gains experience performing tasks jointly with other people. Complex thinking capacities . . . form out of these myriad interactions."[8]

People act in order to learn by using the feedback to influence what they do next. Cognition appears to evolve as our actions and experiences form and fuel our mental lives. We understand others through imitation or with reference to our own experiences: what we think about emerges first through our bodies.

How we physically and emotionally process the world, within the framework of our cognitive maps, guides our decisions, interpretations, and behavior. This is because we have an inner apparatus for creating a familiar nest of experiences, ideas, and locations. Training and rehearsal will encode body memories, and as one study suggests, our biological clocks may be involved as well; that is, there are more eureka moments during the evening or at night. A poll of 1,426 people showed that when seeking inspiration for problem solving, the majority felt uninspired in the afternoon and many made an effort to stay up late to work on creative projects. Nearly half had experienced their aha! moment while in the shower.[9]

Although the subject of body memories is controversial because trauma therapists have adopted the concept to support the existence of repressed memories, there nevertheless is recent evidence for the idea of intelligence—and a primitive memory system—at the cellular level.[10] This means that body memories can become firmly set.

Here's a simple example: Most of us know what it's like when we've tried to change a longtime habit. I moved out of an office I had occupied for two years, going from the second to the first floor, but whenever I'm on the second floor, I automatically start toward where my former office was. The same thing happens when we drive. If we let ourselves fall into automatic habits, we might find ourselves driving to a place that was once routine, even if that's not where we intended to go. Our body "knows" where we should be going. It holds an inner route, and it has not yet replaced that body memory with the new route. Eventually it will, but long-term body memories can leave a lasting trace. Our bodies cocreate our perception from our experience. How we physically and emotionally process the world is based on who we are, and, in turn, it supports our sense of identity.

This finding defies the idea, popular since the French philosopher René Descartes proposed it during the 1700s, that mind and body are separate entities. Essentially, Descartes said that the body takes up physical space and the mind does not, so they must be different types of substance that somehow interact. While many religions accept this philosophical separation so that the ephemeral soul can move on intact, researchers challenge its assumptions. Over the past few decades, work in several areas of medicine indicates that mind and body work as a unit. Dr. Candace Pert is an internationally recognized pharmacologist who has published numerous scientific articles about the role of neuropeptides in the immune system. She served as chief of the section on brain biochemistry of the Clinical Neuroscience Branch of the National Institute of Mental Health and is currently the scientific director of RAPID Pharmaceuticals. Her research demonstrates a biochemical basis for interdependent communication between mind and body, which contributes to the field of psychoneuroimmunology. According to her, the chemicals in our bodies form an information network that links emotional experience with physiological systems. Certain emotions become physically encoded into our cells, forming a "bodymind."[11] If our emotions are chemically based and controlled by an information system that is dynamic, flexible, and adaptable, then our emotions are a component of our bodies. Snaps, then, emerge from how we program our bodies emotionally and informationally.

Typing, once learned, seems automatic. Researchers at Vanderbilt University in Tennessee recruited forty people who showed a typing proficiency of at least forty words per minute, with 90 percent accuracy, using all their fingers (not hunt-and-peck typists). They were assigned to a machine that, unbeknownst to them, introduced errors into 6 percent of the typed words that ended up on the screen. At the same time, the program surreptitiously corrected nearly half of the typists' actual errors. They did not wonder why a word they had typed incorrectly had appeared correctly, but their fingers had: after hitting the wrong key, a typist's speed slowed slightly, even if the error was fixed before the typist noticed it. The brain's motor signal had registered it. The fingers "knew" the error.[12] Presumably similar body knowledge would occur with other trained activities, such as playing a musical instrument. Perhaps it even knows the rhythms of writing a literary work.

A renowned nineteenth-century German philosopher who knew something about body memories—who even attributed his own flash of insight to them—was Friedrich Nietzsche. He sought to reexamine our value systems and devise a new system that better reflected human nature. He believed that to learn important truths about ourselves, we should look back to the time of the early Greeks—before science or Christianity, which he thought had blunted our natural instincts. Nietzsche was intrigued by tales about the drunken, ecstatic rituals that honored the half-man/half-deity Dionysus, the god of the vine. Within this urge to merge with a primal deity, Nietzsche spotted a psychosocial metaphor. He viewed Dionysus as the supreme union of the disparate forces of culture (restraint) and instinct (freedom). Dionysus was both primitive and refined, and Nietzsche thought this image offered a way to revive what seemed to him to be a state of spiritual fatigue in the world around him. Dionysus had sacrificed himself to human ecstasy, torn to pieces, but through his sacrifice, others could participate in unleashed, wanton revelry. He represented the values of nature, where survival of the fittest was the ultimate value and the goal of the elite.

However, it wasn't just Nietzsche's celebration of physical instinct and aggression that made him famous. He also proclaimed the death of God because he witnessed the visible signs of a decline in the power of religion. This was a basis for his notion that, without a higher power in place, human beings must create meaning for themselves, and only the most morally courageous and clear-sighted could rise above the others and devise an appropriate code of morality. Everyone else was part of the herd of humanity—followers who let others think for them.[13]

In 1886, Nietzsche published *Beyond Good and Evil*, in which he stated that absolute notions of good and evil are illusory. He even postulated that crime might be an invigorating condition that helped to strengthen the human species. In other words, life is a "will to power," his title for a more forceful book in which he described the ultimate human ideal as an intense Dionysian affirmation. People who could assimilate the will to power would embrace the aggressive instinct, become leaders, and determine what is good and what is evil. The greatest joy, Nietzsche said, was to "live dangerously," that is, to live on one's own terms. So, let's get to his aha! moment.

Between 1883 and 1885, Nietzsche was hard at work. He composed a philosophical novel, *Thus Spake Zarathustra*, that had four parts. In it, his reclusive character Zarathustra elaborates more fully on Nietzsche's earlier ideas. He proclaims the death of God and predicts the emergence of the "overman" and the superior master race (on which the Nazis unfortunately seized). He also proposes a central tenet, the "eternal recurrence," which means that any given set of circumstances will recur over and over again throughout eternity. The courageous will embrace this "truth," while the meek will fear it. The entire book occurred as a series of inspired moments, beginning with an initial flash of genius.

In August 1881, Nietzsche wrote, he scribbled a hasty phrase, "six thousand feet beyond man and time." He then went for a walk in the woods by Lake Silvaplana in Switzerland, in an Alpine region whose valley floor was at six thousand feet above sea level. He stopped next to a towering rock. Suddenly, he had it. An idea fully formed. He was able to see in his mind's eye exactly how the book should be done. He later described the feeling: "One can hardly reject completely the idea that one is the mere incarnation, or mouthpiece, or medium of some almighty power. The notion of revelation describes the condition quite simply; by which I mean that something profoundly convulsive and disturbing suddenly becomes visible and audible with indescribable definiteness and exactness. One hears—one does not seek; one takes—one does not ask who gives: a thought flashes out like lightning, inevitably without hesitation."[14] He described the "ecstasy whose terrific tension is sometimes released by a flood of tears," and one might become either impetuous or nearly paralyzed. He felt the "infinitude of shuddering thrills" pass throughout his body, accompanied by a profound sense of happiness and an "eruption of freedom, independence, power, and divinity."[15]

Although he did not immediately record his idea, he returned to this same spot a few months later to recapture the sense of that magical moment. There he conceived additional images that gave him more of Zarathustra's story. He then went to work and wrote the first part in ten days. A third part "completed itself" in his mind in a similar manner, and this, too, took about ten days to write. From this experience, Nietzsche recognized that inspiration flowed most freely for him—or, rather "invaded" him—when he was active (walking around) rather than when he was sitting at his desk writing. "The body," he declared, "is inspired."[16] He also surmised that his change in taste for a certain type of music just two months prior to his initial walk was a significant influence. Although he does not fully explain, he seemed to think that absorbing a new creative form had affected his ability to mentally innovate.

So, cognitive maps that influence body memories are representations of our relationship to the world around us. We find our way through imaging and recognition, which becomes part of our mental processing. Although the spatial metaphor of a map is easy to comprehend, a cognitive map is not limited to space. It is a way for us to orient so that we can integrate new information with what we already have learned. Our maps include both conscious and subconscious encodings, which help us to make decisions, plan ahead, organize our thoughts, and solve problems. Thus, because snapping relies on creative selection from our internal database, cognitive maps play a fundamental role in inciting it.

KNOWING THE WAY

Like the rats that ran down the maze with a learned sense of direction, people who snap are often confident of their knowledge, clear about their goals, and engaged with their work in a way that has little cognizance of time or "office hours." They're diligent, able to navigate setbacks, and able to focus for long periods—even years—on the thing that fascinates them. Many creative people are puzzled that they're considered creative; to their mind, they're just engaged in their work. But their doggedness pays off in developing body memories that will serve them well should they come up against an impasse. Those with mental agility will have the best chance to snap an innovative solution.

Contemporary artist Chuck Close has stated that having limitations actually assists the creative process and frees up intuition. In fact, he believes that if one puts oneself into a position in which one is likely to bump into something—paint oneself into a corner, so to speak—the opportunity for a creative leap is more often at hand. He should know. Not only does he suffer from dyslexia and face amnesia, but he also lost the use of his muscles. None of this has impeded him from pursuing what he loves.

Close's dyslexia was so severe as a young man that he'd been advised to forget about college. Too clumsy for sports, his future looked grim. His father, a plumber with a knack for invention, died when Close was eleven, and his mother, an accomplished pianist, was diagnosed with breast cancer. Then he got a bad kidney infection that sidelined him for nearly a year. His only consolation during this terrible time was art—the thing that had called to him since he was four years old. He immersed himself. Not only did he eventually go to college (the University of Washington and Yale) but he also became a renowned artist. His friends always knew him as energetic, even driven. Still, he faced something even more devastating.

On December 7, 1988, Close was present at a ceremony in New York City where his innovative work in photorealism was being honored as a prominent feature of contemporary American art. He was about to step to the podium when his chest began to hurt. He made it through his speech, but the pain was unrelenting. Beth Israel Medical Center was nearby, so he went straight to the emergency room. There he suffered a seizure with violent convulsions. Then the bottom part of his lungs stopped working. His limbs went numb and other organs failed. He couldn't breathe. To his horror, Close was now paralyzed from the neck down. He'd had a spinal artery collapse. Doctors discovered a blood clot in his spinal column, near his neck.

Rather than accept that his art career was over, Close pushed himself into months of rehab. His recovery began in his arms. Then he could take a few small steps, although he had to use a wheelchair. The next task was to figure out how to return to his work. He truly feared that he might never be able to make art again. Instead of giving in to despair, which hovered every day, Close pondered the problem until he snapped on a way to do it.

He knew that there was no going back to the way he'd once painted. Thus, he had to devise something altogether new, both in technique and style. His hands did not work, so he tried painting with his teeth. He had just enough success in a limited space to feel encouraged. Then a physical therapist made a hand-splint to which he could attach a brush. In his typical manner of throwing himself directly at a problem, he learned how to paint again in a whole new way.

He directs an assistant to make grid squares on a canvas. Then he takes on the canvas, one grid at a time, filling them all with a system of dots. Each grid is, in itself, a tiny painting. Viewed from afar, the individual squares merge as a single image that resembles a photo. Today, some of the world's most elite museums hang his work, and Close has been called one of the fifty most influential people in art. Not bad for a kid once called both lazy and dumb. One critic observed that "a ravaged artist has become, in a miracle, one of the greatest colorists and brush wielders of his time."[17]

THE EUREKA EXPERIMENT

Something akin to the aha! moment experience has been documented by Tufts University researchers with an electroencephalograph that registers the moment of clarity. Just to remind you of how it feels, try another puzzle: *I start with an e and end with an e, and I contain only one letter, but I'm not an e. What am I?*

Take a moment to think about it. Don't strain. The subconscious feeds a nonresistant consciousness. You have everything you need in the puzzle and in your experience to see the solution. When you get it, it'll pop. Aha! If you need to, get up and move around a little. Sometimes it's best to just forget it.

Drum roll . . . may I have the envelope, please . . . yes, it's an envelope. That's the answer. Whether it popped before or after I said it, you should have experienced a mental shift. You don't figure this out with reasoning: you *see* it.

Back to the experiment: psychologist Sal Soraci led the way with several colleagues in studying the effects on memory of sudden insight. To locate this phenomenon in the brain, they placed electrodes on the scalps of their subjects and created conditions that they believed would trigger insights. First, they presented sentences that seemed to make no sense, intended to cause the subjects to feel confused. The subject would try to make sense of the material, casting about for something that would help. For example, "The girl spilled her popcorn because the lock broke." How could a person really respond to this? After a few seconds of letting the brain do a bit of futile work, the researchers gave subjects a word or phrase that would provoke comprehension: "lion cage." OK, now they could see the reason why the girl might spill her popcorn. The lock on the lion cage had broken. The keyword phrase, "lion cage," activated a burst of understanding, an insight. Another sentence was "The haystack was important, because the cloth ripped." The meaningful clue was "parachute." With "The notes were sour because the seam split," the hint was "bagpipe." For "The clothes were ruined because the sign vanished," the subjects got the keyword "wet paint." Without the meaningful clues, the brain might grind into gear or race from one possibility to the next, but it would not resolve the confusion on its own. Thus, exposure to the words that made sense of the sentences would have a distinct neural effect. When subjects reported an aha! experience, the electrodes showed activity. About four hundred milliseconds after they saw the meaningful clue, there was an N400 pulse, or spike, in the front of the brain.

These researchers were the first to detect the eureka moment's electrochemical presence. They hypothesized that the more effort the brain initially puts into trying to figure something out (before it gives up or relaxes), the better the chance that it will flash on a meaning, which will assist the person to better remember it.[18]

Other discoveries in neuroscience indicate that cognition is grounded in the interaction of multiple brain systems, which perfect their coordination via training and experience. Challenging tasks help us to become mindfully engaged (top–down attention) rather than being passive participants. Let's look at how this process worked for one of the most iconic thinkers in history.

Albert Einstein said that the ingredients of his effectiveness were curiosity, determination, and hard work. He believed it was important to never stop questioning. Even as a child growing up in Munich, Germany, with educated parents, he exhibited perseverance and determination to get things right. He enjoyed solving puzzles, and he would create elaborate structures from cards and building blocks. He recalled that when he was around the age of four or five, his father told him about a compass, and he wanted to understand exactly what made it work so magically.

Young Albert was a good student, and during playtime he sought out things that would mentally stimulate him. He received a lot of this from industrious relatives, some of whom were engineers, scientists, or mathematicians. He had plenty of willing mentors. By age eleven, he found joy in philosophy and science, reading at a level well beyond that of other kids his age. Then he became enchanted with math, attempting to solve difficult theorems on his own. Einstein adored Euclid and became enchanted with music, especially Mozart, so he took up the violin. He also loved reading Kant, believing that "love is a better teacher than a sense of duty." He recalled the passion of curiosity that had been his constant companion since childhood. He would moreover pursue challenges with a dogged sense of purpose. As a teenager, Einstein knew he wanted to be a scientist. He did not believe he had a special talent for learning; he simply had a greater ability to concentrate. In terms of the neural pathways he was developing, he became habituated to focused periods of abstract reflection.

He experienced extraordinary visual imagery—brain play—that penetrated his thought processes. Images helped him to develop concepts, and they made his thinking more fluid than if he'd developed them according to the rigid rules of language. When he read a theory about light as a student, for example, he imagined himself riding on a light wave through space. This type of creative visualization allowed him to surmount conceptual polarities and play with possibilities. In 1907, while working on a glitch between his special and general theories of relativity, Einstein described a joyful moment of illumination, while daydreaming, from the mental image of a falling man. With it, he solved the problem: he linked accelerated motion with gravity and bridged the gap. Immersed in physics, he would let his mind wander into a visual thought experiment until it snapped the solution. (However, it did take a few years to work out the math that proved it.)[19]

While developing some of his most powerful ideas, Einstein worked in a patent office, which meant he had to investigate, review, and critically appraise others' inventions. It was demanding work, but it was interesting. It also exposed him to a realm of creativity, not to mention the stability to be able to work on his own ideas. It proved to be a time of prodigious creativity, which soon established Einstein as one of the world's leading physicists.[20]

In a letter to Jacques Hadamard, a colleague who was probing the way Einstein arrived at his ideas, Einstein explained that language seemed to play no role in his initial mode of thinking. Instead, he relied on "signs" and "images," which he could produce and combine at will: he allowed them to "play." He believed this was an important early stage prior to logical construction, the "interference" of words, and communicating with others.[21]

Hadamard himself recorded a spontaneous insight upon being awakened one night by a noise. Although he was not thinking at the moment about a problem on which he had been at work, his brain had been processing. When he woke up, it delivered "a solution long searched for."[22] He realized that it was entirely different in quality from the solutions he had devised with rational deliberation.

The good news is that it doesn't require the precise thinking of a mathematician to have such clarity. Three guys with the desire to improve a hobby made it happen, too.

A significant factor in achieving a natural look for a saltwater marine reef aquarium is generating enough water movement inside the tank. "Broad flow is important for any reef aquarist to create a lifelike simulation of the coral reef," said Pat Clasen. "Flow brings nutrients and oxygen to the sessile invertebrates. Without flow, corals will starve and suffocate."[23] Traditionally, pumps have been located inside the tank, but they take up a lot of space and generate heat, which can be an issue. Two students from Lehigh University, Pat Clasen and Tim Marks, joined with Justin Lawyer from the University of Oklahoma to create an innovative new product that would eliminate these issues, the VorTech® pump.

"All three of us have been interested in aquariums," said Marks.

> Justin and I were into reef aquariums in high school and we met each other through Internet discussion forums. Pat and I met through a fraternity at Lehigh. When Justin and I formed the company EcoTech Marine, we were just making equipment we wanted to use to further automate our aquariums. When I met Pat, he brought a lot of energy, and it was obvious he should be brought on board as a partner.[24]

The story of our eureka moment is simple. I went to an aquarium group club meeting in Pottsville. There I met the president of a now out-of-business company in New Jersey. We were talking about different aquarium products. He said he thought the market wanted a DC operated aquarium pump and I told him that this was a project that I and my business partners had on our radar. So he said, "Why don't you come up with a concept and pitch it to us in a couple of weeks?" I brought this information back to Justin and Pat. I said, "We have an opportunity." This is a real company in the industry, and at the time they were doing really well. I said we might have a shot at getting something going.

So we had a brainstorming session, and we put a couple of concepts on table, and Justin said, "I like these concepts but I'm not married to any of them yet. I'm not sold on them. Let me sleep on this." He's one of those late-night kind of guys. His brain goes crazy at night.

The next day, Pat and I were in my office at the Wilber Powerhouse. We started the conference call. At that time we were building a calcium reactor that utilized a magnetic stirring mechanism. So it was a motor with a magnet mounted at the top that spun, and inside the reactor was a plastic coated magnetic pill, so that when the motor spun, the magnetic force went through and into the reactor. Justin said, "Why don't we take that concept and mount it horizontally though the aquarium glass and drive a propeller inside the aquarium?"

I said, "That's it!" I knew it was genius. It would get the motor outside, which would reduce the heat, and it would reduce the size of the part that's inside the aquarium—the propeller section—because normally that would be the entire size of the motor. And it would anchor itself against the glass. You wouldn't need any accessory brackets.

But Pat wasn't sold. He said, "I don't know if we can do this. It sounds a little crazy." But we kept talking, and that was the eureka moment. By the end of the conversation, we were all on board. It was an open brainstorming session. We had two different meetings, and between the first and second meeting, one of us came up with the concept, then one of us caught on immediately, and one was a little more reluctant. We all eventually bought in and we were good to go.

Thinking a lot about something is good, but giving your mind a rest to let it do its natural thing, and waking up in the morning can provide a whole new insight on the situation. We're firm believers of "Let's sleep on it." For engineers, especially—even very creative engineers—the mind is an analytic, linear process. For them, with respect to creativity, the conscious mind is too constrained, but the subconscious mind is not. If I can get out of a conscious linear thought process and into a dream state, that's when better solutions come up. It's easy to get caught inside the box.

An example of a businessman who just happened to see an opportunity rather than setting out to look for one was Hugh Everett Moore. He poked his sense of curiosity into many areas, including philosophy, art, journalism, and law. He was a voracious reader but became a traveling "ad manager"; that is, a salesman for a newspaper, because he hoped to become a journalist. During his second year at Harvard in 1907, Moore was taking a train to New York. Polio was a concern at the time, and he noticed the common drinking facilities with their tin dippers, which posed a health hazard. He snapped on a solution: disposable paper cups would offer an alternative. Thus, the Dixie Cup® was born. Moore left Harvard and his job to found the Individual Drinking Cup Company.[25]

Another train ride was instrumental in another aha! moment of inspiration that served a similar purpose in a different venue. During the late 1890s, problems arose with this era's most prominent method for identifying a criminal, anthropometry, aka *bertillonage*. It was based on an extensive system of head and body measurements that relied on cooperative subjects and competent practitioners, but it was based on faulty methods and ideas. Alphonse Bertillon, who had created it, had tried teaching it, but he could not supervise its use everywhere at once. The method remained inconsistent, clumsy, and wrong. Talk was in the air among law enforcement of an easier method: fingerprints.

Several different people were approaching the idea of using fingerprints as a way to identify unique individuals. Francis Galton had studied bertillonage, but when he decided the system was too complicated, he went to see William Herschel in England to learn more about fingerprints. Herschel, at an impasse, offered everything he had, hopeful that Galton could take it further. Galton set about studying the method for a period of three years, as well as trying to figure out a way to systematize it. He published a paper in the esteemed science journal *Nature*, in 1891, which sparked rage from Henry Faulds, who claimed to have invented the fingerprint technique.

Yet Galton published the first book, *Finger Prints*, proposing that fingerprints bore three primary features from which he could devise sixty thousand classes. But he was stuck on the prospect of completing a practical system. He needed help and was eager for a true collaborator.

Edward R. Henry had tried to create a simplified method of anthropometry but, finding it cumbersome, had then looked into fingerprints. Influenced by Galton's work when he was an inspector-general of police in Nepal, India, Henry had created his own system. He traveled to England, where Galton offered him support. Together they noted the problems in his system, and both were equally stymied about how to make it both effective and efficient. Then in 1896, Henry was riding on a train. He stared out the window at the passing scenery and then looked down at his hand. He turned it over to examine the tips of his fingers. In that moment, the impasse was broken. Henry saw a way to make the fingerprint system simple and manageable: a loop and delta system.

When he arrived at his destination, he set to work. His revised system separated fingerprints into two basic groups: value patterns (whorls) and nonvalue patterns (arches and loops), and described how the ridges could be counted for individualizing a set of finger-prints. With assigned values for different fingers, he formed codes for each set of prints. Thus, the prints were filed via their numeric codes and could easily be retrieved for comparison. This process decreased the time heretofore involved to look them up.[26]

The human body itself assists aha! moments with cognitive maps and perceptual shifts. They prepare us for the next step in our ability to make snaps happen. As long as we retain top–down initiative, we can use body memories as springboards for mental agility.

KEY POINTS

- Our cognitive maps and body memories form habits that can limit our perspective.
- Changing some aspect of our environment or our approach can shift our maps and make our thought processes more flexible.
- Our mental maps can hinder or facilitate our ability to generate snaps, but we can train the brain to springboard from them.

CHAPTER 7

READING BETWEEN THE MINDS

CROSS-FERTILIZATION

Nearly overnight, intertangled snaps for two people who were
initially strangers improved the investigation of crime around
the world. One was a scientist; the other was a cop. Neither anticipated quite the extent of what would happen when their aha! moments converged, but it was significant—locally and internationally.

Dr. Alec Jeffreys was a molecular biologist at the University of
Leicester. He was one of several scientists who had a sudden insight
while handling DNA. (Recall we introduced our initial discussion
with Watson and Crick in chapter 1.) Jeffreys's method examined the
part of human DNA that allows for individual variation. In 1978, he
and several colleagues had isolated a *single nucleotide polymorphism*
of DNA. Furthermore, Jeffreys looked for areas of DNA that would
be more variable. Getting results proved difficult at first, but then he
identified a *minisatellite*—a section of DNA that consists of a short
series of protein bases that repeat in tandem. In September 1984, Jeffreys's team made a radioactive probe that latched onto diverse minisatellites simultaneously and placed the results from different people
onto a blot. When it was ready, Jeffreys and his colleague, Vicky
Wilson, developed an X-ray. On it, they saw patterns that were similar in appearance to bar codes used in grocery stores, and each test
subject's "barcode" was different from every other.

"There was a level of individual specificity," said Dr. Jeffreys, "that was light years beyond anything that had been seen before." He called this a "Eureka!" moment, and so it was. "Standing in front of these pictures in the darkroom, my life took a complete turn."[1] He set to work refining the process to make it more manageable for identifying idiotypes, or patterns specific to all individuals except identical twins. He knew it could soon be used as a human identification system—what he called a genetic fingerprint. With this, he could identity an unknown person, compare samples and identify the donor, and also establish genetic lineage. In one case, he was able to resolve an immigration dispute: a boy from Ghana wanted to prove that a British woman was his mother so that he could live with her. Jeffreys's work made it possible for him to accomplish this beyond any doubt. According to his results, the boy was the woman's son.

Jeffreys and his colleagues received many public honors, and, in a paper published in *Nature* in 1985, they stated that an individual's identifiable DNA pattern was unique and would not be found in any past, present, or future person. This placed Jeffreys's lab in demand for paternity cases.[2] But he would also be contacted from an unexpected source.

Not far from Leicester, in the village of Narborough, Chief Superintendent David Baker had been dealing with a difficult investigation that was at a dead end. He'd been a police officer for over twenty-five years, and it bothered him that he'd failed to find the brutal killer of a young girl.

On November 21, 1983, the year before Jeffreys made his exciting discovery, fifteen-year-old Lynda Mann had been followed as she took a shortcut that skirted the grounds of a psychiatric hospital. Directly after school that day, she had walked to a neighbor's house to babysit. Around 6:45 p.m., Lynda visited several friends. Just before 7:30, she headed home. Apparently, she took a wooded path on the west side of town that locals called the Black Pad. Somewhere on it, Lynda vanished. She never made it home. Although her frantic family, alongside police, searched for her for hours, she was nowhere to be found. At dawn the next day, an employee from the psychiatric hospital came across the body of a young female. It was Lynda Mann. Her jeans, shoes, and tights had been rolled up and cast aside. A scarf covered her neck, but her jacket was pulled up, and her nose was bloodied. Her right leg lay on a three-foot piece of wood.

Chief Baker notified a Home Office pathologist and moved Lynda's body to the morgue. The autopsy revealed that she had been punched and manually strangled. It appeared that she had removed her shoes voluntarily, probably under duress. Seminal stains attested to an attempt at rape, which had not been completed. The rapist proved to be a secretor, so it was possible to identify his blood as type A. There were no leads, so the case went cold.

Nearly two years later, Chief Baker was faced with a similar incident in the neighboring village of Enderby, which connected to Narborough by Ten Pound Lane. On July 31, 1986, Dawn Ashworth, also fifteen, took this lane, walking toward Narborough. She never returned. Her family made an extensive search, but two days passed before police officers found Dawn's body in some weeds. She had been stripped from the waist down, except for her shoes. She lay on her left side, with her knees pulled up. From scratches on her body it appeared that she had been dragged to this area. The pathologist found that Dawn had been hit in the face, penetrated vaginally and anally, and manually strangled. Dawn's body had been left just half a mile from where Lynda Mann had been attacked. Semen removed from both bodies revealed the same blood type.

An officer learned that a seventeen-year-old kitchen porter from the hospital was seen loitering in the area of Ten Pound Lane just after the police had taped it off as a potential crime scene. He was brought in for questioning. Mentally slow, his answers to questions were conflicting. Eventually, he confessed to killing Dawn, but not Lynda. He said he'd been drunk and had not meant to hurt anyone. He couldn't actually recall committing the murder. But then the porter recanted, and his mother offered an alibi, but detectives had turned up several young women who claimed that the suspect had molested them, so he remained in custody.[3]

Investigators believed this young man had killed both girls, and it turned out that he had the right blood type. Detectives thought they could extract a confession that would hold up in court, but the suspect firmly denied everything.

As Chief Baker was reading the newspaper, pondering the problems of his case, he came across an article that featured an interview with Dr. Jeffreys, who had recently spoken at a scientific conference about his work with DNA. In the interview he described how this new technique could offer a breakthrough in many areas, including the identification of criminals. His team required a small sample of biological fluids from the scene of the crime.

Snap! Baker realized that he had biological fluids from both murders, even if one was a bit degraded. It seemed too good to be true that a scientific method for identifying a criminal with what he had was available not far away. Chief Baker thought there was no harm in asking Jeffreys to put his method to the test. If this DNA analysis could prove that their suspect had assaulted and killed both girls, then they could skirt the problems that his confession had raised. They could solve both cases at once. Baker sent a message to Jeffreys right away. To his way of thinking, the lab at Leicester offered just what he needed.

Jeffreys had read about both incidents in the newspaper, so when Baker approached him, he was eager to test the samples. He asked that they be packaged and sent to his lab, along with blood samples from the suspect. However, he warned that the procedure would take a while. At that time, DNA extraction and analysis were painstaking procedures. Baker had no other means for solving these crimes, so he prepared himself to wait. If the method was everything that Jeffreys claimed, his answer was within reach. He already had the suspect. He just needed clear proof.

At the culmination of the analysis, the genetic profile of Lynda Mann's rapist was revealed. However, it was not what Baker and his investigators had expected. When compared to the suspect's blood sample, there was no match. So, perhaps he was telling the truth, which was bad news. The lab work continued for the next "nail-biting" week on comparing the semen removed from Dawn Ashworth to that taken from Lynda Mann. This time there *was* a match: the samples matched each other. This meant that the same person had committed both crimes, so the police were seeking just one offender, but the man they wanted was someone other than their suspect in custody. His blood work matched neither sample—just as he had claimed. This man was duly exonerated, but the police were back to square one. Considerable effort was expended to take blood samples from all local adult males, and although there were some twists in the case, the true offender, Colin Pitchfork, was located, arrested, and convicted. He was a local resident, even a family man, whom no one had suspected. DNA analysis had freed an innocent man and helped to convict a guilty one.

The Pitchfork case sparked international headlines, bringing a great deal of attention to DNA analysis from the law enforcement community. The rush was on to apply it to more crimes. Dr. Jeffreys was knighted, and in 2004, he received a Pride of Britain Award.[4] His moment of insight about lab results, coupled with Baker's aha! moment for practical application, has improved criminal investigation, assisted with the identification of Jane and John Does, exonerated innocent people falsely convicted of crimes,[5] and perhaps changed the future of personal identification.

NEUROAGILITY

The synchronicity of two snaps that, together, can change the world so dramatically seems rather magical. However, it comes from the way the brain evolved. Among other things, Dr. Nancy Andreasen is director of the MIND Institute in New Mexico and winner of the National Medal of Science. As a psychiatrist and an expert on the brain and its functions (as well as a former professor of literature), she studied our most important organ in its creative modes, analyzing such figures as Mozart, Kekulé, and Poincaré. Creativity, she found, is not the same as intelligence. It is the ability to see and shape things in new ways; it becomes *codified* as creativity when the domain or culture affected by the new invention accepts it. There could be lots of examples of creativity that go unrecognized simply because they did not affect culture in the right way or at the right time. For our purposes, we want to know how the brain pushes a creative idea to the surface as a snap, an aha! moment that moves into action. This is part of the creative process.

Andreasen describes how, at the age of twenty-four, Romantic poet Samuel Coleridge was inspired to write the poem *Kubla Khan*, considered among his best work. He had gone to a British farm to recuperate from a bout of illness. One day he was reading a book. In it was a description of Kublai Kahn's magnificent palace. After immersing himself in the details, Coleridge took what many consider to have been a dose of opium and fell asleep. In a hypnogogic state, as images arose in his mind, Coleridge mentally composed several hundred lines of his poem. He claimed he experienced no "consciousness of effort." When he woke up, he set about recapturing in writing what he seemed to have dreamed. However, someone interrupted him for a short period. He rushed back, hoping to reengage with his creative spark, but when he tried to write, he found that he had only vague images at best. They were nothing like the rich, colorful poetry he recalled from his dream-state. He had gotten on paper just one-fourth of what he believed he had produced.[6] He stopped there, disappointed, though having produced a significant work of art.

Verbally agile, Coleridge was not particularly scholarly or accomplished. In fact, he had dropped out of college. However, the convergence of his poetic efforts with his medicated state on this particular day had given his brain the space to do something interesting. "At the time he was reading," says Andreasen, "his brain was experiencing the dreamy sedation caused by opioids. Released from rational control and censorship, he spontaneously, and seemingly instantaneously, produced a convergence of images and metered words that constituted an entire poem."[7] Once he tried to apply conscious effort, the vision dissolved.

Andreasen found that a fresh approach to the world is a foundation for the kind of thinking that engenders a creative impulse in those people who can embrace and use it. Preconceptions play a small role in their lives, and they have little need for the artifice of conceptual structure that gives other people the feeling of comfort and predictability. They can tolerate ambiguity and stay open to new experiences. They can *dare*. "In fact they enjoy living in a world that is filled with unanswered questions and blurry boundaries."[8]

Imposed conventions are ignored. An interesting finding is that creative people who have honed their expertise in an area develop a sensitivity to the nuances of their domain, perhaps more so than their colleagues, and they're usually energetically curious. They persist well past the point where others feel satisfied or give up, and they often need no external validation. They usually work far more hours than others, sometimes day and night, until they're satisfied. They care about their work, especially its quality, so they remain dedicated. They may even slip into dissociative states that open doors to a different sense of reality. They can be flooded with an abundance of thoughts and ideas—even when engaged in conversation. One of the keys to their mental flexibility is that they tend to bypass the self-censoring mechanisms that limit others and just follow their mind wherever it goes.

Composer Peter Ilyich Tchaikovsky affirmed that inspiration, while often sudden, comes from the "disposition to work." He admits that it is difficult to articulate the "immeasurable sense of bliss" that accompanies the sudden awakening of a new idea. "I forget everything and behave like a madman. Everything within me starts pulsing and quivering."[9] Interruptions and the return to normalcy were "dreadful." To him the force of inspiration felt supernatural. However, it does not come to those who sit around waiting. It's top–down, not bottom–up. It comes during the process of mental engagement.

In simple terms, the brain has four lobes with specific functions. The occipital lobes help to process vision, the temporal lobes assist auditory perception and the development of language, the parietal lobes relate to spatial perception, while the frontal lobes generally assist with executive reasoning and decision making. The association cortex includes areas of the cerebral cortex that are not sensory or motor in the traditional sense but are associated with advanced stages of sensory information processing, multisensory integration, or sensorimotor integration. Neurons cover the lobes in six layers and integrate information processing throughout the brain. The complex organization, via multiple connections, allows us to perform complicated mental activities in seemingly effortless ways. Andreasen suggests that the brain is a self-organizing system of feedback loops that constantly generates new thoughts—sometimes spontaneously. At times, its thinking processes can therefore be nonlinear.[10]

Andreasen studied random episodic silent thinking (the brain *not* performing a task), which she believed could provide a neural basis for the unconscious. Using positron emission tomography scans, which measured regionalized blood flow in the brain, she found a great deal of activity in the association cortex, where information is integrated. "Apparently, when the brain/mind thinks in a free and unencumbered fashion, it uses its most human and complex parts."[11] The association cortex makes it possible to gather a lot of information together and thereby creates the conditions for novel associations. It makes sense, then, that when snapping occurs, the idea seems to arrive fully formed and ready for action. Andreasen believes that during these flashes of genius the brain is working as a self-organizing system, and what it delivers during inspiration depends on its information input.[12] A musician's snap is loaded for musical composition, a chess player's, for chess moves, and a mathematician's, for theorems and equations. Poincaré even described the feeling as that of ideas interlocking.

Recall the experiments from chapter 1 in which Dr. Joel Katz and his team took medical students to an art museum to improve their process of observation. This proved so successful that he expanded his work to other personnel.

"We have two other courses that utilize art museums as a teaching stage," he said. "One of them is for interns in medicine. They're now official doctors. The problem they face is that the rigors of their schedule and the enormous responsibilities they face, often with consequences that are outside their control, tend to erode the humanism. Our goal has been to create a humanistic curriculum to try to help first-year physicians preserve and grow the humanistic attributes that brought them into medicine. It's a longitudinal series of workshops that run the entire year. One is in the art museum."[13]

Working with Dr. Katz, Dr. Moriah Quinn heads the humanistic curriculum. It involves ten workshops, the purpose of which is to increase a sense of community, diminish isolation, and create a professional support network. "For one three-hour session," Katz explains,

we take them to the Boston Museum of Fine Arts. We have a dinner and then group observation sessions, with facilitated discussions by professional art educators in the galleries. We have a warmup activity: we take them to Paul Gauguin's painting *Where Do We Come From? What Are We? Where Are We Going?* It encourages them to find their own areas of observation but also to consider other people's ideas.

Then we take them to a second one, such as Copley's *Watson and the Shark*. This activity is about drawing metaphors about life. It's about an incident that happened in Cuba where a man fell overboard, was attacked by a shark, and was rescued. We ask them how this piece relates to their work in medicine. Some relate to the person being attacked, some relate to the shark, some to the rescuers, and some relate to the bystanders who are watching, without any control.

The third activity is about difficult conversations, and we take them to an Etruscan sarcophagus. It's a beautiful carved limestone on the outside of a casket of a husband and wife. This presents an opportunity for the interns to talk about conversations they've had about patients who died or about family members who weren't able to let their patients die. The central idea is how they relate to the dying patient.

The fourth session is about self-care and renewal, and we take them into the Buddhist Temple Room and lead them through a guided relaxation exercise. It's a very peaceful room.

The results are being analyzed, but it's clear to Katz and his team from day-to-day observations that the participants in this curriculum have developed greater clarity and mental agility in their approach to their primary work.

Psychologist Howard Gruber searched for the creative spark in the set of notebooks that Charles Darwin kept from 1837 through 1839, when he made some of his most significant discoveries. What Gruber discovered affirms the type of preparation needed. Darwin had a gift for mindful engagement and intense focus. He kept lists of his observations, sketches, and ideas, going over them again and again to consider them within different organizational schemes. He might abandon one line of interpretation, only to return to it later for reconsideration. His process of mental examination is akin to the persistent novelist's constant revision of a manuscript: try this, try that. He used a central metaphor to help with organization, which changed as he found one that better suited his purposes. In addition, he kept in mind his guiding purpose, which fueled the determination to continually monitor his progress and remain alert to nuances he had not yet noticed. He remained on course, without letting up, and the work became so much a part of him it was second nature. He could remember many aspects of his projects with ease. His reward, as Gruber's cognitive mapping shows, was illumination on nearly a daily basis. Gruber viewed Darwin as a skilled juggler who could keep many things in the air at once while always looking to add something fresh.[14]

"The associations are occurring freely," says Andreasen. "They are running unchecked, not subject to any of the reality principles that normally govern them."[15] Andreasen believes that the brain operates according to certain stages. First, it disorganizes its information. Then it links words or objects not previously linked for a new form of self-organization. "Possessors of extraordinary creativity are apparently blessed with brains that are more facile at creating free association."[16] They can perceive the world in unique and unusual ways.

This is a good place to say something about mental flexibility as a way to develop agility. Flexibility is the skill of thinking beyond what we have been trained to do, defying traditional thinking and coming up with unique perspectives. *Agility* is being able to offer perspectives that include a plan of action. You apply mental flexibility to actual situations, coming up with several options to achieve some result. Whenever we prejudge a situation or cling to habit, we blind ourselves to other possibilities. Mental agility requires flexibility followed by a creative approach and a course of action. You need first to realize that almost any situation can be viewed in more than one way and, second, to be able to think of some of those possible ways.

Here's an example: rags were in short supply in mid-seventeenth-century Europe, and since paper was made from cottons and linens, paper producers grew desperate. England had even banned people from burying their dead in cotton garments to preserve the paper supply. In the midst of this shortage, René-Antoine Ferchault de Réaumur, a French chemist who was affected by it, was walking in the woods. He spotted a whitish wasp nest. He stopped and looked more closely. When he examined its paperlike composition, he snapped on the solution to Europe's problem: wasps made paper by chewing wood and plants. His idea was the first step toward making paper from wood pulp.[17]

In 1906, a fictional detective caught America's interest because he examined difficult thought puzzles from unique and surprising angles (which meant that the author who created him was able to do this, too). The author, Jacques Futrelle, introduced in *The Thinking Machine*, the character Professor Augustus S. F. X. Van Dusen, whom a multitude of universities and scientific institutions had honored for his extraordinary cerebral skills. Although Futrelle went down with the *Titanic* in 1912, he left a series of stories that demonstrated how science, ingenuity, and logic could solve seemingly impossible dilemmas. In his most famous tale, "The Problem of Cell 13," Professor Van Dusen accepts a dare to be locked inside a secure prison cell and, without tools, to think his way out. He had just one week. In a MacGyver-like manner, he ponders unique uses for everything he sees and relies on a rat, a drainpipe, his shirt and socks, a passerby, a wire, tooth powder, shoe blackener, and several dollar bills to assist his successful escape. He tells his awed audience that "anything is possible in the hands of a man who knows how to use it." Futrelle's stories had nearly as great an influence on popular ideas about investigation during this era as did Sherlock Holmes.[18]

Exercising similar flexibility, Wilbur and Orville Wright used a damaged tombstone and buggy parts to build a printing press for their newspaper. In 1893, they opened a bicycle shop and created their own bicycles. Later that decade, Wilbur read everything he could find about aviation. He noticed problems that had plagued other inventors, sometimes fatally, so he carefully considered what he would need to do to invent a successful flying machine. Wilbur watched birds in flight, and noticed how they banked and turned. He believed that the secret of their control lay in the way they twisted their wing tips. He knew that to make a machine take off in flight it would have to be able to roll right and left. One day at the bike shop, Wilbur began twisting an inner tube box with the ends removed. He snapped on an idea about how to achieve the control he wanted for flight: twisting the wing would change its position in the oncoming wind. Wilbur and Orville built a box kite and braced the wings with wires so they could be twisted in opposite directions. It worked. They called this "wing warping," and with it they managed to launch a small glider from a dune in North Carolina. Next, they built an engine and in 1903 made aviation history.[19]

SLEIGHT OF BRAIN

Brain processing is complex, but within its mysteries—even its apparent vulnerabilities—we can create the conditions for snaps. Many people who have dramatically experienced creative aha! moments describe them as magical, and they're not far off the mark. In fact, the way that magicians exploit the brain gives us other clues about how to launch some snaps.

The human visual system was built to focus attention. It's a survival mechanism. We need to see important things much more than we need to see *everything*. Over the past decade, neuroscientists have come to understand that the mechanisms of focus and attention are involved in illusions, and by devising experiments that duplicate stage illusions, they have discovered how our brains' perceptual loopholes make magic possible. For example, we have neurons that respond to motion. When they also attend to the terminal point of a stick that is moving in a rapid bouncing manner, it can appear to be flexible, bending in the middle. This is a *spatial mislocalization*. With spatial mislocalization, a magician can appear to bend a metal spoon. Visual persistence means that when we look at an object that is then removed from the visual field, its image will briefly persist as an after-image. In addition, objects to which we attend have more solidity (salience) in our perceptual field than objects in the same field to which we do not attend. As the task of processing grows more complex or difficult, essential information is enhanced at the expense of processing nonessential information. The latter is more actively suppressed.[20]

A famous pickpocket discovered that his ability to deflect attention succeeded only when he moved his distracting hand in an arc. Cognitive scientists believe that eye movements that precede decisions about the direction of our gaze, called *saccades*, cause this effect. The hand movement tricks the saccades. When the hand moves in a straight line, we look at the end point. It's automatic. But when the hand moves in an arc or semicircle, the saccades cannot decipher where the hand is going, so they fixate on the *hand*, not on its direction. Cognitive scientists view this phenomenon as a vulnerability in the way humans perceive motion.[21]

A neuroimaging study undertaken by neuroscientists Stephen Macknik and Susanna Martinez-Conde (husband and wife) after a trip to Las Vegas gave them an aha! moment that provided a new direction for their work, as well as some unexpected colleagues. They were trying to bring attention to their research on visual neuroscience at the Barrow Neurological Institute in Phoenix, Arizona. In particular, they wanted to find a way to intrigue people outside their area of specialization. They had thought up a contest to find the best illusion of the year, which proved to be successful. Soon they were invited to chair a conference in Las Vegas for the Association for the Scientific Study of Consciousness. They went out to Vegas to look for an appropriate venue. But they faced a problem: they had already run a contest, so what could they do as a follow-up that would be provocative and original? Macknik and Martinez-Conde walked up and down the famous strip, looking at one hotel after another. Many, they noticed, were advertising magicians performing stage tricks. They had a flash of insight: these performers knew all about illusions. They, too, worked on observer susceptibility to deception. "The idea rapidly took shape," they later wrote. "We would bring scientists and magicians together so scientists could learn the magicians' techniques and harness their powers."[22]

Thus Macknik and Martinez-Conde created a new field of psychology: neuromagic. They realized that magicians had a studied grasp of how to trick mental processing, perhaps a better grasp than neuroscientists had. Despite the code of silence among professional magicians, several agreed to join the project, including James Randi, Apollo Robbins, and the team of Penn & Teller. Interested themselves in cognitive science, the magicians demonstrated and then described optical, mechanical, and psychological methods for magic. By tricking their audiences into making normal but erroneous assumptions and focusing on distractions, they could effectively operate in the perceptual shadows. The observing psychologists decided that the greatest magic show on earth was inside the brain, thanks, in part, to the way our visual system functions.

Information from the external world moves through our retinas and forms patterns in the brain. We make sense of them according to our inner representations of the world. Different cortical regions extract information from electrochemical impulses, so we can perceive objects as lines, surfaces, textures, colors, motions, and contrasts. Different sets of neurons respond to different things. For example, some are there to detect upward motion; some to respond to downward motion. We can focus our attention mindfully, and when the object is particularly salient, our focus narrows even more, resisting distraction from other parts of the visual field.

One study shows that people with highly developed working memories can dissociate more easily from background noise; that is, they can resist "sensory capture"; however, because their attention is so fixed, they are more vulnerable to the type of attuned focus that can easily be deceived.[23]

The perceptual system resolves apparent ambiguity by interpreting sensations within a context. The brain fills in gaps to provide a rich visual experience. This also means it can be deceived into including erroneous information. Macknik and Martinez-Conde describe the magician's working arena as a "frame." They are attention managers. They create a context for drawing focus to whatever they want, knowing that their audience will automatically follow. They then use motion, lighting, novelty, surprise, timing, knowledge about typical human assumptions, and a context to keep control over their audience's perception. One might keep up a constant patter to draw attention or to trigger a dramatic or fast device. They set up their tricks as part of a natural action, such as touching their hat, so it won't draw attention.

As we watch a magician perform sleight-of-hand tricks, different neurons operate in contrasting ways that defy ordinary logic. It seems to us that successful tricks, such as having our watch surreptitiously removed while we're watching, are impossible. But Macknik and Martinez-Conde have studied illusions—the experience of something that fails to match reality—so they know something about brain slippage. A common experience is the waterfall illusion. When we focus on a waterfall for a full minute and then look at the rocks off to the side, the rocks appear to move in an upward direction. The researchers say this is because the brain neurons for downward motion have adapted and relaxed, going into a less active mode. When we shift our attention to the rocks, we throw off the neural balance and, for a moment, the neurons that focus on upward direction come to the fore. We "see" upward motion that is not really occurring.[24]

When people watch a magician, one group of neurons enhances focus and another group actively represses attention to anything else. In light of the main event, any other events are deemed irrelevant. Thus, they fail to get processed into memory. Magicians have calculated how to draw and maximize focus on a deflection so that they can effectively work their tricks in the attentional shadows. This provides neurological disbelief, the experience of surprise and awe. Studies that track eye movement (a scan track) during a trick indicate that the eye can see the trick, but the brain apparently does not register it. (The magician manipulates attention by misdirecting it.) There appear to be separate mechanisms for visual motor control and for perception, which is partially constructed from social cues and expectations. Brain scans pick up a dramatic level of activity in the left hemisphere as the trick occurs, suggesting that the brain is working overtime to make sense of what just happened: "That's impossible, but it must be possible; it just happened."[25] Magicians can even induce false memories by using suggestion, unspoken innuendo, and misinformation after an effect has been witnessed. What they imply, especially regarding intentionality and cause-and-effect, can become part of the observer's memory. For example, they repeat an action several times to induce the observer to believe that every time they do this action, they get the same effect. However, they can short-change and thereby fool the observer: throwing a ball into the air three times makes observers expect that the fourth time the magician "tosses," the ball must have gone into the air. They "see" and remember it, even though it did not occur. He kept the ball in his hand.

The brain is wired for illusion, because it apparently fails to self-reflect. "Magic tricks work because humans have a hardwired process of attention and awareness that is hackable."[26] That is, the brain constructs our reality based on our experiences, which creates our expectations. When we get used to a certain cause-and-effect scenario, we anticipate how it will work, so we expect and we stop focusing. Thus, we fail to see everything in our perceptual field. We fall into a cognitive stupor that shuts out a lot of information because we "know" what happens next. This opens the door for illusionists, who can play off any of a number of perceptual habits. They can turn an observer's attention against itself through misdirection, such as directing viewers toward a dramatic distraction that draws attention (e.g., a flying white bird). At the same time, they shield what they're actually doing, like shoving another bird up their sleeve.

There is also a perceptual phenomenon called lateral inhibition. Two bars line up on either side of a target bar. As they are moved closer to the middle bar, it seems to vanish: while the conscious brain no longer sees it, the retinas do. Now we see it, now we don't—simultaneously. Another way to make a trick work is to gaze at viewers while performing it, because most people will look into eyes that are looking at them.

"People take reality for granted," says Teller of the Penn & Teller magician team. "Reality seems so simple. We just open our eyes and there it is. But that doesn't mean it is simple."[27] Penn & Teller use stage magic to awaken people to the tricks of their own perceptual processing. They know that the brain cannot see everything, so it uses perceptual shortcuts to simplify the picture. Teller believes that each time he performs a trick, he's engaging in a psychological experiment. "If the audience asks, 'How the hell did he do that?' then the experiment was successful. I've exploited the efficiencies of your mind."[28]

Aside from visual and optical illusions are cognitive illusions. These usually rely on the way our attention functions, and on how we make causal attributions. Back in the 1970s, Ulric Neisser and his scientific colleagues were aware that people failed to recall the content of a speech presented to one ear while focusing on speech with their other ear. This suggested that the brain does not multitask very well (despite what texting drivers want to believe!). It appears to have some perceptual shadows.[29]

These researchers also studied what happens to attention when an unexpected event occurs. The setup was this: subjects viewed two superimposed videos of people playing a game. Then something unexpected would occur in one of them, such as the game players suddenly stopping to shake hands. If the viewers had focused on the other video, most missed the unexpected event entirely.

The observing brain tries to reconcile the conflict between what is seen and what seems possible. An object might be right in front of us, but if the brain focuses firmly (turns its spotlight) on something else, a blind spot can form in the perceptual field, producing *inattentional blindness*. We see something right in front of us, but we don't process it as information.

Arien Mack and Irvin Rock, who researched the effect of divided attention on perception, coined the term *inattentional blindness* for this phenomenon. In one experiment, they had subjects view a cross that appeared briefly on a computer screen and report whether the horizontal or vertical bar was longer. During one of the trials, another shape appeared as well. At the end of the trials, the researchers queried subjects about whether they had noticed it. As many as three out of four had failed to see it, even when it was a unique color.[30]

The most celebrated experiment of this nature ended up on

YouTube®. Daniel Simons and Christopher Chabris took it to the basketball court. They had observers watch a video and count how many times the players in white passed a basketball to one another. As subjects concentrated on this task for a full minute, intentionally ignoring the passes made by players wearing black, a man dressed in a gorilla suit ambled to the center of the court, faced the camera, and pounded on his chest before exiting. Approximately 50 percent of the subjects failed to see the gorilla. Common sense says they should have noticed such a thing, but the brain has its own sense. While it is true that the gorilla blended well with the dark-shirted players, and thus the contrast often necessary for clear perception was absent, an experiment with a woman dressed as a witch instead of a gorilla produced the same results.[31] So did adding a red gorilla.

This finding can be applied to sudden insight. When we focus on one thing, the attentional field narrows. Our expectations assist to makes sense of what we're seeing so that unexpected incidents or objects fail to register. We've seen examples of how people focused a great deal of effort on a problem but solved it only when they pulled away and relaxed. In chapter 5, Poincaré articulated the phenomenon. The brain was processing a solution, but it lay outside the attentional spotlight. It might have been as close as the gorilla facing the camera, on the tip of the tongue, so to speak, but it remained in the blind spot. To be able to see an innovation in an unexpected event involves not just stepping away but being mentally agile enough to refocus.

For example, Charles Goodyear had an obsession with rubber. He knew it could erase pencil marks and keep us dry in a rainstorm, but he was determined to find more substantial ways to apply it. He saw two hurdles: rubber melted at high temperatures and became brittle at low ones. For over a decade, Goodyear applied himself, mixing the smelly substance in his improvised kitchen lab with various chemicals. But it wasn't his thinking process that yielded the discovery that changed the lives of people worldwide. Rather, it was Goodyear's flash of insight after he accidentally dropped one mixture on the hot stove. He'd mixed rubber with sulphur and white lead, and it hardened into a unique and practical material. Among other things, Goodyear's discovery sparked the invention of tires.[32]

The left brain works on one type of information, and our focus follows a coherent route: we can make sense of how we got from point A to point B. However, the right hemisphere has a more holistic way of processing, and it's most effective when the left brain goes blind. The right hemisphere performs the trick. A significant factor in this type of success is mental agility: the brain must relax, play, dance. The perceiver must be able to refocus expectations and agendas.

DANCE FAVORS THE PREPARED MIND

Daniel Tammet, a linguist with autism who holds the record for reciting the first 22,514 digits of the mathematical constant pi, says that he does not "crunch numbers," he "dances with them."[33] That is, he creates the conditions for a playful convergence of brain processes, and he has hit on just what makes a snap actually snap: it's the free flow of right- and left-brain processes that work together—and play together—on a problem. It feels exciting and energizing, like a dance choreographed to include the opportunity for unpredictable spontaneity. "In my mind," he said in an interview, "numbers and words are far more than squiggles of ink on a page. They have form, color, texture, and so on. They come alive to me. . . . The information is not static."[34] Tammet points out in his book *Embracing the Wide Sky* that visualizing information makes it easier to remember, and his creative talents offer an increased ability to chunk words and numbers.

Tammet admits that no one had viewed him as intelligent when he was a child because his autistic behavior was rigid and repetitive. He believes that his brain developed differently, and that his epileptic seizures offered "hyperconductivity" to his thoughts. This provided a greater degree of communication among the separate parts than most people have. "My theory," he said, "is that rare forms of creative imagination are the result of an extraordinary convergence of normally disconnected thoughts, memories, feelings, and ideas."[35]

Although it's not necessary to actually start dancing with ideas or information, it just might work. Pop singer Michael Jackson, known for his unique dance routines, began his ascent to the top of international pop culture in the late 1960s as the youngest and most visible member of the Jackson 5. His aspiration for success as a solo artist was realized during the following decade with the release of his albums *Off the Wall*, *Thriller*, and *Bad*. After his multi-record-breaking success, many viewed him as largely responsible for rescuing the music business. He then changed the music video industry. A perfectionist with visions of greatness, Jackson kept ripping through the envelope to create videos of his music that would surprise viewers and set new standards. In an interview for MTV, he insisted that he had wanted to avoid being just another can on an assembly line: he wanted to take music and dance a step forward, so he was vigilant about spotting innovative ways to achieve this. He took a top–down approach.

Jackson often defied the music industry's conventions by doing something so compelling that people *had* to notice. At a time when music videos relied on basic videography, he enriched his products with storylines and complex dance moves, including group dances. He offered them as more than just a PR tool; they were an art form. As a result, Jackson became the first black entertainer to become a favorite with the crossover audience of the so-called MTV generation of the 1980s. He understood that surprise, extravagance, and entertainment were significant features for getting people to return for more. From his single white glove to the perceptual illusion of his "moonwalk" dance step to a group choreography for zombies, Jackson never ceased to test and push past boundaries. In the process of doing this, he broke through many racial barriers as well. "He would come up with great ideas," his producer said, "and then say, 'Now how can we make this better?'"

In 1991, for example, the music video for "Black or White" used a new type of "morphing" technology to produce a special effect that blended people of all races seamlessly into and out of each other. Jackson morphed himself into a black panther, an idea on which he had snapped while talking with his sister, Janet, also a successful singer. It was a groundbreaking flourish. He later described how he found his moves for this video as he was creating them: "In the dance, I let go." The seemingly impossible forward lean in "Smooth Criminal" that Jackson and his team of dancers performed came from an innovative engineering feat. To achieve the 45-degree angle, they wore special shoes with a triangular cutout in the heel. When the time arrived for them to make the move, a peg-like aperture emerged from the dance floor onto which they could hook the heel, anchoring them sufficiently so they could lean much farther forward than gravity would typically allow.

Even beyond his musical aesthetic, Jackson's innovations extended from short film to choreography to fashion. Among his goals was to put together the best group of people he could find and then inspire them to go to new places. "I want to use my gifts," he once said, "to help others figure out what their gifts are."[36] He was a pathfinder, the light on the path, and the one at the rear who kept others moving. For his final concert in 2009, *This Is It*, which he choreographed just before he died from heart failure, his team created an enormous 3-D LCD screen for a stage prop. The goal was to blend the stage show via illusion with the most astonishing visuals. The same performers were filmed in various depictions from a haunted house in "Thriller" to mobster scenes for "Smooth Criminal," so that it would appear that they had walked out of the film onto the stage. Nothing like it had ever been done before. As Jackson would constantly say, "We gotta find something new." He found it within a dance, an image, a musical instrument, or something heretofore wholly unrelated to music.[37]

While Jackson used physical movement to snap, others have "danced" in their sleep; that is, they found a solution to a problem while dreaming. Friedrich Kekulé, a Belgian chemist, had spent years on a special designation of a molecular structure. Feeling defeated, he gave up. One day he fell asleep by the fireplace. When he woke up, he remembered his dream of a snake with its tail in its mouth. Kekulé understood, using the image as the foundation for the benzene ring.[38]

Otto Loewi, an Austrian neuroscientist, even got his famous life-changing dream to repeat itself. He was at work on the notion of chemical transmission of nerve impulses. He'd been experimenting on a frog heart but was getting poor results. He worried about it and had trouble relaxing. At night he often lay awake. One night, he had a vision of what he needed to do, so in the middle of the night he scribbled some notes. Then he went to sleep, finally able to let go. However, in the morning, he could not read his handwriting. He spent the entire day trying to recall the dream, because he thought it was the key to designing an experiment that would appropriately test his hypothesis. As hours passed, he grew desperate. Finally, worn out, he went to bed. Around 3:00 a.m., the images recurred. This time when he awoke, he got dressed and went right to his lab and performed the experiment on a pair of frogs. For his discovery that nerve impulses are chemically transmitted, he earned the Nobel Prize in 1936.[39] (The award money saved his life when the Germans arrested him in 1938; it was sufficient to bribe them to let him go.)

It's important for enhancing mental agility to create a playful or relaxing mental space in which the mind can freely invent. We've already seen how the right brain takes over during an impasse. However, certain activities can facilitate it. Many innovators insist that part of the process is to just get away from the workspace and take their minds off the issue. Some go for a walk or take a nap. Others have described more unique contexts:

- Dr. Jonas Salk was working on a cure for polio in a dark basement in Pittsburgh. He failed to get what he wanted, so he traveled to Italy to walk around for a while in a monastery.

There, he experienced a rush of ideas, including the one that led to the polio vaccine.[40]

- Art Fry, an employee of 3M, had spotted a weak type of glue in the course of his work, but only when he was singing in church did he see an application. He wanted a bookmark that would stay in place without damaging the hymnal, and he went on to invent the Post-It® note.[41]

- Poet Hart Crane liked to scribble snippets of verse and put them aside, collecting them for months, even years, before they all came together as inspiration for a poem. Taking his cue from a friend who liked to hunt animals by "charming" them into the open with a harmonica, Crane used music, laughter, and drinking to coax his ideas out of their hiding place in his subconscious.[42]

- Rudyard Kipling insisted that "when your daemon is in charge, try not to think consciously. Drift, wait, obey. . . ."[43]

- Sir Paul McCartney of the Beatles claimed to have woken up one morning with a melody fully developed in his head. He thought that perhaps he had heard it somewhere, but he could not identify a song like it, nor could his friends and musical associates. He worked on lyrics and came up with a title, "Yesterday." It went on to be one of the most recorded songs in history.[44]

- Philo Farnsworth envisioned the first electronic television while plowing a field.[45]

- Poet John Keats found that stopping his work when he felt blocked and getting dressed in his best clothes helped him find his muse.[46]

- Richard Feynman—a physicist instrumental in developing quantum electrodynamics—usually went to a topless bar to relax (although his most seminal insight occurred when he saw a tossed plate fly through the air in Cornell University's cafeteria).[47]

- Math professor Darren Crowdy let his mind wander while listening to a lecture; suddenly he knew the solution to a long-unsolved math puzzle. "It just clicked," he said, "and I stood up and left the room. I was so excited I had to get to work on it then and there."[48]

- Author J. K. Rowling was on a train pondering the plot of an adult novel when she snapped on a child wizard. "I had been writing almost continuously since the age of six," she wrote, "but I had never been so excited about an idea before. I simply sat and thought, for four (delayed train) hours, and all the details bubbled up in my brain, and this scrawny, black-haired, bespectacled boy who did not know he was a wizard became more and more real to me."[49]

Our culture firmly supports the notion that conscious effort will produce our best work because it is based on transparent rationality. We can articulate and evaluate the steps. However, this approach can actually hinder our best work. Snaps emerge most often from people who exercise and develop the association cortex. They gain a greater sense of connection among seemingly distinct brain functions. They don't mind "behaving like a mad man," as Tchaikovsky put it, because they're eager to experience their bliss in its fullest expression, to dance with their ideas into nonlinear arenas, come what may. Thus, they exercise and expand their mental agility among the brain's many neural systems.

The attentional structure that makes us vulnerable to a magician's illusions works to our benefit for mental flexibility. We need only understand that the perceptual shadows also contain things. In fact, the more we develop the spotlight of focus, the more likely it is that we will be able to immerse in our field, notice its nuances, cross-fertilize with other fields in the most innovative ways, and then allow innovation to snap.

KEY POINTS

- Alertness that produces a snap coordinates with mental agility.
- The best conditions for a snap involve work that feels like play.
- Snappers learn the best conditions for idea incubation.
- Some brain cells enhance focus while others operate under the radar of left-brain consciousness.
- Our best work may arise from neural blind spots and thus defy rational explanation.

CHAPTER 8

THE TAO OF DATA MINING

NEW PERCEPTIONS

Physicist Gordon Gould had worked on amplified optics for two decades, struggling to develop a laser when, during a relaxed Saturday night, he envisioned it: "The whole thing suddenly popped into my head," he said.[1] He went right to work sketching the components for a model and listing the practical applications, which eventually included weapons systems, supermarket scanners, and even DVD players. Gould had the answer the whole time in the type of data he'd collected over the course of his career. He just needed to mine it in the right way.

Try this puzzle and see if you can find the pattern.

Which is the next word in this sequence? *Base, Minor, Upstart, Helicon, Curate.* Choose from *Flute, Icon, Hexagon, Meridian,* and *Tumbler.*

Give it a moment—remember, relaxing the brain lets it feel safe to play a little. Everything you need is right in front of you. Don't peek until you've given this a try, because this chapter is about the ability to pull out answers from the data you know.

OK, here's the answer: the five vowels repeat through the words in alphabetical order. The next word, then, would be *icon.*

Data mining is the process of extracting hidden patterns from information—seeing or organizing it in a unique new way, usually for decision making, marketing, or prediction. This generally involves sorting through large caches of information so as to efficiently retrieve the information needed. Fortunately our brains are equipped to perform this task. To achieve effective mining for a specific purpose, we must usually analyze data from a variety of different perspectives. Computers have software for this purpose, which allows users to access information from many different angles, categorize it, and summarize the relationships among different aspects or types. Technically, data mining is the process of finding correlations or patterns among dozens of fields in large relational databases. For example, companies use computers to sift through volumes of supermarket scanner data to create market research reports. In the business world, data mining has identified successful employees and customer habits. It has also yielded numerous discoveries in medicine, education, and bioinformatics. Snapping relies on effective data mining, and effective snappers have plenty of data available from their training and experience. Once they succeed with invention, they keep looking for ways to do it again—especially when they appreciate how snapping works.

Many myths surround the figure of Eugène François Vidocq, the founder of the world's first undercover agency. But his ability to effectively transform data from his experience and from wherever his curiosity led him is beyond dispute. He went from a convict with a hopeless life sentence to one of the world's most respected law enforcement officials, first by being inventive with opportunity and then by being vigilant in his occupation. He was a top–down type of guy. Such novelists as Victor Hugo, Alexandre Dumas, and Honoré de Balzac celebrated his exploits, as well as Edgar Allan Poe, whom he also inspired.

A resourceful visionary, Vidocq insisted in his memoir that his prison experience had given him advantages that had one day made him successful. Born in Arras, France, on July 23, 1775, Vidocq was the son of a baker. Still, from a young age he yearned for adventure. One day, he killed a man in a duel. Since King Louis XVI and Queen

Marie Antoinette were in need of an army to resist the movement for a new republic, Vidocq was given a choice: go to prison or join the military. He chose the latter, but his impetuous nature got him arrested again . . . several times.

During his first actual prison stint, Vidocq met a farmer who had been arrested and incarcerated for stealing grain to feed his family. Taking pity on him, Vidocq forged a pardon. Prison officials discovered the deception and increased Vidocq's sentence to eight years. Incensed, he escaped, was caught, and escaped again. The challenge became a game to him, and he became quite adept at charming, deceiving, and eluding his guards, often with clever disguises. At one point, his reputation for breaking out was so great that officials forbade him any excursions from his cell. Still, he got past them. Yet for all his escapes, he was no good on the run, and each time Vidocq was caught, his sentence increased in severity. Finally, he was sentenced to life in a corrections hellhole so brutal that many men who were sent there buckled from the treatment and died. Vidocq remained hopeful that he could rely on his reason to prevent this from happening to him.

According to one tale, Vidocq managed to get an audience with the prefecture of police at Lyons. He claimed that his original offense did not merit such harsh treatment, and he wanted a chance to prove that he could go straight. He offered something that could help reduce crime in the city: he could be an informant. He knew French criminals better than anyone, having lived among them for so many years. He was familiar with their gang associations, their plans for future crimes, and their associates on the outside. As the story goes, the prefecture said he had no choice but to send Vidocq to prison, so Vidocq snapped on an idea and proposed a deal: if he should succeed in escaping, he would show he meant business by returning to the prefecture's office. In this way, he would demonstrate his honesty and cleverness at the same time. The prefecture agreed but then added extra guards to escort Vidocq to prison. Vidocq was soon back in his office.

In a less imaginative account, Vidocq explained his plight to the head of the Lyons police, Jean-Pierre Dubois. When Dubois looked into the matter, he decided that Vidocq was guilty of a minor misdeed, so he (not Vidocq) offered the deal for him to become a police informant in exchange for freedom. No matter who came up with the plan, Vidocq was quick to grasp his advantages. He could move freely among criminals, who knew him as one of them, listening to them brag about crimes and learning the details of their future plans. These he reported to Dubois, and the arrest rate greatly improved.[2]

Eventually Vidocq moved to Paris, where Napoleon reigned, and in 1809 continued there as an informant for the Criminal Division of the prefecture of police. His work gained him an audience with Napoleon, who encouraged Vidocq to continue as an undercover informant. He agreed to be "arrested" so he could gain access to the hardened offenders in La Force prison. From there, he made regular reports and even solved several murders. After nearly two years, Vidocq, who wanted a street assignment, was taken out in irons and managed to "escape." He merged seamlessly into the Parisian underworld and surreptitiously offered information for hundreds of arrests.

But he aspired to do something much more ambitious, and he created one innovation after another. Vidocq proposed a bureau of undercover informants like himself. When he got the green light, he snapped a quick succession of ideas, mined from his experience, with which he could improve law enforcement. He organized the first-ever card file system on offenders and required his agents to file written reports. He also included women as agents because he realized that they could get into places and get information that male agents could not. The operation proved to be a success. In October 1812, Napoleon signed a decree that made Vidocq's *Brigade de la Sûreté* into the world's first national security force. The Sûreté brought respect to law enforcement in Paris, and branches were soon established in other areas of France.[3]

Teaching his associates that "observation is the first rule of investigation," Vidocq mined his background to snap a system of clever techniques for acquiring information. By this time, the criminal underground had caught on to who Vidocq was, so he invented other tactics: he and his agents went among criminals in various disguises. He also exaggerated his reputation for getting men to talk, hoping to influence a perception of his skill that could provoke confessions. In addition, Vidocq used deception. When he arrived to search a place, he might fabricate the reason he was there so as to give the suspect false confidence that Vidocq was on the wrong trail. Once inside, Vidocq would then look for evidence of the actual crime.

His focus on a systematic approach inspired several forensic inventions that are still in use today: he kept detailed records, he performed bullet comparisons, he preserved footprint impressions with plaster of paris, he compared samples of handwriting to forged notes, and he suggested that fingerprints might be a viable form of identification. Vidocq also created forge-proof paper and indelible ink, and for the courts, he invented a form of plea bargaining. In other words, he was always attentive for ways to make his knowledge and experience produce something that would improve his profession.

Even after he resigned in 1833, Vidocq hardly retired. The following year, he established *Le Bureau des Renseignements*, the world's first private detective agency. Having no trouble attracting clients, he remained active until he was eighty years old. Despite the resistance among established law enforcement to Vidocq's "new" ways, he made such an impression and was so successful that he inspired many novelists—and thus, became the archetype of the forensic sleuth.[4] As a resourceful data miner, he left a powerful legacy.

THE SPEED OF THOUGHT

When psychologist Nancy Koehn studied entrepreneurs, she noted that they keep learning throughout their lives, in whatever situations they find themselves.[5] They are perpetually collecting and processing; they see the same things that others see, but they *notice* more and are more apt to make some use of the information. As a result, they gain perspective that illuminates new patterns in the information at hand. They're also more inventive than the average person. It's the difference between the person who tosses the can after drinking the juice inside and the person who turns the can into a vase, a planter, or some other useful object.

Take James Watt, for example. From his expertise as an ordinary mechanic for the University of Glasgow, his brain was able to mine the data and extract something that he instantly recognized as a brilliant idea and a much-needed invention. Although the story is told secondhand, from what we know about aha! moments, there is no reason to disbelieve that the experience happened as reported.

Watt was taking a walk one Sunday afternoon in 1765 around Glasgow, Scotland. From Charlotte Street, he went through a gate into the Glasgow Green and passed a washing house. All the while, Watt was pondering a repair he'd been asked to make to a Newcomen steam engine, invented fifty years earlier. The machine used vacuum power inside a cylinder when steam was condensed to liquid form. The resulting pumping action had made it possible to remove water from mines. But the machine was inefficient. To make it work to produce cycles of heating and cooling required a lot of fuel, because the same cylinder that contained the steam also condensed it.

Suddenly, Watt snapped on a more efficient device: use *two* cylinders: one to heat water to steam and the other to cool steam to water. They could thereby cut their fuel use by half. "The idea came into my mind, that as steam was an elastic body it would rush into a vacuum, and if a communication was made between the cylinder and an exhausted vessel, it would rush into it, and it might be there condensed without cooling the cylinder."[6] He realized exactly what he needed to do. "I had not walked farther than the Golf-house when the whole thing was arranged in my mind."

With this new technique, Watt was able not just to double the efficiency of the steam engine but also to make it more useful in many other applications. What he knew about the engine had provided the data he had needed to see and understand the contraption and then view it from a different angle. This had allowed him to envision a separate condenser. His *tacit* knowledge, given a bit of space, had popped forth. As philosopher of science Michael Polanyi said in *The Tacit Dimension*, we know more than we can tell.[7] Watt was walking around with the engine's mechanisms in his head, as well as with the need to repair one. He was apparently also concerned enough about the engine's design to mull it over. From this, a new way of seeing had evolved faster than the speed of thought—something Watt knew, but did not know that he knew, until it emerged as a full-blown idea.

Watt also demonstrated another principle that we have seen throughout this book: when he was in a relaxed mode, daydreaming, his brain generated the insight.

MINING MINDS

In *Rhetoric*, Aristotle said that ordinary words convey only what we know already. He viewed metaphor as the best medium for seeing things in a fresh way.

What happens in the brain when we're inspired to see beyond the surface of what we know to extract something fresh? We've seen in earlier chapters how the brain is set up, how it relies on focus and expectation, and how it gathers its resources for the pop of inspiration. Now we'll add to this.

Neurologist Alice Flaherty teaches at Harvard Medical School and specializes in mood and movement disorders at Massachusetts General Hospital in Boston. She has studied the biology of creativity and produced a book on the intriguing subject of hypergraphia, or the overwhelming compulsion to write (from which she unexpectedly suffered following a tragic incident in her life). In the process of writing, she developed an appreciation for the ability to generate metaphors as "one of the most magical aspects of language."[8] With metaphors, we realize similarities among otherwise disparate things. In Greek, the word means "transfer," and it is this ability to transfer that inspires creative data mining. This enhances the ability to generate a new perspective on a problem.

"Synetics" is the process of connecting seemingly unrelated elements while searching for a creative solution to a problem. To achieve this, we might imagine ourselves playing a role in finding a solution to a problem. Watt, for example, could have imagined himself as the single cylinder. Another person might ignore all restrictions and imagine that the impossible is now possible, looking for a solution in fantasy (as Martin Cooper did in chapter 5). Symbolic analogies help people view the thing on which they're working as something else altogether.[9]

Creating metaphors involves the linguistic cognitive brain and the emotional brain, as well as the infusion of excitement over novelty. Metaphor brings together the two important elements of a snap in that playful manner discussed in chapter 7—the dance. Creating an enlivening metaphor engages the limbic system's emotional music with the cognitive system's knowledge of the steps. To attract the muse, the brain must connect in the right way. Otherwise, it could produce substandard work or inhibit creative expression altogether.

Flaherty's own snap, which inspired her book on hypergraphia, occurred during physical activity that directly followed immersion in her work. She had been at her lab one morning and was bicycling back home. Around her, she felt a sense of harmony that filled her with joy. "Suddenly by the Charles River Dam," she wrote, "the phrase 'the opposite of writer's block' came into my head. I was immediately convinced that I had to write a book about hypergraphia. The words of my revelation . . . seemed to me as if they came from some higher power. . . . Some limbic force still believes it absolutely and has driven me to work on the manuscript nearly every day for the past four years, with a single-mindedness that seems abnormal even to me."[10] She produced a singular work on a rare disorder that shed new light for clinicians, physicians, and sufferers. It also illuminated the writing process in a unique new way, especially for the most prolific.

The temporal lobes assist with language comprehension, especially its emotional layers, as well as the perception of music and visual objects. It connects to the limbic system, where emotions are generated. The frontal lobes, which on the left recognize speech, appear to help screen, organize, and edit content. On the right, they recognize melody and assist in visuospatial thinking. Functional MRI (fMRI) scans, which measure oxygen use in various brain areas, show the brain's activities. In addition, some researchers are using repetitive transcranial magnetic stimulation (rTMS) to cause neurons to depolarize, which makes the cell membrane more positive or less negative and thus alters activity in different parts of the brain. With a handheld magnetic device, they use low frequencies to inhibit brain activity (sometimes to block inhibitions) and high frequencies to stimulate it. They are attempting to find out how rTMS affects inspiration, mood, and logical calculations.

Researcher Allan Snyder, director of the Centre for the Mind in Sydney, Australia, and fellow of the Royal Society of London, has expertise in biology, neuroscience, optical physics, and information technology. He received the Marconi International Prize in 2001 for his ideas about optical fibers for telecommunication. (He points out, like a good data miner, that this insight came not from engineering or communications but from his research on animals eyes.) "It seems that the more different pictures you have of the world, the better," he said in an interview. "Somehow our mind unconsciously juggles these different pictures, rearranging them for a new synthesis."[11]

In some circles, Snyder's work with rTMS has led to predictions of a revolution in our understanding of the human brain. He has envisioned the invention of a thinking cap that would improve our memory, remove perceptual blinders, and inspire creativity—the aha! moment. He believes that savants have better access than most to information before it gets taken up into the more holistic thinking processes that normal brains perform. Savants may not filter their thoughts as much, which gives them access to more information in the brain. In Snyder's lab, scientists have induced savant-like performances, from art to math, in ordinary subjects, who also show a reduced susceptibility to false memories. The researchers use rTMS and transcranial direct current stimulation (tDCS) to inhibit the anterior temporal lobe, which is important for processing concepts, semantics, labels, and categories. The aim is to reverse inhibition, which allows subjects greater access to more literal detail. They eclipse the neurons that apply meaning in order to see just how the process occurs at the unconscious level. That is, we tend to build knowledge via the Big Picture, which is a good survival mechanism for quick anticipation and decision making. However, this can prejudice information toward a certain perspective and shut off access to flexibility and even creativity. Thus, switching off parts of the brain allows others to activate, producing skills that were not otherwise exercised. They call this "paradoxical functional facilitation."

Snyder views the holistic approach to knowledge as a bottleneck to our ability to focus on literal details, which we might otherwise join in novel ways. "We have a predisposition to impose prior connections," he explained. "But, creativity would seem to require that we, at least momentarily, free ourselves of previous interpretations, enabling us to link disparate ideas into a new synthesis."[12] Snyder points to Leonardo da Vinci as the exemplar of the person who seemed to be able to switch between holistic conceptual ways of thinking and unfettered literal ways of knowing. This might arise, Snyder believes, from da Vinci's immersion in so many different fields. In fact, many of those who have experienced aha! moments have cultivated such flexibility.

ALWAYS AWARE

Dr. Joseph Bell was Queen Victoria's personal physician whenever she was in Scotland because she liked the way he ran his wards. In addition to his surgeries at the Royal Infirmary, he taught medical students at the University of Edinburgh. He gained renown among them for what he called "the Method"—a disciplined approach to deducing subtle facts about patients through nothing more than keen observation. Arthur Conan Doyle became a student and assistant of Bell's in 1877. He was sufficiently impressed to turn his mentor into a fictional character: Sherlock Holmes. In Conan Doyle's only filmed interview, he firmly attested to Bell's influence, and in a letter to Bell he once wrote, "It is most certainly to you that I owe Sherlock Holmes." Bell even wore a cloaked coat and deerstalker cap.[13]

Bell grew up during the mid-1800s in a medical family and became protégé to a renowned Scottish physician, Dr. James Syme. He understood the art of cross-fertilization of information, as when he was not at work, he practiced several avocations. He was an amateur poet, bird-watcher, and avid shooter. Aware of the needs of patients, he organized systematic lectures for nurses and agreed to defy considerable prejudice to teach the first female medical students.

Bell was quite effective at gathering data from which to mine his insights about patients. As he developed his medical practice, he noticed the kinds of people who came to him, so he set himself the task of learning about their habits and occupations. He made a study of tattoos. He also read everything possible about skin disorders, scar shapes, the use of tobacco, how the habitual use of different implements made marks on hands, and even subjects as seemingly mundane as the different types of soil around Scotland. Bell knew as much about disease as any of his colleagues, and he worked long hours at matching behaviors, postures, facial expressions, and other subtle clues to physical ailments. He also devoted considerable time to handwriting analysis and the identification of accents, linguistic oddities, and speech patterns.

As he grew adept, he left the interviewing of patients to his students. They would ask questions and take notes, but to their surprise, Bell could spot the problem with a patient without asking a single question. Invariably, he was correct. In other words, he had educated and trained himself sufficiently to prepare his brain to snap to a diagnosis. From within his studied expertise, he had created the conditions for an aha! experience with nearly every patient.

For twenty-three years, Bell edited the *Edinburgh Medical Journal* as a firm proponent of science, and he authored several medical texts. This work, too, enhanced his mental database. The successful diagnosis, he believed, derived from three things: "Observe carefully, deduce shrewdly, and confirm with evidence." For him, the Method—the "accurate and rapid appreciation of small points in which the diseased differs from the healthy state"—was one of the most important things he could impart to young medical minds. It was paramount, then, to make a study of people.[14]

One day a woman came to Bell's clinic and handed him a vial. It had a stopper, around which was wound a bit of black thread. Bell commented that her husband was a tailor and asked her how long he had been ill. She confirmed that it was her husband who was sick, and after she left, Bell's students wanted to know how he had deduced this. He told them that she was too healthy to be the patient, and that she wore a wedding ring but not a widow's dress. She had plugged the vial with a stopper made of paper—the same kind a tailor uses for thread. In fact, some thread was still on it. None of the deductions was difficult for an observant person. He urged the students to use their eyes, ears, brain, and power of deduction.

"Nearly every handicraft writes its sign-manual on the hands," Bell once stated. "The scars of the miner differ from those of the quarryman. The carpenter's callosities are not those of the mason. The soldier and sailor are different in gait."[15] Ornaments, tattoos, and clothing added more dimension, as did posture and demeanor. However, "mere acuteness of the senses" was not sufficient to achieve this degree of expertise. One had to study in minute detail, and with great diligence, those subjects that would aid in making distinctions: the diverse odors of poison, for example, or of tobacco or different perfumes.

Bell would walk energetically around the crowded lecture room, urging students to recognize the importance of performing a close and critical study before diagnosis. There was always a danger of jumping too soon to a conclusion that could be wrong. To demonstrate, he would ask an assistant like Conan Doyle to escort one of his waiting out-patients into the room. This would be someone he had not yet met. He would then demonstrate the Method: from many different clues, Bell would describe the person's occupation and health status, perhaps his or her family concerns or recent activities. In one case, Bell discussed what he could see on an elderly woman. She said nothing. He then asked her, "Where is your cutty pipe?" Startled, she stared at him and then dug into her purse and brought one out. The students wanted to know how Bell had known she would have a pipe at all, let alone this particular kind of pipe, and he told them that he had seen an ulcer on her lower lip. Coupled with a smooth scar on her cheek where the pipe would curve in, he had rightly surmised from what he knew about the various implements used for smoking and the marks they made that she smoked a short-stemmed pipe.

Bell asserted that nothing was more useful to medical work than finely honed sensory observation, guided toward a specific purpose. Whenever he called on students to try the Method, he'd urge them not to touch a patient, but to "use your eyes, sir, use your ears, use your brain, your bump of perception . . ." and "never neglect to ratify your deductions."[16] What he meant was that after they had deduced something, they had to check each notion with the patient.

To keep students on their toes, Bell had a few tricks. One story holds that he would bring in an amber-colored fluid, which he described as a potent drug that tasted quite bitter. He would offer a preamble about the need to sometimes engage in unpleasant acts to develop one's knowledge. Among them was to smell and taste things they might not like. He would then tell them to follow his example. Bell would dip a finger into the fluid, stir it a little, and bring it to his mouth to taste it. He would make a face to show them that what he had said about the fluid was true: it wasn't sugar-water. As the students looked at each other, Bell would pass it to the first one and urge him to taste it. Of course he would, and Bell was right. The fluid was foul. One student after another dipped a finger in and tasted. When the flask made its way around the room, with Bell ensuring that each student obeyed, he would take it back. Then Bell would inform them that they had missed the most important part of the experiment: observation. He'd shown them that he'd used one finger to dip into the liquid, but had then placed an unaffected finger into his mouth. They had seen but had not "truly observed" him.

Although Bell's skills were primarily in the surgery, in 1892, he admitted in an interview to a reporter that the Crown had engaged him on numerous occasions in medical jurisprudence—the investigation of crimes. One such case involved Elizabeth Dyer. Because Bell did such an extraordinary job with vigilant observation, he spotted some key items that helped to solve it.

Dyer had been a fifteen-year-old student of Eugene Marie Chantrelle, a French immigrant, who had seduced her and was then forced to marry her. He abused her for ten years, often threatening to kill her. In 1877, Chantrelle insured Elizabeth for a considerable sum. Three months later, she fell ill. Alone in her room, she might have died if her maid had not discovered her and run for the doctor. When they entered, Chantrelle was in the room, standing at the window. The observant maid noticed that a half-full glass of lemonade was now empty and several orange segments were gone, although Elizabeth had not moved. Also, there was now a strong smell of coal gas in the air.

The doctor surmised that Elizabeth had suffered from accidental coal gas poisoning. She later died without ever waking up. The maid confided her suspicions, so the doctor invited a toxicologist from the university, Sir Henry Littlejohn, who in turn invited Bell. They thought Elizabeth's symptoms were more consistent with narcotic poisoning, so Chantrelle was soon under arrest. But the officials needed proof.

Littlejohn and Bell returned to Elizabeth's room and collected vomit from the pillow, as well as from the nightgown she had worn when she died. Under microscopic analysis, it appeared to contain a solid form of opium. The police learned that Chantrelle had recently purchased thirty doses of opium. Protesting his innocence, he said that when he'd entered the room, he had smelled gas. The maid's report backed him up, and an employee from the gas company located a broken gas pipe just outside the victim's bedroom window.

Now Bell went into action. He snapped on another idea, mined from what he knew about illnesses and people. He located a gasfitter who had once repaired this very pipe under Chantrelle's watchful eye. The man described Chantrelle's interest in how it worked. This testimony strengthened the charge of murder: insurance, opium, symptoms of narcotic overdose, and Chantrelle's awareness of how the pipe under the window worked. The circumstances seemed clear: Chantrelle had staged his wife's "accidental death" from a burst gas pipe. If not for Bell's firm command of symptomology, coupled with his study of behavior, the murderer might have gone free. After a four-day trial, Chantrelle was convicted.

Bell's legacy, immortalized in the stories of Sherlock Holmes, keeps his method and his concern about tunnel vision alive for students of many generations. The Joseph Bell Centre for Forensic Statistics and Legal Reasoning in Edinburgh honors the late pathologist and promotes his ideas.

Vigilance like that advocated by Bell and demonstrated by Gould, Watt, and Vidocq, is a habit of intentionality. Most people relax their focus until they need it, whereas people who notice nuances practice mindful engagement with the world around them. They do so with a sense of purpose, often fueled by curiosity. After a while, it becomes second nature, and their reward is heightened preparation for an aha! moment. Chance favors the prepared mind, and they're always ready. They're the first to see opportunities, first to ponder possibilities, and first to move toward them. Often, they're also bolder and more optimistic about the outcome than less mindful individuals.

Yet solitary study goes only so far; interacting with others, especially across disciplines, is a significant factor in snapping. Next, we'll explore this component.

KEY POINTS

- Data mining extracts hidden patterns from data, which offers new information.
- Entrepreneurs perpetually collect and process: their radar for innovation is turned on 24/7.
- Aha! is not the end point; it's just the beginning.

CHAPTER 9

PSYCHO-ENTANGLEMENT

COLLABORATION PLUS SYNCHRONICITY

Rick Arlow is a graduate student at Case Western Reserve University, getting an MD and a PhD in biomedical engineering. In his research, Rick is focusing on the process of deep brain stimulation—not just how to do it, but how to do it *better*. His confidence comes from going through the entrepreneurial process with a fellow student, Zach Bloom, at Lehigh University in Bethlehem, Pennsylvania. They were taking a course in integrated product development, which helped inspire them to develop a new method for obtaining better surgical airways in critically ill patients, called the SMART (Seldinger-Modified Airway Rescue Tracheotomy) Technique. When they met, Rick was an emergency medical technician, so he knew the world of emergency medicine. He and Zach began working toward the goal of redesigning the process of airway management in the field and hospital to increase patient safety and control high associated costs. That is, they sought to safely increase the adoption of a more challenging, yet beneficial, procedure for patients in the field and at their bedside through innovative design. Their design, serendipitously based on a viper fang, succeeds. The path was difficult, and marketing will be a challenge, but as they kept at it, they had a few eureka experiences.

Explaining one such breakthrough, Arlow said,

It came from me and Zach getting to know each other. We brought different backgrounds and areas of expertise. I was studying biomedical engineering and taking a class at Lehigh: Integrated Product Development. It's about the intersection of business and product development in early stage projects. Zach's was half biomedical engineering major and half economics major, and he was taking classes in how to do the business aspects, so he got involved in the entrepreneurial community at Lehigh.[1]

After an exam, we got together and decided to hang out and just play some guitar, because we both play music. I didn't know him before that, and afterward we started talking about what we were both interested in. At that point, we started thinking about trying to do a company ourselves. I was working as a student, setting up a project for a company that was a noninvasive lactic acid monitoring device. We didn't really know how the process worked or what we were getting into, but we decided to jump in and try it.

We had ideas initially that ultimately weren't close to what we finally decided to look into, which was a tracheotomy device. But that initial willingness to jump on board and start throwing out ideas, start balancing the time we had to regularly throw ideas off each other and other people, and eventually go ask the medical community. That was the way the aha! moment started for us. We realized this was something feasible, we each had professors who could help, and we knew students who were doing similar things as start-ups. We both knew this is what we wanted to be doing.

Being in that location [Lehigh's Baker Institute], and in that type of environment, I was able to see that this is something realistic that we could do, if I just put my mind to it and worked with Zach and found other people. Slowly we learned how to do the process. We learned how a medical device goes from conception to realization. It was the pairing of two people with complementary and overlapping skill sets, both deciding to work together. A lot of it was being in that environment at Lehigh. They had faculty members who were on board to be that type of advisor and to spend time talking with us.

Since then, we had an aha! moment about the product. We'd have these "idea dumps," where we'd try to bring drawings or modifications of what we were working on. Zach had been reading a lot about bio-mimicry, and he'd looked at other products that had used it. He would come in with different pictures of animal parts, like fangs or a rhino [horn]. At the same time, the person who was giving us lab space in the biology building for testing our prototypes told us that he had an office downstairs, and if we need him we should just come down there. We asked him what he did in his office and he said, "I'm a snakebite expert." He had a whole lair of snakes, and had slow-motion footage of how a snake bites, with all the components.

I've had a lot of aha! moments that didn't work. When we started, I had a list of twenty ideas, and Zach had his list, and most of them were pretty bad ideas, which wouldn't work out clinically or be economically viable. The better aha! moments, I think, correlate to how long you've been working in that field and thinking in that way and meeting those types of people. It doesn't have an immediate benefit. People spend most of their time doing nonurgent things, hearing other people's stories, going to different events, and seeing entrepreneurs do their thing. The more I meet with people in the field and work on the project, the better aha! moments I have. The ideas I have now for another device are better, faster, and more clear. I see better what's valuable.

SPOOKY ACTIONS

Although Einstein is often pictured alone when having an aha! moment, a significant one occurred as the result of an ongoing engagement with a friend whose expertise lay in a different field. Einstein had been pondering several ideas related to Galileo's approach to the velocity of light and energy. For over a year, he had tried to reconcile what seemed to be incompatible concepts. Often he would talk to a few close colleagues who grasped the physics involved. One was Michele Besso. This man, six years older than Einstein, shared with him a propensity for playing the violin. He was studying to become an electrical engineer. Einstein appreciated Besso's "sharp mind," "outstanding intelligence," and "elegance of thought."[2] He also noticed that Besso had a difficult time focusing on specific tasks, and, while delighted with Besso's apparent disorderliness, Einstein valued him most for his ability to listen to and grasp complex issues. They often talked for many hours at a stretch. For someone as self-directed in his studies as Einstein, Besso proved to be an invaluable sounding board.

Early in 1905, they walked together on what Einstein recalled as a beautiful day. He was quite direct about his desire that day to engage Besso in a discussion about theoretical questions that had become prickly. As they pondered the issues concerning motion, with Einstein laying out his various futile approaches thus far, he experienced an illuminated moment—the proverbial lightbulb. He had envisioned the solution to the problem. "With this new concept, I could resolve all the difficulties completely for the first time," he later said.[3] Within five weeks he had completed a paper on his special theory of relativity, "On the Electrodynamics of Moving Bodies." In it, he acknowledged Besso's "valuable" suggestions. He told someone else that, in the whole of Europe, he could not have found anyone better with whom to try out his ideas. The evidence for this lies in their ongoing correspondence, which lasted half a century. (They even died three weeks apart.) Besso often could not comprehend how Einstein had gleaned the meaning that he did from "inadvertent statements," but that is often the nature of creative collaborations: one person says or does something that another person filters into a different context, giving it a new spin.

About two years after Einstein published this famous paper, he was trying to push past it to address gravity. This effort found a soft spot in the wall of mental resistance to erupt in another flash. "I was sitting in a chair in the patent office at Bern," he stated years later, "when all of a sudden a thought occurred to me: 'If a person falls freely, he will not feel his own weight.' I was startled. This simple thought made a deep impression on me."[4] It led to his general theory of relativity, which revised Newton's laws and launched theoretical cosmology and quantum theory.

Among Einstein's other acquaintances who stimulated his thinking were his wife, Mileva Maric, mathematician Marcel Grossman, and medical student Max Talmey. They provided him with images from other arenas that served as elements in his thought experiments. He was able to imaginatively create a milieu that allowed him to visually play with physical relationships until they made sense to him. Einstein also developed a respectful friendship with Niels Bohr, a Danish physicist who would make important contributions to the evolution of quantum physics. The two men strongly disagreed on certain fundamental concepts, but they sustained an intense debate that mutually fed their minds. Einstein valued clarity and simplicity, while Bohr was just as comfortable with the loose ends of ambiguity and complexity. He did not mind weirdness. Perhaps this came from his exposure to the existential notions espoused by his countryman Søren Kierkegaard, a nineteenth-century philosopher.

Regarded as a founding father of existentialism, Kierkegaard had observed that, for limited human beings, "truth is subjectivity," and he had conceived of a "lived" dialectical tension in which a thesis (a condition) and its opposite could coexist without resolving into a transcending synthesis.[5] Seemingly opposing things could both be true. Bohr appreciated this possibility, and some researchers believe it influenced the ideas he proposed in 1927 about complementarity. That is, something can exhibit certain properties under one set of conditions but also exhibit contradictory properties under others. No single representation provides a complete description of quantum phenomena. "In other words, if you design an experiment to see if electrons are waves, you get waves. If you design an experiment to test whether electrons are particles, you get particles."[6]

Conflict and dispute, Bohr believed, offered ways to see all sides.

Ideas could be rigorously defined by including aspects that might upset original views. He often constructed these notions—including solutions to puzzles—while engaged in a dialogue. "He loved to be contradicted in order to get deeper into the subject, but he progressed best when the person with whom he thrashed had the same attitude as himself, not only in approaching the problem but also in needing to penetrate its depth to the uttermost."[7]

Bohr understood the value of surrounding himself with fertile, competent minds. During the mid-1920s, along with Erwin Schrödinger and Werner Heisenberg, he became one of the leaders in developing the framework of quantum reality. The task proved difficult and confusing, and the men engaged in sustained and exhausting debates. Bohr compared this group to mountain climbers moving through fog. They all knew they could not create a new paradigm without mutual cooperation. Bohr accepted conceptual conflict as a necessary part of the process and stated that he performed his best thinking during debates with equals. Through collaboration, they took on problems and found solutions that, as individuals, none had noted. While at Bohr's Institute in Copenhagen, Heisenberg proposed his famous uncertainty principle regarding the limits of experimental information—one can't precisely measure certain pairs of properties (position and momentum) at the same time. He used a unique representational mode to overcome the limits of visualization and to propose that electrons can exist in many locations simultaneously. How much other thinkers contributed to this idea is unclear, but these men were productively interdependent. The intellectual enterprise of each, they acknowledged, deepened and broadened that of the others.[8]

Not only did they tackle the complexities of ever-deepening scientific approaches from the Western world, but they also incorporated new ideas from the East. Einstein started the ball rolling, but Bohr and others moved it along toward a more holistic sense of reality. While seeming to be solid, they found, the world is actually made of vibrating molecules, atoms, and atomic subparticles;

showers of high energy continually bombard Earth's atmosphere. Mysticism's awareness of fluid reality had something to contribute to help dissolve the rigid boundaries of mechanism.

Throughout the history of science, ideological foundations have been shattered and rebuilt as anomalous facts revolutionize perspectives. Classical physics had been defined within the seemingly concrete world of solid substance and uniform order. It was Aristotle who had organized and systematized concepts about the physical world. By the seventeenth century, French philosopher René Descartes had divided reality distinctly into mind and matter, further entrenching our perceptions in dualism. The material world, he'd determined, was like a machine. Shortly thereafter, Isaac Newton made this notion the foundation for formulating his ideas—among them the laws of motion. Going into the twentieth century, Newtonian mechanics had defined scientific reality: mass was essentially passive, and its behavior could be predicted with certainty, because the laws of the universe were invariable.

In the East, views of reality evolved in a different direction. For them, spiritual principles grounded reality. Their philosophers, mostly mystics, viewed everything as interrelated. They tried to avoid the distortion of concepts by using meditation, metaphor, and paradox to access immediate experience. Truths were intuitive, elusive, and subjective. Although these mystics had very little, if any, influence on modern science, they valued paradoxical expression for communicating reality. Physicists, in studying the behavior of light, have discovered its paradoxical nature. Can light be both wave and particle? It seemed that it must be.

Physicists set about to relearn their discipline with an expanded awareness and new ways of thinking. With sophisticated technology, they intuited that the building blocks of nature were beyond sensory perception and could thus be known only indirectly. This came with uncertainty, which forced a change in many traditional assumptions. Not only could nothing be definitively measured at the subatomic level, but the observers were so uncertain that they wondered if the act of observation was *creating* the thing they thought they were observing. Probability replaced a solid sense of cause and effect.

All this brings us to our central metaphor for this chapter. Another physicist in this group of mountain climbers, Erwin Schrödinger, proposed entanglement theory (which also irked Einstein). With several collaborators, Einstein had proposed a thought experiment, which in turn inspired this idea. When two objects interact in a certain way, they become connected; so, measuring one particle affected another that could be a great distance away. Laboratories around the world now create such entanglements to study and to apply to technology and informatics. It's still weird and mysterious, but thanks to collaborative efforts from many different fields, it's become more manageable.

ONE AFFECTS OTHERS

Back to snaps: in physics, entanglement theory predicts that, under certain circumstances, seemingly isolated particles are actually instantaneously connected through space and time. In psychology, this might suggest that minds are similarly entangled, and in fact, many "snap" moments arise from rubbing elbows in a professional field.

During the early 1880s, Carl Koller graduated from the medical school of Vienna with Sigmund Freud. They had been classmates and remained friends and colleagues. Freud was experimenting with cocaine and in 1884 had published a monograph extolling its virtues as a way to cure morphine addiction. He invited Koller to collaborate with him on the effect of cocaine on muscle strength. Koller had already noticed the numbing effects of cocaine on the tongue, but it was not until a specific incident that he snapped on a practical application.

Koller had spent the summer in his lab, working on the treatments in ophthalmology. He was aware of the need to numb specific areas for closer work, but thus far, no one had discovered a substance for local anesthesia. A colleague placed some cocaine on his tongue and remarked about its effects. Koller agreed. But then he realized: *this* was the substance they were looking for! He had it in his pocket.

He went directly to his lab and urged his assistant to dissolve some grains of the cocaine powder into distilled water. They dripped this solution into the eye of a frog. They let it set before touching the eye with the sharp tip of a needle. When the frog did not react, they tried it on a dog and a rabbit. Then they tried it on themselves. It worked! They could not feel a thing. Koller's hydrochlorate of cocaine soon made international news in the medical world.[9]

Another story demonstrates a similar effect in spite of the central character's firm belief that solitude was the only way to work out solutions to difficult problems. Mathematician Andrew Wiles believed that his famous solution to a long-standing mystery was the result of working completely on his own, but it's clear from his process that he was immersed at all times in the framework of a community of minds.

For three centuries, Fermat's last theorem—an unknown proof for a mathematical proposition—had vexed mathematicians worldwide. Wiles came across it while reading in a library when he was ten years old. Fermat had written just one vexing thing about it: "I have a truly marvelous demonstration of this proposition which this margin is too narrow to contain." Wiles soon became obsessed with it, inspiring his career in mathematics. He found that many others before him had tried to solve it for some three hundred years, so he studied each approach. However, the solution eluded him as well. He put the problem aside to do other work until he heard that a colleague had linked "Fermat" to a related math mystery.

"At the end of the summer in 1986," Wiles told an interviewer, "I was sipping iced tea at the house of friend. Casually, in the idle of a conversation, this friend told me that Ken Ribet had proved a link between Taniyama-Shimura and Fermat's Last Theorem. I was electrified. I knew that moment that the course of my life was changing. . . . My childhood dream was now a respectable thing to work on. I just knew that I could never let that go."[10]

The theorem now seemed solvable. Wiles's obsession returned, and he withdrew into seclusion. He believed that one had to stay totally focused, in isolation, to fully brainstorm such a monolith. But over the course of seven long years, he experienced many setbacks. Sometimes he would go for a walk to let his subconscious work on its own, but this did not get him through his impasse. He described it as moving through a dark mansion: "You enter the first room of the mansion, and it's completely dark. You stumble around bumping into furniture, but gradually you learn where each piece of furniture is. Finally . . . you find the light switch. You turn it on and suddenly . . . you can see where you were. Then you move into the next room."[11]

It was only when he came out of intellectual seclusion from time to time that he found a few pieces to this puzzle. On several occasions, Wiles was reading other papers or talking with colleagues when he'd recognize how something offered one of the missing pieces. This would send him back to work with a fresh perspective. One day in 1993, he was certain he had achieved his goal. He submitted his work to a review board, but after lengthy consideration, its members showed him a subtle error. Another setback.

Wiles sought out a former student to assist him in correcting the error, but both came up short. It was intensely frustrating. It appeared to Wiles that this obsession might have cost him many years of his life. He considered giving up. But he decided to give it one last try.

In September 1994, Wiles went to his desk and sat down. He looked through his papers. It felt as if the answer was there, somewhere. He just couldn't quite articulate it. Then he stopped and sat still.

"Suddenly, totally unexpectedly, I had this incredible revelation," he reported. "It was the most important moment of my working life. It was so indescribably beautiful, it was so simple and elegant, I just stared in disbelief for twenty minutes."

But he did not want to get his hopes up. He slept on it and looked again in the morning. Then he knew: "I got it!"[12] And he had.

However, it was not total isolation that made the solution pop. Despite his periods of focused solitude, Wiles had stayed in touch with the mathematical community. He had read what others were doing, and he had brainstormed with a trusted friend. Clearly, the work of other mathematicians had assisted him, offering one piece after another, toward finally proving Fermat's last theorem.

Something very basic in our brains appears to be at the heart of these entanglements. While we often think of brilliant researchers being alone for hours, days, or months in their labs or offices, there is a social dimension to aha! moments that we should not overlook. In fact, a flash of insight was part of this very discovery of a social dimension: the existence of mirror neurons. These brain cells become active when subjects are observing others in the same way they would when they'd actually performed this action themselves.

In Italy during the early 1990s, Giacomo Rizzolatti, a neuroscientist at the University of Parma, placed electrodes in the ventral premotor cortex of a monkey to study the neurological mechanisms involved in hand and mouth movements. One day, a graduate student lifting an ice cream cone noticed that the monkey's brain showed activity even when the monkey that was watching him did not move. Inspired, the researchers set up experiments to examine what was occurring in the brain when monkeys observed others engaged in specific behaviors. Rizzolatti discovered that the same brain cells fired when the monkey was watching an activity as when the monkey performed the activity. He dubbed the neural mechanism "mirror neurons." By this, he meant that certain brain cells start processing sensory information when a monkey sees or hears an action that its own body can perform. According to brain scans with fMRI, which monitor human brain activity indirectly, humans appear to possess mirror neurons as well.

Mirror neuron systems in humans that respond to behavior and intention are located in the inferior parietal lobula and the ventral premotor cortex, while a mirror neuron system in the insula responds to emotional situations. In one experiment, researchers asked participants to infer an intention from someone performing an act. There were three conditions, which conveyed a context, an act, and an intention:

1. Objects were arranged on a table as if ready for someone to drink tea or as if someone had just finished;
2. a hand grasped a mug without any context;
3. a hand grasped a mug to drink or to clear the table.

The mirror systems activated in contexts where the intention to act was evident, as well as when a specific identifiable action occurred. Since this brain activity is similar to what we see in primate research, and primate research directly monitors specific mirror neurons via implants in the brain, we can apply the conclusions from primate research to humans.[13]

Thus, our brains appear to be capable of understanding and empathizing with another person's actions and emotions. Imitation makes culture possible, including research projects that produce snaps. Through interaction, we're experiencing not just what others are doing but how they view what we're doing. That is, we can see ourselves through others' eyes. Mirror neurons make socialization possible on many different levels. We recognize others' emotions as simulations of our own emotions.

"The same neural structures involved in the unconscious modeling of our acting body in space," writes researcher Vittorio Gallese, "also contribute to our awareness of the lived body and of the objects that the world contains. Neuroscientific research also shows that there are neural mechanisms mediating between the multilevel personal experience we entertain of our lived body, and the implicit certainties we simultaneously hold about others. Such personal and body-related experiential knowledge enables us to understand the actions performed by others, and to directly decode the emotions and sensations they experience."[14] Because we have a shared neural substrate, we don't just see an action when we observe it, we experience it as if we're doing it, too.

SNAP, CRACKLE, POP

The research team that combines the art appreciation with medical training has also looked at group dynamics. Mary Thorndike leads a workshop directed at team thinking, in which Joel Katz participates when he can.

"The issue we address is that medicine is becoming a team activity," says Katz.

We take these participants to the Sackler Museum in Cambridge. We invite an entire team—the senior physician, the resident, the intern, the med students, the nurses, the social workers, and the physical therapists. We focus on team-building skills, such as communication, interdisciplinary relationships, and decision making. The exercises focus around visual arts. We might start with *Pan and Psyche* by Sir Edward Burne-Jones. It shows Pan and Psyche in an ambiguous pose, with a lot of vulnerability. We use it to talk about hierarchy and relationships. Then we take them to a Rembrandt painting, *Portrait of an Old Man*, and have them pretend this is their patient, or their father as a patient. They talk in subgroups about what's going on. Each gets to say one thing to the other groups. Then they put a poem together about it.

The concluding event is to take them to a modern abstract piece of work called *I'm with Stupid*, by Rachel Harrison. There's a lot going on in this piece, and it's hard to interpret. Whenever you think you know what's going on, you see that something else is going on.

Participants discover in these workshops that every member of the team has something valuable to contribute. They learn about team dynamics. Then we [the researchers] observe markers, or outcomes, of team functioning, like how quickly they [make] round[s], and how many phone calls are required after rounds to clarify points. We do this before and after the sessions, to see if there are measurable improvements in the ability of that group to function as a team. We find that this exercise helps people work better as a team.[15]

Other groups have devised intriguing group exercises as well. The aim of 6-3-5 Brainwriting, developed in Germany in 1969 for a structured approach to creative advertising, is to gather six people and have them generate 108 new ideas in half an hour. The ideas do not need to be good. The important aspect is to keep them flowing, with each person offering three every five minutes. The starting person writes three ideas on one line on a sheet of paper. Then she passes the paper to the next person, who reads them and generates three more, either working off these or adding something else. The participants are encouraged to find inspiration in something someone else might have said, taking it further or applying it in a different way. All participants are active, no moderator is required, no discussions close off avenues, and the pressure generates energy. (It might also inspire anxiety, however.)

"Rolestorming" is another fun approach to generating ideas in a group. In this, a group gathers to think about a problem together, but each takes on a role. For example, the "superheroes" method involves addressing a problem the way Superman, Spiderman, Thor, or Wonder Woman might. Group members might facilitate this by wearing masks or costumes, but the goal is to adopt a perspective different from one's own: "What would Superman think about this?" Literary or fictional character rolestorming groups work as well: "How would Sherlock Holmes approach this?" Or, "What might King Arthur do?"

Psychologist Howard Gardner, who conceptualized multiple intelligences, believes that creative breakthroughs in such settings or communities are highly charged and need support. He compared the process to the development of a new language. To survive and flourish, there must be committed communicators who provide opportunities to practice and learn.[16] Cognitive scientist, Nobel laureate, and polymath Herbert A. Simon, who relied on an interdisciplinary approach for his greatest contributions, stated, "To make interesting scientific discoveries, you should acquire as many good friends as possible who are energetic, intelligent, and knowledgeable as they can be. Then sit back and relax. You will find that all the programs you need are stored in your friends, and will execute creatively and productively as long as you don't interfere too much."[17]

Despite distinct individuals being credited with important discoveries, most realize that teamwork, brainstorming, and even just the inarticulate absorption of the professional culture have contributed to their insights. No matter how reclusive an inventor might be, as we saw with one of the most extreme examples in Andrew Wiles, no one works entirely alone. Crossing paths can spark any number of ideas, even if you weren't thinking of anything specific at the time.

THE SURPRISE FACTOR

Frances Glessner Lee was the daughter of John Jacob Glessner and thus heir to the International Harvester fortune. Born March 25, 1878, in Chicago, "Fanny" was raised in privilege and privately tutored. As she grew up, she hoped to study law or medicine, but her father would not hear of her going to a university. She had to watch her brother George study at Harvard while she remained home to learn the domestic skills expected of a wealthy young lady. She was disappointed. Little did she realize then that one of her talents would be at the heart of a significant contribution. She would find her bliss as well as improve medicolegal education for many.

The Glessners had a thousand-acre summer home in New Hampshire's White Mountains called "the Rocks." Fanny was there during a school holiday when her brother brought home a friend, George Burgess Magrath. He was studying in the field of legal medicine with a focus on death investigation, and his tales excited the young woman. She told her father about it, but he declared that no member of his family would get involved in such a sordid subject.

Still, Magrath's tales about medicine, investigation, and death continued to fire Fanny's imagination. Whenever she had the opportunity, she took him aside to learn whatever she could. In addition, she loved reading Sherlock Holmes stories, especially how a single clue might completely change how to interpret the circumstances. Fanny enjoyed the surprise factor.

When she was twenty, Fanny married Blewett Lee, an attorney and law professor at Northwestern University. They had three children before the marriage failed and they divorced.

A common pastime during this era for women of means was to make miniatures. Fanny was artistic, and as a gift to her music-loving mother, she created a miniature replica of the Chicago Symphony Orchestra. She spent two months crafting ninety tiny musicians, all fully garbed and each with a musical score and instrument. Her mother was delighted, so Fanny tried another one. She created a chamber orchestra of four musicians but concentrated on them in such detail that the project took two years. The musicians on whom she had based it were astonished by the resemblance.

Yet this was not what Fanny wanted to do with her life. Her father died when she was fifty-two, leaving her quite wealthy—and determined to pursue her own interests. Magrath had become the chief medical examiner for Suffolk County (Boston), and he confided to Fanny the need for better training for death investigators. Although a Medicolegal Society had formed in Massachusetts, passionate physicians like Magrath had to pick up the torch.

She was disturbed about crimes that went unsolved or unpunished. With her usual industry, Fanny set about to become an expert in the field, and, despite being a woman, she came to be viewed as an authoritative consultant. In the years to come, she would receive an honorary appointment as a captain of the New Hampshire State Police, would become the first woman to be invited to the initial meetings of the American Academy of Forensic Sciences, and would become the first female invited into the International Association for the Chiefs of Police.

In part, Fanny achieved these recognitions because of her innovations in the medicolegal field. Convinced that she had found her calling—had, in fact, known it all along—Fanny urged Magrath to tell her what she could do. He suggested that she found a medicolegal department, with an endowed chair, at Harvard.

Fanny was ready. At the Rocks, she created a home close to Boston. Fanny helped to establish a department at Harvard for the teaching of legal medicine, with Magrath as its first chair, and paid the salary of its first professor. In Magrath's name, she donated a library of more than a thousand books and manuscripts that she had collected from around the world. However, after developing the Department of Legal Medicine with Fanny, Magrath died in 1938. Fanny was heartbroken, but she continued to support Magrath's vision.

Soon, she would have her flash of insight. Fanny had noticed during the course of her studies that police officers often made mistakes when trying to determine whether a death was the result of an accident, a natural event, a suicide, or a homicide. Too often they simply missed clues. She thought that something concrete and practical should be done to mitigate this.

Then she realized: she knew exactly what to do! She had made those musicians, with their instruments, music sheets, and chairs. She could make dolls like that again, but stick them into miniature crime scenes. They could be made to scale and include items found in actual crime scenes. Fanny knew plenty of crime stories and had been on ride-alongs with police, as well as to morgues and autopsy suites. To get more material, she had but to call on friends she had made among detectives. She had everything she needed to make it happen, including a spacious work area at the Rocks.

Fanny set aside the second floor of her mansion, filling one room entirely with miniature furniture. Some pieces she picked up during her travels, but she hired a carpenter to make others. He (and later his son) also made the dollhouses, which Fanny christened the Nutshell Studies of Unexplained Death. (Her inspiration came from a phrase used by police: "Convict the guilty, clear the innocent, and find the truth in a nutshell.") To create each diorama, Fanny blended several stories, sometimes going with police officers to crime scenes, sometimes reading reports in the newspapers, and sometimes utilizing fiction. She might even interview witnesses.

Fanny spent an enormous amount of time on each Nutshell, making many of the items herself. The project combined her interest in interior design, her talent for detail, her interest in crime, and her eye for antiques. Each doll was made by hand: "She began with loose bisque heads, upper torsos, hands meant for German dolls, and with carved wooden feet and legs. She attached these loose body parts to a cloth body stuffed with cotton and BB gun pellets for weight and flexibility. She carefully painted the faces in colors and tones that indicated how long the person had been dead."[18] Fanny added sweaters and socks that she'd knitted with great difficulty on straight pins and items of clothing that were meticulously handsewn. Once the dolls were ready, Fanny would decide just how each should "die," and proceed to stick knives in them, hang them from nooses, burn them, and paint signs of decomposition on their skin.

The little crime scenes, from cabins to three-room apartments to garages, were also her design, built on a scale of one inch to one foot. Each one cost about the same amount as an average house at that time. Fanny did not care. It seemed to her the best way to use her inheritance.

Once Fanny had several "dollhouses of death" completed, she used them as part of the weeklong seminars she sponsored at Harvard twice a year for the many different professionals involved in law enforcement. One day of each week was set aside to showcase the Nutshells, which were kept in a temperature-controlled room. Participants were granted a limited period of time to look at each scenario, take notes, and report back to the others. The point was not to "solve" the crime but to notice important evidence that could affect investigative decisions. The exercise was meant to help instill an appreciation for the art of vigilance and to help exercise it as a skill. By the time Fanny finished her ambitious project, she had nine-teen detailed Nutshells (which are still preserved).

Her vision was finally realized. By 1949, some several thousand doctors and lawyers had been educated at the Harvard Department of Legal Medicine, and thousands of state troopers, detectives, coro-ners, district attorneys, insurance agents, and crime reporters had attended Fanny's seminars.[19] Fanny had found her calling, merging a skill from one context to enhance another. The convergence in her life of an acquaintance, a keen passion, plenty of money, and an opportunity had transformed her preparation for tranquil domes-ticity into a satisfying enterprise that effectively tapped her knowl-edge and experience. Thanks largely to her years of conversations with Magrath and her exposure to the world of medicolegal educa-tion, Fanny had been prepped to snap a unique innovation. In this case, what seemed to be serendipity was actually synchronicity. She had only to be attuned to it with sufficient vigilance to act on oppor-tunity. Like the others who accepted inspiration from contact with others, Fanny had used this medium to pursue her passion and bene-fit the group.[20]

KEY POINTS

- Among effective ways to snap is with a group of like-minded people with a common vision and the passion to work toward it.
- Brainstorming with others can offer surprising eureka dividends.
- Groups with a common vision support members' creativity.
- Snaps can arise from the serendipity of diverse disciplines crossing paths.
- The appreciation for cross-fertilization and the vigilance for fresh ideas are significant factors.

SOLVE

CHAPTER 10

RISK AND INCENTIVE

OBEDIENT TO THE END

The momentum to snap awakens when trust in our inner resources outweighs the perceived risk. When faced with a hurdle—even a life-threatening one—confident people who trust their instincts can often snap an innovative solution. They set their eye on a goal and learn what it takes to get there. If they learn that they're not yet prepared, they find out what this means and rectify it. They keep moving forward, focusing on what they want and watching for ways to achieve it. Any person or situation can present an opportunity, even when it looks like anything but.

Even as a child, Stanley Milgram stood out. Everyone who knew him believed he'd accomplish something great. He was driven, even exceptional, in everything in which he took an interest, and he was a keen observer of small details. He had that "edge-of-the-seat" attitude about life, and by the age of twenty-eight, he had changed the way the world thinks about what ordinary people are willing to do for an authority figure. Despite the considerable risk he was taking to a career he'd work hard to build, he expected to accomplish something important and extraordinary. To achieve this was worth whatever cost it exacted.

Born into a family of Jewish bakers, Milgram pushed himself hard to excel. He took on the subject of political science but grew disenchanted with the apparent muddle of methods and information. When he learned about an education grant in 1954 that encouraged students to enter the behavioral sciences, he liked the possibilities implied. He read a catalog for the courses offered in Harvard's Department of Social Relations and decided to apply there for graduate school. This was bold, considering that he had little background as an undergraduate and he was trying to enter one of the most hallowed institutions in the country.

Indeed, the admissions committee responded that he lacked adequate preparation. Instead of accepting the decision or wallowing in disappointment, Milgram demonstrated his penchant for challenge: there was always a way, he believed, to get what he wanted. He proposed to the graduate chair, the esteemed Gordon Allport, that he take intensive summer courses, but Allport thought this was not sufficient. Still, he was impressed enough with Milgram's persistence that he offered another route: he advised Milgram to apply as a "special student" so he could make up his deficits during his first year with a load of undergraduate courses. It was a generous gesture, but Milgram spotted its potential for setback. He thanked Allport and proceeded with his own plan. That summer he enrolled in six undergraduate courses in three different colleges in New York, auditing two and taking four for credit. It was an enormous load, but Milgram completed these courses with straight As. This allowed him to enter Harvard that fall on equal footing with other grad students, as well as showing its "gatekeepers" that he meant business. It was not the last time he'd face such obstacles, but Milgram would approach all future tasks with this kind of bold determination.

In fact, when he moved into the dormitory, Perkins Hall, he found the common phone to be a nuisance. It rang endlessly, prohibiting him from focusing on his studies, so to stop the constant distraction, Milgram invented a system for the other residents to follow: for each incoming call for them, each student must answer the phone twice. "He had created a norm, a guideline for appropriate conduct," wrote his biographer Thomas Blass, "in what previously had been a behavioral vacuum."[1] It worked; even after Milgram left, the residents continued to use this rule.

During the fall of 1955, Milgram received a momentous assignment. He was to be a teaching and research assistant to a visiting psychologist from Swarthmore College, Dr. Solomon Asch. Known for his ability to make complex ideas simple for research purposes, Asch had a passion for studying modes of conformity. The fashion of social psychology during this time focused on situational influences, especially those from other people. Thus, Asch had made a name in the field, and Milgram was impressed.

Asch had created an experimental design that was producing some surprising results. The core experiment involved this: he would place an individual subject among seven other people and ask him to participate in a series of exercises that involved a perceptual judgment. The subject would believe that everyone was all doing the same thing, but in fact the other seven people were confederates whose job was to make erroneous judgments. The research tested how strong the influence of others' opinions was versus one's own judgment.

The study involved eighteen trials per subject. In each trial, Asch would show different sets of four vertical lines of varying lengths, two of which matched. The subjects had a simple task—to identify the matching lines. Each would announce his response to the others. On the first two trials, everyone made the correct call, but on the third trial, the confederates gave a response that research subjects could clearly see was an error. At this point, the subject had to make a decision: say what he could clearly see or agree with the group, despite believing the answer to be wrong. This same scenario occurred twelve out of the eighteen trials, forcing the subject to question his judgment again and again.

When he designed the experiment, Asch had believed that most people would go against the group and respond with the right answer, but to his surprise, about one-third of the research subjects agreed with the group. This inspired Asch to design more experiments on conformity with variations on this same design. He hoped to pinpoint the nature of the group pressure that elicited conformity, even when conforming seemed wrong or absurd. Sometimes, he instructed one confederate to be the subject's ally to see if this diminished the rate of conformity. From these data, he worked on a theory about the individual and the group.

Milgram was sufficiently impressed to design his doctoral work around conformity studies, hoping to compare the results from other countries against those from the United States. But first, he had to prove himself once more. He had failed the required statistical examination, so his doctoral committee questioned his ability to carry out solid research. They said, in fact, that without a solid grasp of statistics, writing a dissertation in this field was impossible. Milgram dismissed this concern. He believed that this test was not indicative of his ability. He told the committee as much, and he prepared a detailed report that convinced them that he was right. He passed.

Milgram selected Norway and France for comparison, finding that Norway's rates of conformity were nearly the same as those of the United States, but in France, where group pressure was culturally less imposing, the experiments showed a lower rate. More interesting, Milgram took the experiment in a direction that Asch had not yet done, and it laid the groundwork for his flash of genius. Sensing that something was missing, he added consequences for the responses that subjects gave. He told them that information from the study would be used to assist in designing safety signals for airplanes. Believing that people would reconsider group cohesion in light of the potential of contributing to an unsafe airplane design, Milgram was surprised to find that this item reduced the level of conformity by only a small increment. More than half the subjects still yielded to peer pressure. Milgram thought that maybe they were embarrassed by the public nature of the experiment: because they stated their response to everyone else in the room, they didn't want to be the odd man out.

Next, Milgram rigged an intercom system so that the subjects could hear the confederates' responses, but they could not hear what a subject said. While the rate of conformity dropped a little more, it remained near the 50 percent level. Again, Milgram was surprised, and he attributed his results to the role of pervasive cultural pressures to conform. Although this data would not be much more for Milgram than a dissertation topic, the two years he spent on the experiments prepared him for intense focus and innovative thinking. It also opened up a life-changing opportunity. When Asch invited Milgram to be his research assistant at the Institute for Advanced Study in Princeton, New Jersey, he accepted. Located near the Ivy League university and next to a woodsy nature preserve with extensive walking paths, the institute was a center for theoretical research —an idea hatchery. It had hosted the likes of Albert Einstein, John von Neumann, and Kurt Gödel. In this idyllic setting, select researchers were able to pursue their goals without distraction, but opportunities were also available to meet other intellectuals of note—historians, philosophers, mathematicians, scientists—and perhaps to find stimulation in their work. This think tank was a rare place for intellectual inquiry and the meeting of minds.

Milgram arrived with great expectations of scholarly camaraderie, but in his opinion Asch kept him in the shadows, using Milgram's efforts without proper credit to complete a book on conformity. Asch also gave Milgram precious little time to work on his dissertation. Although Milgram was frustrated with this unexpected roadblock, being at the institute was good for him. He had dinner conversations with the likes of physicist J. Robert Oppenheimer and historian George F. Kennan. But his heart was in Cambridge, and only the correspondences with his friends and mentors there kept him buoyed. The anonymity, along with his loneliness, inspired him to work on a subject that would have "great consequence" and win him a name equal to or greater than any of his mentors. The institute also provided Milgram with the setting for what he described as his "incandescent moment."

It occurred during the spring of 1960. Milgram had promised a draft of his dissertation to his committee but had found it difficult to meet his goals. He'd been offered a teaching position at Yale, and he already knew that his interest in conformity had formed during that Cold War era into an interest in why people obey authorities. "Obedience is as basic an element in the structure of social life," he would later write, "as one can point to. Every power system implies a structure of command and action in response to the command."[2] He identified with the Jewish suffering in the Holocaust, and he wanted to understand why ordinary German people had colluded with the Nazis to help commit genocide. As a Jew, he felt pressured by the possibility that such a thing could occur again. But he knew he would need an experimental design as elegant as the one that Asch had created. That was the rub—how does one set up conditions to get people to obey an authority figure who clearly demands that they do something unconscionable?

He describes what led up to his aha! moment in letters, as well as in a book he later wrote, *Individual in a Social World*. Contemplating Asch's experimental design for conformity, Milgram had thought that too little was at stake. He wondered whether group influence could push someone toward an act in which a subject would knowingly behave aggressively toward others. This upped the stakes. It wasn't just observing four lines and going along with the majority; it was actually *acting*, and doing so in an improper manner. Milgram realized that to make a comparison that would reveal the group's influence, he would first have to know how the person would perform away from the group. As he looked each day across the wide expanse of the institute's manicured lawn, with trees budding with leaves or flowers, he considered the problem from different angles. At first, nothing clicked. Still, he sensed something was *there*. He just had not yet figured it out. Then one day it hit him. In an exciting fast-action flash, the design budded and bloomed.

"At that instant, my thought shifted," Milgram recalled, "zeroing in on this experimental control. Just how far would a person go under the experimenter's orders? It was an incandescent moment."[3]

He sensed that he had a brilliant idea that could command international attention and give him lasting fame, but he exercised restraint and kept it to himself. On the day he said good-bye to Asch, he mentioned in a low-key manner that he planned to study obedience. He gave little hint of the scheme he had in mind, but as he prepared to join the ranks of academic professors, he contemplated what lay before him. He offered the pilot project to his graduate students, and they accepted. Milgram polished it and began the project in earnest.

He believed that the subject had to be ordered to perform specific acts, and that the acts should be personally significant to the subjects, as well as having some association with important social themes. Thus, he could win notice beyond the walls of academia. To achieve this, Milgram designed a "shock box" prop and a set of commands that he considered appropriate within a laboratory setting.

The setup was this: Milgram placed an ad in the *New Haven Register* to request participation in research at Yale University; he also mailed his request to people he'd randomly selected from the phone book. For an hour of their time, he offered $4.00, plus fifty cents for travel. He selected adult male volunteers between the ages of twenty and fifty (although a later experiment included some females). They ranged in profession from blue to white collar, and all received a check prior to the experiment, which they could keep, no matter what transpired. (Thus, the fee would not be the primary motivator.)

During the summer of 1961, Milgram had set up four rounds of his experiment. The subjects were told they would be participating in an experiment about learning and memory, specifically to test a theory that people learned best when punished for mistakes. They met a fortyish confederate named "Mr. Wallace," who posed as another volunteer. Although the assignment of teacher and learner was preset, the scientist in the gray lab coat who paid the subjects and explained the experiment pretended to make a random assignment.

Each "teacher" would be seated in front of the prop's three-foot-long control panel, which consisted of a row of thirty switches, each of which progressed in severity in fifteen-volt increments. In addition, all the switches were labeled according to their shock level, starting with *Slight Shock* and ending just after *Severe Shock* with the 450-volt sign, *XXX*. None was actually attached to a shock mechanism, but the subjects heard the accompanying buzzer, saw a red light, and watched the voltage meter dial move, so they thought the prop was real. In fact, each "teacher" was allowed to feel a 45-volt shock. Subjects were to administer shocks to the "learner" (whom they had seen strapped to a chair in another room) whenever he got an answer wrong, ramping up the voltage each time. When he failed or refused to answer, they were to count this as a wrong answer and continue to administer shocks. The learner was not actually hooked up to the shock mechanism, but his script offered wrong answers at preset intervals, and a tape of his reactions was played. As the shocks grew stronger, his responses grew more agonized and hysterical. He'd shout about his heart condition, demand to be released, pound on the wall, and then go silent.

Once the subject hesitated or resisted (which Milgram anticipated), the authority figure—the stern scientist wearing a gray lab coat—would insist that he continue. This "scientist" had a succession of standard scripts, all of which were designed to exert authority and to remind the subject of his commitment. If the teacher made it all the way to 450 volts, the scientist told him to administer that same charge two more times.

Although Milgram's colleagues (including a group of psychiatrists) had predicted that only the rare sadist would go to the most extreme levels—less than 1 percent—they were mistaken. Even Milgram was surprised. No subject refused to participate in an experiment involving electric shocks, and none stopped until the level had reached 300 volts, the first time the learner showed real distress. Yet only five ended it. Over 65 percent obeyed the scientist and inflicted what they believed were painful shocks. Although some of these subjects showed symptoms of anxiety and nervous strain, they nevertheless obeyed the command to continue.

Over eight hundred subjects participated in the full range of experiments, and Milgram found no variation when he included women. They, too, obeyed. He varied the design, and in one, the learner sat next to the teacher, who was required to physically place the learner's hand on a shock plate. Predictably, there was a lower rate of compliance, but 30 percent of the subjects still went the distance. Milgram reported that he found it quite disturbing, since the learner was crying out and strenuously resisting.

Of course, when published, this study roused great controversy over the ethics of subjecting people to such a cruel deception. Some reviewers were certain that psychological scars would remain for a lifetime, but Milgram sent questionnaires to all the subjects to see what they might say. With a 92 percent response rate, over 85 percent were happy they had participated, and none expressed any sense of having been harmed by it.

However, Milgram's bold pursuit of his own curiosity did have risks. Considered one of the most controversial figures in social psychology, he lost his tenure bid at Harvard (having been lured there from Yale), and this decision meant that he had to leave. To his surprise, no other Ivy League university stepped up to claim him—a serious blow to his ego. However, he landed on his feet. Thanks to a colleague's intervention, the City University of New York offered him a home and the directorship of a new graduate program, as well as a considerable amount of space to conduct research. He was in the midst of a flourishing career there when he had a heart attack at the age of fifty-one. He died late in the afternoon of December 20, 1984. Despite the controversy he raised, he is still considered one of the most important social psychologists in the history of the discipline. "Milgram sensitized us to the hidden workings of the social world," biographer Thomas Blass states.[4]

Milgram once told an interviewer, "I believe that Pandora's box lies just below the surface of everyday life, so it is often worthwhile to challenge what you most take for granted."[5] It was this attitude that led the way for most of his groundbreaking projects. For our purposes, Milgram provides a great study. Like a tunneling mole that hits a rock, he would rapidly shift paths and keep going. Intrinsically motivated, he had a rich imagination, kept detailed track of whatever he was thinking for reevaluation, and pursued many interests simultaneously. He also mingled with other profound thinkers and nurtured a sense of humor, even about himself. He wrote fiction and poetry alongside his science and kept his eyes open for new ideas. He understood that his creative impulses had sometimes run contrary to his professional career, and he responded to them anyway. Milgram was an intellectual risk taker. His "incandescent moment" was a guiding light that led him into a thorny place but ultimately enlightened the world and gave him a lasting legacy.

AUDENTES FORTUNA JUVAT

Developing motivation as its own reward is the central feature of snapping. Innate abilities and gifts mean nothing if the person does not engage them toward a meaningful purpose. Along the way, decisions must be made about how best to use time and resources, and the more expertise one develops, the faster these decisions are resolved. However, it often takes a person who not only knows what to do but also has the audacity to *snap* to the occasion. The military would certainly appreciate a person like this, especially when the outcome of a battle depends on it.

Some interpretations of the Civil War's pivotal battle in Gettysburg in the summer of 1863 hold that General Robert E. Lee made some bad decisions during an off day. Others say he simply underestimated the enemy or overestimated his own strength. Thus, his army suffered a stunning defeat. Most notable was the high level of casualties from General Pickett's ill-fated charge across a mile-wide open field that included the hurdle of climbing over a fence. Lee mentioned later that the attack had not been supported as he'd intended, but he'd left his meaning open to interpretation.

Several historians believe that Lee's plan included an attack from General J. E. B. Stuart's cavalry, which was to come in from what is now known as East Cavalry Battlefield. Historian Tom Carhart offers a version of events in which we find a seemingly suicidal snap-against-all-odds that features none other than the flamboyant George Armstrong Custer.

In fact, Carhart himself had an aha! experience that launched his idea. "During the mid-nineties," he wrote,

I was in the West Point library stacks, researching West Point–related issues in the [nineteenth] century for my dissertation. And somehow, I stumbled over some Civil War maps made by Jedediah Hotchkiss. I knew that Hotchkiss had made maps for Lee after Stonewall Jackson died, and I wondered how good his maps of Gettysburg were. So I looked. Parenthetically, I had always wondered why J. E. B. Stuart had ever fought on East Cavalry Field in the first place—he even started the fight himself. But why? Even if he had won, as you can see on any map, there would be no way for him to get back to Lee on the main battlefield off to his southwest, as his passage would be completely blocked by Lake Heritage, one mile north-to-south and a quarter mile east-to-west.[6]

Then I found Hotchkiss's Gettysburg maps, which were, for the time, quite excellent. But, to my great surprise, Lake Heritage appears on none of them. Rather, at the heart of the space now taken up by that lake was Bonnaughtown Road, leading southwest from East Cavalry Field to Baltimore Pike and then up into the Union rear! Aha! So *that's* what they were trying to do! And everywhere I turned I found more evidence supporting the idea and virtually nothing precluding it. Bonnaughtown Road, of course, was covered by man-made Lake Heritage in 1965. So what a stroke of luck it was for me to see that Hotchkiss map! And when that happened, how the scales did fall.

We know George A. Custer best for a tragically poor set of calculations he made later in his career at Little Big Horn in Montana, which ended his life and wiped out his command, but on this day in 1863, his rapid insight during the heat of a three-hour battle could not have been more surprising—especially for the other side. Although to carry it out Custer defied a direct order, his action was later considered one of the most gallant cavalry charges of this war.

Seventy thousand troops from the Army of Northern Virginia—the Confederates—had advanced through southern Pennsylvania that June, apparently moving with aggressive intent toward Harrisburg. President Lincoln, alarmed, sought a buffer of safety for Washington, DC, so he put General George Meade in charge of the Army of the Potomac—the Union—and urged him to move forth. They, too, marched toward Gettysburg. On the hills and in the fields surrounding the small community, the armies converged, Lee from the north and west, and Meade from the south.

Fighting commenced on July 1. Two days later, Carhart and others surmise, on Lee's orders, General Stuart was to lead his cavalry division (over 4,800 strong) around the Union lines. Coming in from the east, he was to break through in the center and join General Pickett's divisions, which would already be on the main field of battle. If successful, this strategy would cut the Union line in half, making each side of it more vulnerable. (While no officer's notes spelled out this plan, none contradicts it, and those on East Cavalry Field had witnessed Stuart moving a large column of mounted soldiers in the direction of the main battle just as it had commenced.)

At one point near the Rummel farmstead, Stuart ran into an enemy contingent. Since his men outnumbered them, he led a charge to breeze past them. As he'd anticipated, they pulled back. All of them, that is, except Custer and his four hundred troops from the First Michigan. Despite being outnumbered ten to one, they were lined up in fifteen columns, ready to go.

Custer was an unusual leader, and how he arrived at this daring moment deserves examination, because his personal development demonstrates the traits and behaviors that lay a foundation for effective snaps. Not much of a thinker, he had plenty of high-spirited gumption. He was also a keen observer, courageous, and prepared for opportunity. For him, life was a series of forward motions, being alert for each new opportunity.

Born in 1839 into a large family, the mischievous little "Autie" was a pampered boy. His father, a blacksmith, had a hard time keeping the children fed, so he sent the boy, then ten years old, to live in Michigan with his married half-sister. Custer was able to attend a prestigious school, and it was here that he developed a love for military biographies, history, and fiction. He excelled as a student, which later helped him to win an appointment to West Point, the US Military Academy. This was a rare and highly valued opportunity, as well as a free education among America's elite. While there were considerable hurdles for him to acquire the requisite congressional recommendation, Custer persisted until he succeeded. Despite the fact that his father was a staunch Democrat, he persuaded a Republican congressman to sponsor him. Just seventeen, he made it through the rigorous screening to become one of sixty-eight recruits in his entering class. That was the easy part.

Lest anyone has the impression that snaps come only to those who work hard all the time, Custer is a clear counterexample. A zealous young man, he could be impulsive and reckless, but he had a great sense of humor that won loyalty. For four years, Custer did what he must to get by in his classes, but he still found time to pull pranks on fellow cadets or plan ways to test the school's many rules. He had a way with people and soon became one of the most popular cadets at West Point, though his impetuous nature often pushed him into trouble. Custer's record of demerits stands as one of the worst in West Point history, but during each six-month accounting period, he always managed to stop short of the number that would ensure his expulsion. He was determined to graduate and become an officer, so he was able to control himself when it counted. Although he was a perpetual disciplinary problem, once he faced the dire circumstances of combat, this same temperament would be his strength. He was bold, quick, and charismatic, a natural leader who took initiative and loved the spotlight.

Custer was at West Point when the War between the States broke out with the 1861 attack on Fort Sumter. Although Custer's mediocre academic performance and list of demerits had ranked him last in his class (not to mention a de facto court-martial for a broken rule that detained him on his very last day), he became in July that year a second lieutenant in the Second Calvary. His exuberance was such that he told his sister that if it were his lot to lay down his life, he would do so as freely as if he had a thousand lives to give. He'd been preparing hard over the past four years for an opportunity like this, and he intended to experience it to the fullest.

Unexpectedly, if one judges by his past performance, Custer distinguished himself several times during the war, rising quickly in rank and responsibility. Before he even got to the battlefield, he proved himself to General Winfield Scott. Upon Custer's arrival in Washington, DC, he met Scott, who asked whether he would rather train new troops in a safe place or get close to battle. Without missing a beat, he chose the latter. When it proved difficult to find a horse to take him to his first assignment, he worked out a deal with a West Point acquaintance to ride a horse that was being taken to Manassas. Thus, he proved himself to be enterprising and alert. In addition, if he had to change his ways to achieve a goal, he did so. On temporary sick leave in Michigan, he met Elizabeth Bacon, daughter of a judge. Custer hoped to woo her, but during one drunken evening he made a fool of himself in front of both of them. Thereafter, he vowed he would never drink again. He kept this pledge.

With a reputation for being both fierce and fearless, Custer had no trouble transferring his flamboyance to the battlefield. The first time he led his troops occurred after he received an order to push back a line of Confederate pickets. He requested the honor of fulfilling it, which meant taking his men directly against the enemy. His request was granted. Eagerly, he led the way. When he saw Confederates in disguise up on a ridge, he ordered his men to spread out and walk their horses forward side by side, spread over several hundred yards. He urged them to keep moving forward, despite gunfire that whistled uncomfortably close. To prevent his men from using pistols that might thwart a charge, he told them to fire one shot and then holster their weapons. Drawing his saber, he told them to do the same. Then he spurred his horse forward with a bold command, "Charge!" They raced in a line up the ridge, went over, and came down the other side. To their surprise (and relief), the enemy had vanished behind bushes. Although gunfire ensued, no one was hurt. Custer had accomplished with distinction, and without mishap, his first mission under fire. Excited by his success, he remained alert to more such opportunities. In fact, when riding as a scout, he spotted a burning bridge before anyone else noticed and rushed to save it, even as Confederates shot at him.

Custer found the battlefield quite stimulating, writing to a friend that despite the carnage he would be sorry to see the war end. He wished he could be in a battle every single day. For him it was quite the sport, and he seemed to have enormous luck escaping death even as numerous horses were shot out from under him. He envisioned himself winning fame and honor and could think of no better way than valor in warfare. He took this to an extreme at times, but it worked for him.

During one encounter with the boys in gray, Custer saved the day. General Winfield Hancock's brigade froze as Confederates charged at them with their piercing rebel yell. Hancock could not get them to fix bayonets and move, so Custer rode directly into the path of the approaching enemy, making himself a clear target, and urged the Union soldiers to follow him into battle. They did, and since the South was outnumbered, the rebels' finest retreated in haste. On that day, the North captured its first enemy flag.

Custer enjoyed being singled out for honors, and thanks to the luck that accompanied his bold spirit—dubbed "Custer's luck" by his friends—he continued to find opportunities. Now a regular scout, he honed his observational skills and accepted the enormous load of responsibility for spotting the most subtle telltale sign of the Army of Northern Virginia. He enjoyed the honor.

In May of 1862, the Union took the banks of the Chickahominy River across from Richmond, Virginia. Rumor had it that in places the river was shallow enough to ford on foot, and Custer was now the go-to guy for daring exploits. He readily agreed to test the waters. Holding his pistol over his head, he waded in. The rushing water came up to his waist, his chest, his shoulders, but his head and the pistol in his hand remained dry. He kept going. When he reached the other side, he moved into the woods and looked around for weakness in the enemy's picket line. Finding it, he waded back and reported to General McClellan a strategy that he believed would work with minimum casualties for the North.

McClellan sent Custer back across with the Fourth Michigan Infantry. They managed to capture thirty-seven enemy soldiers while losing only two of their own men, and Custer received his first promotion. Becoming a captain, he also gained a post on McClellan's staff.

On June 9, 1863, when his commanding officer was killed during the Battle of Brandy Station, Custer took charge at once and led an aggressive saber charge at the Confederates. (He adored the image of the saber-wielding cavalry officer.) The unerring sense of timing he'd developed as a prankster served him well in battle, as did his honed athleticism. But he was also an observant man, writing down everything in the narcissistic belief that others would want to know what he saw and felt. This kept his senses prepared and ready.

That same month, Lincoln had given General Meade the authority to promote anyone he wanted, so at the young age of twenty-three, Custer had gathered enough attention for his feats of bravery to rise to the rank of brigadier general; he was the youngest general in the Union Army. On June 29, he received his star and took command of the Michigan Calvary Brigade—a group that he'd recruited himself while on leave. In just three days, he'd face his greatest challenge in Gettysburg. The boy general, nicknamed "Curly," couldn't have been more elated.

Now that he was a general, he could wear a uniform of his own design. So to help his soldiers spot him in battle (and attract attention from reporters), he wore his blond curls long and donned a black velvet uniform with rows of gold buttons and wide gold lace at the wrists. Topping it off, he chose a wide-brimmed hat and wore a crimson cravat around his neck—a "red flag" of visibility. Although his men were initially uncertain what to think of him (some called him a circus rider), he proved himself cool in the hottest of circumstances and asked nothing of them that he would not do himself. Within days, he had won their respect and devotion. (They still thought he was a bit strange, though.) And there was never any mistaking where he was—usually at the head of the charge. Custer knew that his visibility was a factor in maintaining morale.

Fighting began the very day after Custer's promotion with skirmishes here and there, mounted and dismounted. His brigade consisted of the First, Fifth, Sixth, and Seventh Michigan, totaling about 1,800 soldiers. As usual, he led with ease, looking for "sport." He arrived on the George Rummel farm outside Gettysburg to support other Union regiments. A brigade of two thousand, including the First Michigan, were the first to clash with Stuart's cavalry. The Yankees held the ground, but eventually Stuart forced them to retreat to the southern end of the field.

Custer sent the Fifth Michigan out against Stuart on foot. They held for a while until Stuart ordered a charge. Custer was not about to let the Confederates succeed, so he mounted a horse and rode in all his velvet glory in front of the men of the Seventh Michigan. He drew his saber from its scabbard and held it high. Above the persistent rattle of gunfire, he shouted, "Come on, you wolverines!" He spurred his horse into action, trotting four lengths ahead, visible and vulnerable. His men followed. They rode as eighty horsemen abreast, five rows deep, an intimidating sight. However, at the Rummel barn, a solid fence stopped them. As the horsemen in back moved in, they were all squeezed together in a chaotic mass. Confederates took advantage, firing at this stationary target. Custer led those who survived to safer ground, disheartened at this embarrassing rout. But he did not let it demoralize him. He watched for his next opportunity. Vigilant, eager, and aware of his command, he was about to enter the aha! arena.

Stuart gathered his forces into a long and intimidating column. He could see clusters of Union troops at various places around the open field, but none seemed threatening. Most were dismounted. Stuart's column came at a trot, in rigid formation, and the Union soldiers who were in their path pulled back. The Union artillery made a few dents, but like a self-healing wound, Confederates closed the holes.

Custer saw this spectacle advancing toward him and recognized the opportunity. He had the First Michigan in reserve, standing ready. He could see well enough that he was vastly outnumbered, but he also knew it was not the first time in history that a battle had presented such terrible odds.

At West Point he'd studied many successful military strategists who had beat overwhelming numbers. They hadn't backed down; instead, they'd gotten creative. Carhart suggests that Custer was inspired by an incident from 331 BCE. Alexander the Great had faced the enormous Persian army of Darius III at the Battle of Gaugamela (200,000 men to his 47,000), and his chance of success had looked impossible. But he'd anticipated what Darius would likely expect him to do in response to Darius's movements, so he'd figured out a way to do the unexpected. Darius bore down, expecting Alexander to meet his army straight on as most enemy armies would, but instead Alexander moved to the right. This threw Darius's advancing army off balance when it could not maneuver as quickly as Alexander's smaller force. This presented a brief opportunity at their weakened center, which Alexander had exploited. Despite the enormous odds against him, he'd won.[7]

Likewise, as Custer watched the tight formation of an enormous column of Confederate cavalry approach, he snapped a plan: create an illusion that would surprise them and allow him to use the same trick. With fewer troopers, he had more flexibility, so he could try to throw the larger force off-balance.

Custer raced to the front of the First Michigan, saber raised again, and once more shouted encouragement, "Come on, you wolverines!" They fell into columns of sixteen abreast as he galloped ahead of them straight at the wall of enemy soldiers. Just a few hundred yards from a seemingly inevitable wipeout, Custer ordered the columns to spread out, with some in the back coming forward, so that his formation appeared to enemy eyes to be three times its actual number. He retained his flexibility while presenting an imposing facade.

"As the charge was ordered," a colonel who had watched this attack later wrote, "the speed increased, every horse on the jump, every man yelling like a demon. . . . Staggered by the fearful execution from the two batteries, the men in the front of the Confederate column drew in their horses and wavered. Some turned, and the column fanned out to the right and left . . . Custer, seeing the front men hesitate, waved his saber and shouted, 'Come on, you wolverines!' and with a fearful yell at the First Michigan rushed on."[8]

This wild attack took the Confederates by surprise. Sections of the First Michigan hit them head-on, while others raced down either side, firing their weapons. As the Confederates tried to make a responding maneuver, they lost their balance and momentum, similar to what had happened to Darius. Custer's men raced into the exposed cracks, supported by the remounted Fifth, Sixth, and Seventh Michigan, which came at the enemy's flanks.

By this time, Union regiments from Pennsylvania and New Jersey had recognized Custer's ploy and rallied, attacking the massive Confederate column from other angles. The column disintegrated as individual soldiers defended themselves. One participant later recorded that the Confederates resembled a herd of sheep looking for a hole through which to escape. Although Custer's own horse was shot out from under him during the fierce engagement, he had effectively delayed Stuart from crossing the field. What had seemed a suicidal assault had in fact been brilliant, snapped in a split second when military training converged with desperate reality. As the enemy divisions fought hand-to-hand, distant cannon sounded, signaling to Stuart that Pickett's charge was underway. If there were some plan for him to assist, Stuart would have known he was now too late. In any event, Custer had stalled him from joining Lee's efforts in any form. After a stretch of fighting, he withdrew his men back to the ridge from whence he'd come, and the Yankees took control of the field at Rummel's farm. On the main battlefield, Pickett's charge became a bloodbath with over 50 percent casualties, and Lee realized that he was losing the Battle of Gettysburg.

Custer received numerous commendations, and by the age of twenty-five, he'd been promoted to major-general. He had also won the heart of the woman he loved. When the war ended in 1865, Custer and his new wife received the surrender table from the Appomattox Court House, a gift from General Sheridan.

Risk analysis can be a time- and energy-consuming process of sorting through options. However, the idea of "snapping" involves such a deep trust in one's perceptual set that decision-making becomes instinctive. One accrues a feeling for the right direction and can snap it faster than the speed of ordinary thinking. *Audentes fortuna juvat*: fortune favors the bold. Custer, for all his crazy stunts, was certainly in this category.

INTO THE FRAY

Also at the Battle of Gettysburg, another Union officer should be recognized for his flash of genius. Another man who had diligently prepared, Joshua Chamberlain had been a passionate student of military strategy. Once he received his commission, he read whatever he could get his hands on, asked questions of his superiors, watched what they did, and listened to their instruction or advice. He had told the governor of Maine that whatever he did not know, he knew how to learn. Not one to sit passively for whatever lessons were dished out, he seized them with gusto. Like Custer, he took a top–down approach. A firm believer in a united government, Chamberlain had developed a passion for the Union's cause, leaving his teaching post at Bowdoin College to become a soldier. His colleagues had scoffed and thought he lacked the right stuff to be a proper soldier. When they learned that he'd received the rank of lieutenant colonel, they'd been astonished.

Joining the army in 1862, Chamberlain gained command of the Twentieth Maine Infantry in May 1863. This regiment had started with one thousand soldiers, but after five major engagements, they were down to just over one-third of that number. In short order, Chamberlain received charge of 120 disgruntled mutineers. A humanitarian, he listened to their grudges, fed them, and hoped they might yield to his leadership. By the afternoon of July 2, they were all engaged together in a fight for their lives.

As both armies marched toward Gettysburg, Chamberlain's men took over the high ground on a hill called Little Round Top, placing them at the extreme left of the Union line. Some seven hundred troops from the Fifteenth Alabama, who had aimed to take that hill, attacked within twenty minutes. They came at the Twentieth Maine in successive waves, so Chamberlain spread his men out farther to protect the flank. Although this surprised the Confederate commander, he urged his men to keep at it. Both sides gained and gave back ground as bodies piled up and ammunition ran low. Within two hours, the Confederates had rushed up the hill five times. Their fury was astonishing, but each time the Twentieth Maine beat them back.

As evening approached, Chamberlain realized that some of his men had only their bayonets, and yet the soldiers in gray or butternut showed no sign of retreat. He knew they were preparing for yet another assault—one that could well succeed. He'd lost one-third of his soldiers, and very few had even one bullet left. But retreat was out of the question. Chamberlain considered his dire position. In the midst of a "medley of monstrous noises," he heard the undulating rebel yell that sent chills down his spine. The Fifteenth Alabama charged up the hill through the trees. Bullets ricocheted every which way. Then another force of confederates charged from a different angle. Chamberlain's men were outnumbered, and their only advantage was being uphill. Some of them scrambled among the dead to find whatever ammunition they could. Many looked to him for a solution. If he failed to offer a workable plan, they would all die.

"The roar of all this tumult reaches us on the left," he later recorded, "and heightened the intensity of our resolve."[9]

Chamberlain flashed through several maneuvers but dismissed each. He waited, unsure. Then he snapped on a strategy—straight from a textbook. He was ready. They would take the offensive.

Quickly, he gathered his officers and ordered them to charge down the hill with the only thing they had left—their bayonets. But they couldn't just charge in a line, because they might get separated. He told them that the right end of the line would remain fixed in place while the left wing swung toward the Confederates like a giant hinged gate on a post. Thus, in this "right wheel" formation, the remaining two hundred soldiers would come together and sweep down into the enemy line at a right angle.

There was no time to debate. They had to *move*. The officers shouted orders. The troops responded. Against all odds, the charge succeeded, surprising the Confederates. Many retreated, but Chamberlain took several hundred prisoners. More important, he had preserved the Union's line. His spontaneous decision contributed significantly to the ultimate Union victory, and he later won a Congressional Medal of Honor.

Chamberlain, Custer, and Milgram had been voracious learners and disciplined thinkers. They had trusted fully in their knowledge and training. Even under the most dire of circumstances, without a shred of self-doubt, they could choreograph risky maneuvers that paid off.

KEY POINTS

- Satisfaction in one's work is important for effective snaps.
- The desire to improve or discover something new in one's field drives momentum.
- The more one succeeds with new ideas, the more trust one builds in one's judgments.
- Self-trust assists innovation and fuels aha! moments that pop into strategies.

CHAPTER 11

SNAPS ON DEMAND

RECALCULATING ROUTES

Percy Spencer was immersed in radar research one day when he grabbed the candy bar he'd pocketed that morning and found a chocolate mess. Then a light came on. He realized that low-level microwaves surrounding him had melted the candy—and this snapped an idea. Spencer quickly filed for a patent and invented the microwave oven. It just takes "seeing more" and being ready to roll.[1]

Johannes Gutenberg reportedly went to a wine festival around the time that he was trying to figure out a way to mass-produce books. He had created moveable type but had not solved the problem of how to keep pressure on the plate to allow for repeated printing. At the festival, he was watching a wine press squeeze juice from grapes when he snapped on the design he needed. He went on to create the printing press.[2]

Anyone who has traveled with a global positioning system knows the familiar voice that speaks whenever there's an unexpected move. The GPS has directed a left turn, but you go straight. In short order, the system assesses how to get back on track: "Recalculating route!" This resembles the quick-strike decisions involved in a snap: the brain knows where it needs to go, and, if allowed, recalculates.

Napoleon may have been the first person to use "embedded advertising," which came to him when faced with the crisis of over-

239

crowded cemeteries in Paris: decomposed bodies were bursting through the cellar walls of adjacent businesses. He purchased a beautiful park named Père Lachaise outside the city. However, Parisians thought it was too far to go to bury and visit their dead, so the land lay unused. To make the place more appealing, Napoleon transferred the remains of such famous people as Molière, but this did not work either. However, when the popular novelist Balzac "buried" his characters in Père Lachaise after they "died," the place drew curious readers. Napoleon *snapped*. He "recalculated," and planted more such "ads." Soon Parisians viewed the park as a potential cemetery, especially as they saw artistic monuments housing the likes of Oscar Wilde, Frédéric Chopin, and Marcel Proust. Today, Père Lachaise is one of the most impressive— and crowded—cemeteries in the world.[3]

As we have already seen, some people incubate their problems for recalculation by sleeping on them. Others take a walk, work on puzzles, change their environment, or play with their kids. They learn what works with their inner GPS and set the conditions to improve the process, trusting it even when other ways seem more sensible or obvious. Isaac Asimov, a preeminent science fiction writer, knew that it was useless to force the issue when he experienced writer's block. He would go see a movie and allow his unconscious to process in its own way. Once he returned to his work, he had dissolved his impasse.[4]

Snapping can occur from a chance word or encounter; it can arise from a challenge; or it might require a long process of immersion and incubation. When Thomas Edison was criticized for taking so long to adapt lightbulbs for home use, he reportedly said that he had not failed; he'd merely found ten thousand ways that would not work. But he did eventually snap the solution. Although snaps can occur serendipitously, even without much prep, we can improve the chances of provoking them by preparing.

PRACTICAL MATTERS

Brain studies on creativity all support the fact that mental flexibility is the foundation for developing the mental agility of a snap—and this often comes down to attitude. Many businesses realize that innovative thinking, as unpredictable as it might be, trumps sticking to the rules. Pondering a children's educational toy, an ordinary globe, Jim Marggraff created the interactive Odyssey Atlasphere, which made learning world geography more fun. He also invented the LeapPad reading platform and Leapfrog's Fly talking pen—and for this latter device he relied on a "board" of children, who discussed its design over ice cream. Marggraff also devised the Pulse Smartpen, which records audio while tracking what the pen writes. He attributes his innovations to considering something familiar from new angles. But he also takes his work to bed with him.

"Typically, I go to bed chewing on it," he says, "and I'll wake up at four in the morning with some sort of solution."[5] When an idea pops, he figures out a way to create and market it.

The perceptual shift that launches a snap relies on knowing when to keep thinking versus when to quit. It begins not with mere awareness of a problem that needs to be solved, but with being curious enough to pursue learning for its own sake. For this, I propose the Joseph Bell approach: figure out what best draws your attention and learn as much as you can about it and about other areas associated with it.

Remember the art experience for Harvard medical students? Because Joel Katz knew the area, as well as what was missing, he was able to see a new approach. The more you know about a given subject, the better your chance of spotting a need or problem that should be addressed—especially if you're alert. You will also be in a good position to snap a solution or a new approach. Although snaps can happen any time, for any reason, they arise most often from incubation, which allows the subconscious to absorb and redistribute information into an internal template or database. Then, when a snap occurs, you can move into action, testing it to ensure that it's viable. (In a life-threatening situation like those that Sullenberger, Custer, and Dodge faced, the test is immediate.)

A regular habit of mindful meditation appears to develop areas of the brain involved in agility. Researchers at Massachusetts General Hospital and Harvard Medical School found that people who meditate for half an hour every day have measurable differences in their gray matter—especially in the association cortex, which integrates information processing. They also noted increased density in the hippocampus, which is responsible for memory and learning. Meditation improves the ability to focus and pay attention for longer periods.[6]

A study involving Buddhist monks confirmed this. They had more "gamma power" in the frontal, parietal, and temporal association cortices. This indicates that people can improve their brains' functioning with training. Dr. Nancy Andreasen, who studies creativity, offers an alternative to Westerners of the Eastern practice of emptying the mind. Instead, she says to practice "random episodic silent thought." To do this, dissociate yourself from external input and allow your mind to wander freely, to any subject. This is like conscious dreaming. The ideas themselves, as they rise to the surface, might connect into a snap—as has happened for many inventors, writers, and scientists.[7]

FIND WHAT WORKS

Research at Northwestern University revealed that people are better problem solvers and use insight more often than methodical calculations when they're in a good mood.[8] Seventy-nine participants completed mood state inventories just before they performed the experimental task, which involved word completion tasks like those described in chapter 5. Thirty participants were scanned with an fMRI. Brain activity in the association cortex was consistent with conditions conducive to finding insight solutions. These results confirm the approach of companies like Google that urge employees to take time for recreation. The better their mood, the more productive and creative they tend to be. The researchers suggested that a positive mood broadened the scope of attention, both externally and internally. However, a good mood is just the start, like setting the table before a grand feast.

Professor Nancy Koehn of Harvard Business School has studied entrepreneurs. She noticed that the most successful ones keep their "antennae" out all the time. They don't restrict themselves to workday hours or stipulated assignments. They look for new information in everything with which they connect. "They have," she states, "lots of internal disk space."[9]

Among the things from which they readily learn are their own mistakes. Far from interpreting errors as failures, they see the valuable lessons they have learned. They also know how to partner with people who make great sounding boards or who enhance their thinking. Staples became the first office supply "supermarket," thanks to how Tom Stemberg combined his expertise in the grocery distribution business with a mentor's challenge to be more creative.[10]

John Knific experienced his aha! moment in a dorm room.[11] Although it took two years of dedication to make it work, that initial creative spark kept him and his partners going. Knific and his roommate, Marc Plotkin, were music majors at Case Western Reserve in Ohio. Both of Knific's parents are professional musicians, and he is a jazz pianist. To this expertise he added Internet technology, which played a role in his innovation. Knific was surfing around on different websites one day, trying to find a platform for establishing a professional Internet presence, but he didn't like anything he found. He'd already tried MySpace® Music, as well as several others, but he had disappointing results.

"It dawned on me that I didn't like any of them," said Knific. "I wondered why there wasn't one that appealed to me. I thought that I wasn't that different from any other young professional musicians trying to promote themselves. I knocked on Marc's door and asked, 'What do you think of the services out there?' He had the same opinion, and I thought, 'Why don't we try to change that?' This was the initial spark."

Knific was excited about the idea. "I was pacing around and thinking a mile a minute. You immediately think everything is figured out and you just have to start working on it. But then you start backpedaling and stripping it down and you realize that the core of the idea works, but everything else has to be figured out."

Knific put the idea aside for a while to study abroad, but when he returned he started mulling it over again. It still seemed like a good idea—a sort of LinkedIn for musicians. "During my senior year, Marc and I decided to take it seriously. We raised $100,000 in grant money and asked a friend, Eric Neuman, who was a talented programmer, to be the lead developer. So I set up a team and decided, let's make a go of this." Although Knific was accepted into medical school, he decided to devote himself to the company. However, like many others who began with great ideas, the path to production and success was not easy. In fact, their initial idea failed to pan out.

"It wasn't until we actually sat down and tried to do it that we realized it wasn't going to work. When you entertain it in your mind, of course, everything's rosy. But the problems don't come up until you're at the execution stage." In fact, they were insurmountable. There appeared to be no market. "It wasn't until May 2010 that we ended the social network angle." But they weren't willing to declare their idea a total failure.

A fortuitous engagement offered the next aha! leap. They were beta testing their product at the Cleveland Institute of Music. "While I was demoing it," Knific recalls, "an administrator raised his hand and asked, 'Can people submit these for auditions?' When it was clear that this could be done, he said, 'Hey guys, is there any way we could use this for the admissions process?' He had this aha! thought before us, but we immediately said yes. Whatever it was going to take, we were going meet that need. We rebuilt the entire product in less than three months and relaunched in August 2010."

The result was CitizenGroove, a Web-based company that partners with music programs to assist with digital recruitment by offering student musicians a way to create audition tapes for a digital portfolio. "It's a platform designed to process media-intensive applications," Knific explains, "and we found our biggest clients to be music and arts programs, places where you have thousands of incoming audio and video files, and you need an efficient way to screen that material. Instead of receiving DVDs and paper portfolios, we manage everything electronically, from submission to review to the decision-making."

Knific acknowledges that it took two years and teamwork to create a company from the initial idea, and everyone involved came onboard as an officer. "This is not a one-person vision driven company," he says. "It's three cofounders and support from the business community in northeast Ohio. It worked, in part, because they broadened the notion of 'social' and were thus able to recognize other possibilities. I think there's a lot of interesting interactions you can facilitate using asynchronous video, as in video messaging, video posting, and how you can leverage that into different workflow solutions. Video is an upgrade from having just messages or photos."

Looking back, Knific appreciates that illuminated moment and feels kinship with other entrepreneurs who've kept their candles burning. "There's a core motivation that keeps them going through bad times because they understand what the vision can be. The execution part—the people who are very methodical about it but still keep that high trajectory—they seem to be the successful ones who can weather the bad days."

For Knific and his crew, the dark days appear to be past. *BusinessWeek* ranked them among the top twenty-five entrepreneurs under age twenty-five in the country.

❄❄❄❄❄

So, let's look at some practical things that you can do to improve your snapping abilities. Although it's true that snaps can occur almost any time simply as the result of a perceptual shift or fortuitous encounter, to enhance your ability to make them happen with some regularity, you might try any of the following:

1. Practice being observant. Really *look* at things you pass each day or take a walk in a new place. Try describing it or even forming what you see into poetic metaphors. The more you exercise your brain in new ways, the more flexible and agile it will become. Einstein once said that you can't use the same thinking to solve a problem that you used to produce the problem. In other words, let the brainpower of subconscious assimilation get into gear.

2. One way to fuel a truly innovative snap is through cross-fertilization. Expose yourself to a diversity of subjects because the most creative snaps arise from combining seemingly unrelated ideas into something new. We've seen examples of "polymaths," or people who know many things. Recall that most, if not all, were driven by edge-of-your-seat curiosity. Develop the habit of top–down initiating. Keep exposing yourself to new ideas. The less an enterprise has already crossed into your field of expertise, the more potential it has for generating a truly unique aha! moment. Psychologist Shelley Carson, who teaches people to be creative, endorses this idea. She urges us to absorb information from a variety of sources, to listen to others, read magazines and newspapers, find out what others have done in similar situations, and then "dance" with all the subconscious material.[12]

3. Put yourself mentally into a situation or instead envision yourself achieving a goal. Imagine noises, smells, and bodily sensations. Make it as real as possible to try to build up a body memory. The more vivid it is, the more effective it will be. As we saw with the research on mimetic cells, when you

imagine doing something in a certain way, the brain tends to accept this as a real experience.

4. Try writing down what you know about your problem just before going to sleep, taking a shower, meditating, playing the piano, or going for a walk. Instruct your brain to work on it. Then leave it alone.

5. Exploit drowsy or hypnogogic states: you may not feel like doing anything, but the brain waves associated with drowsiness can be highly creative.

6. Change activities, as James Watson (of Watson and Crick) would do. He reported flashes of insight while daydreaming, conversing, riding a bus, walking, watching a film, doodling, and falling asleep. Stepping away will not necessarily generate an aha! moment, but when you find an "other" activity that works, make it a regular habit. Your mind–body will learn your rhythms through cognitive maps and will often deliver.

7. Have someone guide you in an imagery exercise that involves the following steps: you write down the problem on which you're working and then have your friend read it to you while you relax. In other words, let this person speak it to your subconscious. See what you get.

8. Ask three people who have different areas of expertise their opinions on your problem, and just listen. Let your brain process the information you receive.

9. Write down all ideas associated with your problem that occur to you in the space of thirty minutes and then read your list before putting it aside.

10. Study the habits of people who have included the pursuit of eureka experiences into their work. This is especially effective for inspiring aha! moments in children.

11. Absorb information from exposure to a variety of sources.

SNAPS ARE FOR KIDS

Rick and Lauren Altman have run an online company since 2007. They let their six-year-old daughter Hannah name their product— decorative zipper pulls to hang on coats and suitcases. She called them CoolZips. When Hannah was nine, her family went to a restaurant one day, and she noticed a vending machine that contained pencil top toys. She wanted one, but her father thought it was a waste of money. Hannah insisted, so he gave her a quarter. She was so intrigued with the gimmick that she dreamed up a website to sell these "squishies" to other kids. Thus was "Hannah's Cool World" born. At the age of ten, after watching her parents become Internet entrepreneurs, Hannah became CEO of her own international operation, with thousands of customers.[13]

Children can be taught to experience the joy of snap experiences. Offering them problems involving an interesting challenge that is rigorous enough to feel like fun but not intimidating provides opportunities for mental play. When they succeed, they want more. They can also be taught through the role models of successful snappers. And as they develop, they will recognize the conditions that work best for them. One result is better self-esteem; another is self-trust. The key is to blend mental work and relaxation or play in such a way that you provoke their curiosity; give them a series of successes along the path toward a larger goal; reinforce their mindful activity; and encourage them to keep reaching. Often, like the Polgár sisters, they will invent their own skill-enhancing games.

EUREKA PRODUCERS

A Boston software company hopes to make the eureka moment accessible by computer.[14] Invention Machine's Goldfire® application is designed to sustain innovation. Users choose a task, and Goldfire's wizard interface assists them to select a methodology to work out their needs. The users determine the reasons why their existing system has failed, and they then develop a new conceptual design. The software tracks system activity and offers ideas about specific projects. Although the company has been successful in at least twenty-five countries, it hasn't managed to replace the excitement of a snap. It also depends on people to think up the options, so it's limited to their ideas. It also cannot help with inventions with unknown parameters or with rapid decision making in a crisis.

Companies that encourage employees to move beyond traditional methods are more likely to spark insight. In fact, the Dexter F. Baker Institute for Entrepreneurship, Creativity, and Innovation at Lehigh University in Pennsylvania awards grant money via annual Eureka! competitions to young entrepreneurs. Eureka moments are not always the spark of inspiration, but sometimes they are. Lisa Getzler-Linn, the administrative director of the Baker Institute for Entrepreneurship, Creativity, and Innovation and the Integrated Product Development Program described the institute's approach.

"When we engage students in the process of innovation-related activities and creative problem solving," she said,

> we talk to them about their passion and their recognition of a problem to be solved as an opportunity to create value. In terms of students who have pursued their dream and created a sustainable business, we have seen a couple every year. The mission of the Baker Institute includes producing a greater number of sustainable student ventures and, equally as important, to reach students across the university to show them that innovation and creativity offer a pathway to creating value regardless of one's discipline.[15]

The Institute itself has been in existence only since March 2010, although there have been many nationally recognized programs at Lehigh that teach and promote the entrepreneurial mindset, creating a fertile ground for eureka moments to occur. The Integrated Product Development Program was founded in the mid-1990s and has been working with large and small companies on developing new products and processes by leveraging the sponsoring company's expertise and resources to help us guide student teams through the process of technical innovation.

The Dexter F. and Dorothy M. Baker Foundation is our funding organization. Every fall, we set ourselves up as "innovation central" to make students aware that we're going to be holding this series of competitions. It's called the Eureka Series because we have categories in which students can make their proposals specific to what they're doing. We have a social venture competition, a general entrepreneurship area, an advanced technology competition, and the series will be expanding into environmental proposals. We'd like to expand into the arts as well.

We don't require a team, but when it's not [a team], one of the first things we help student innovators recognize is the idea that they probably can't do it alone. Within Integrated Product Development, we have spent time developing measures around interdisciplinary teamwork and a team climate, and [we] can show evidence that it provides fertile ground for innovation to occur. We provide mentorship throughout the proposal development period. We do presentations in the classes across campus to pique the interest of all types of students. It's a student venture proposal, and the more they know their product, and their market, and their stakeholders, the better they do.

We also have the Lehigh Entrepreneurs Network, primarily alumni, which is willing to help our students move their venture to the next level. Sometimes they partner with the students. We cultivate their entrepreneurial mindset and their willingness to immerse themselves in this process. One young woman, an International Relations major, has been working on developing a way for villages in Tanzania to fix the broken well pumps that have been installed by NGOs. This year's winning social entrepreneur is building and distributing composting toilets in the third world, and she's trying it out here in the South Side Initiative's community garden.

In terms of creativity, Dexter Baker's mantra is that without creative thinking, there is no innovation, and without innovation, there is no future for our economy. That's one of our guiding principles. Students who aren't starting companies are just as important to us, as they learn to be creative and entrepreneurial. We provide examples, role models, opportunities, and skills that will help them to achieve this goal.

Research on over one hundred companies' brainstorming sessions produced techniques with potential:

1. Team people together who have diverse perspectives and skills to create scenarios of future markets.
2. Build a website that invites ideas from other sections of a company or even from nonemployees—and offer rewards.
3. "Deep dive," or immerse yourself like an anthropologist, to learn more about consumers and their culture than you think you need to know.
4. Study possibilities in markets that the company has not envisioned.
5. Bring an outsider into a brainstorming session to force employees to make their plans and ideas clear or to challenge their assumptions.
6. Encourage different departments to talk to one another.
7. Create "play areas," like Google's famous table tennis tables, for relaxation.
8. Encourage employees to break away from the routines and distractions of the office. Different environments and experiences—a walk in the park, a trip to a local coffee shop—can stimulate new thoughts.
9. Write down the problem, then find a second and third way to express it.
10. Imagine mounting your current project in a different country and culture.

Note: it's not about putting six people around a table in a brain-storming session, it's about encouraging unique, untested, even "disruptive" activities. Individuals without access to other employees can do solitary exercises in creativity, such as considering what an object in their home might add to solving a problem. The point is to shift the thinking process and add more perspectives than what are typically utilized. This is the vigilance advantage.

In sum, a person's preparatory brain state prior to encountering a problem influences whether the solution will snap. It's like driving a car: you need to put fuel into it, keep it in running condition, and turn the key to spark the process. You don't have to understand how it works. You need only do your part. Prior training or experience incubates potential ideas. And when we intersperse discipline and effort with relaxation, we make the best use of the brain's range of resources. We accept despair, frustration, and impasse as part of the process. This is the time during which the brain can produce something other than what methodical left-brain routes can achieve. Clenching won't help. We must allow the areas in which the brain choreographs associations to make diverse connections and introduce the surprise climax. So, *scan* the environment for learning opportunities and let the brain *sift* through what you load into your internal hard drive to *solve* the problem or meet the need. "All that we know, all that we are," said Tim Berners-Lee, "comes from the way our neurons are connected."[16]

Teaching children to blend purpose and goals with a sense of adventure can get the ball rolling early, but adults can transform their habits, too. A sense of direction that feels right develops trust in our abilities. We can then tap into our inner GPS and become more vigilant about opportunities. This produces a dopamine rush that results in joy and excitement, especially when ideas snap.

Although it feels magical, it's not. Science has demonstrated what happens. How much you prime your brain is up to you. How much you learn, how widely you set your antennae, and how willing you are to remain at the edge of your seat will all assist the brain to incubate, associate, and deliver. As Stephen Hawking said, it feels like sexual pleasure, but it lasts longer. It can only enrich our lives, so the earlier we start, the better.

KEY POINTS

- Frustration coupled with goal-driven behavior offers conditions for a snap.
- During an impasse, successful snappers relax and let the brain do its work with their internal database.
- Like a magician's trick, a snap occurs in the gap between the brain's articulate thinking and its subconscious processing.
- The brain rewards itself during an aha! with a rush of pleasure.
- Successful snappers recognize how they generated flashes of insight and will replicate those conditions.

GLOSSARY

aha! moment—the sense of discovery, an epiphany or a brainstorm. It feels qualitatively different from the typical thinking process and usually occurs quite suddenly.

chunking—organizing a lot of information into meaningful groups for better short-term memory retention.

cognitive map—a set of habits and beliefs that influence how we perceive and interpret our environment and experience. It helps us to move easily through our world but can also limit us from discovery unless we keep expanding it.

data mining—searching for new patterns in a grouping of data.

dopamine—the neurotransmitter that floods the brain with pleasure during the experience of anticipation.

entanglement—the idea that we rub shoulders with so many people and partake of their ideas that we absorb influences that feed a eureka discovery.

entelechy—Aristotle's notion that our life's purpose is already contained within us.

flow—the experience of being so attuned with a project or activity that you fail to perceive the passage of time or other external clues. Often, we produce our best work during flow.

long-term memory—enduring memories that are stored for later retrieval, whether minutes or years later.

mental flexibility—the ability to see things from different angles, which can be developed and strengthened with practice.

perceptual shift—the experience of seeing something differently from your first impression due to new information that changes the context.

scan—the automatic habit of watching for opportunities or ideas.

snap—a flash of inspirational brilliance, a brainstorm, the "aha! moment," or a "eureka" experience, which launches a sense of direction and a desire or need for action.

vigilance advantage—what people gain who mindfully scan information for opportunities or new ideas.

working memory—short-term memory that allows us to process information quickly and retain a small number of items for a brief time.

NOTES

CHAPTER 1: PASTEUR'S PROPOSAL

1. James Watson, *The Double Helix* (New York: Atheneum, 1968), p. 167.

2. Marlene Wagman-Geller, *Eureka: The Surprising Stories that Shaped the World* (New York: Perigee, 2010), pp. 33–39.

3. Alan Hirshfeld, *Eureka Man: The Life and Legacy of Archimedes* (New York: Walker, 2009).

4. Isaac Asimov, "The Eureka Phenomenon," *Magazine of Science Fiction and Fantasy*, 1971.

5. Visual Thinking Strategies, "History," http://www.vtshome .org/pages/history (accessed April 11, 2011).

6. Sheila Naghshineh et al., "Formal Art Observation Training Improves Medical Students' Visual Diagnostic Skills," *Journal of General Internal Medicine* 23, no. 7 (2008): 991–97.

7. "BWH Research Finds Formal Art Observation Training Improves Medical Students' Visual Literacy and Diagnostic Skills," Brigham and Women's Hospital press release, July 10, 2010, http:// www.brighamandwomens.org/about_bwh/publicaffairs/news/press releases/PressRelease.aspx?sub=0&PageID=385 (accessed September 25, 2010).

8. Joel Katz, interview with author, March 22, 2011.

9. Great-Quotes.com, "Louis Pasteur," 2011, http://www.great -quotes.com/quote/1374936 (accessed December 12, 2010).

10. Rick Beyer, *The Greatest Stories Science Never Told* (New York: HarperCollins, 2000), pp. 40–41.

11. "Hawking Extols Joy of Discovery," BBC News, January 11, 2002, http://news.bbc.co.uk/2/hi/science/nature/1755683.stm (accessed November 5, 2010).

12. Robin Marantz Henig, "Understanding the Anxious Mind," *New York Times*, September 29, 2009, http://www.nytimes.com/2009/10/04/magazine/04anxiety-t.html (accessed April 10, 2011).

13. Michael Useem, *The Leadership Moment* (New York: Random House, 1998), pp. 43–64.

14. Ibid., p. 57.

15. K. A. Ericsson, R. T. Krampe, and C. Tesch-Römer, "The Role of Deliberate Practice in the Acquisition of Expert Performance," *Psychological Review* 100 (2008): 363–406.

16. Mihaly Csikszentmihalyi, *Finding Flow: The Psychology of Engagement with Everyday Life* (New York: Basic Books, 1997), p. 3.

17. Ibid., p. 2.

18. Geoff Williams, "ManCan's Hart Main: A 13-Year-Old Entrepreneur Invents Candles for Men," http://smallbusiness.aol.com/2011/05/10/mancans-hart-main-a-13-year-old-entrepreneur-invents-candles-f/ (accessed May 10, 2011).

19. Albert van Helden, *The Invention of the Telescope* (Philadelphia: American Philosophical Society, 1977), p. 40.

20. Richard Platt, *Eureka! Great Inventions and How They Happened* (Boston: Kingfisher, 2003), pp. 44–45.

CHAPTER 2: PRIME MOVERS

1. Eric Estrin, "CSI's Zuiker: I Owe My Career to a Bookie Runner," *Wrap*, April 13, 2010, http://www.thewrap.com/television/column-post/csis-zuiker-i-owe-my-career-bookie-runner-16268 (accessed September 25, 2010).

2. Bill Carter, *Desperate Networks* (New York: Doubleday, 2006), pp. 114–21.

3. Michelle Nichols, "'Digi-Novel' Combines Book, Movie and Website," Reuters, September 2, 2009, http://www.reuters.com/article/2009/09/02/us-books-digital-idUSTRE58135120090902 (accessed September 25, 2010).

4. Nathaniel Brandon, "Our Urgent Need for Self-Esteem," *Excellence*, May 14, 1994.

5. Aristotle, *De Anima*, bk. 2, chap. 1, 412a.9.

6. Joseph Campbell, *Joseph Campbell and the Power of Myth with Bill Moyers*, ed. Betty Sue Flowers (New York: Doubleday, 1988), p. 113.

7. P. D. James, "Let Me Tell You a Story: My Life in Crime Fiction," *Mailonline*, http://www.dailymail.co.uk/home/moslive/article-1381149/P-D-James-My-life-crime-fiction.html (accessed April 30, 2011).

8. John T. Richardson, "How Dean Kamen's Magical Water Machine Could Save the World," http://www.Esquire.com/features/Dean-kamen-1208 (accessed January 27, 2010).

9. Michael Inbar, "Welcome to the Secret Island of the Eccentric Genius," *Today Show*, October 21, 2010, http://today.msnbc.msn.com/id/39775733/ns/today-today_tech/t/welcome-secret-island-eccentric-genius (accessed November 5, 2010).

10. Ibid.

11. Anne Driscoll, "Armless Piano Player Moves 'China's Got Talent' Audience to Tears," Tonic, August 18, 2010, http://www.tonic.com/p/armless-piano-player-moves-chinas-got-talent-audience-to-tears/ (accessed December 14, 2010).

12. Mihaly Csikszentmihalyi, *Finding Flow: The Psychology of Engagement with Everyday Life* (New York: Basic Books, 1997), p. 124.

13. Gail Buchalter, "A Power Will Guide You—If You Let It," *Parade*, April 4, 1999, pp. 4–6.

14. Ibid.

15. Nathaniel Wright Stevenson, *Lincoln* (New York: Echo, 2006), p. 12.

16. Carl Jung, *Synchronicity: An Acausal Connecting Principle* (London: Routledge and Kegan Paul, 1972).

17. Josh Berman, interviews with author, January 2011.

18. Ibid.

19. Howard Gardner, *Frames of Mind: The Theory of Multiple Intelligences*, 2nd ed. (New York: Basic Books, 1993), p. ix.

20. Ibid., p. x.

21. Annie Dillard, *Pilgrim at Tinker Creek* (New York: Buccaneer Books, 1998).

CHAPTER 3: THE MASTER'S ZONE

1. Susan Polgár, *Breaking Through: How the Polgár Sisters Changed the Game of Chess* (London: Gloucester, 2005), p. 6.

2. Ibid., p. 7.

3. Carlin Flora, "The Grandmaster Experiment," *Psychology Today*, June 14, 2005, http://www.psychologytoday.com/articles/200506/the-grandmaster-experiment (accessed October 18, 2010).

4. Polgár, *Breaking Through*, p. 15.

5. Ibid., p. 41.

6. Flora, "Grandmaster Experiment."

7. Ibid.

8. Ibid.

9. George Miller, "The Magical Number Seven, Plus or Minus Two: Some Limits on Our Capacity for Processing Information," *Psychological Review* 63 (1956): 81–97.

10. Ibid., p. 83.

11. Ibid., p. 95.

12. Joshua Foer, *Moonwalking with Einstein* (New York: Penguin, 2011).

13. Beryl Lieff Benderly, "Everyday Intuition," *Psychology Today*, September 1989, pp. 35–38.

14. D. A. Rosenbaum et al., "Hierarchical Control of Rapid Movement Sequences," *Journal of Experimental Psychology* 9 (1983): 86–102.

15. F. Gobet and H. Simon, "Exert Chess Memory: Revisiting the Chunking Hypothesis," *Memory* 6 (1998): 225–55.

16. Ibid., p. 250.

17. Christopher Chabris and Daniel Simons, *The Invisible Gorilla* (New York: Crown, 2010), pp. 210–11.

18. Ibid., p. 211.

19. Ibid., p. 212.

20. Howard Gardner, *Art, Mind, and Brain* (New York: Basic Books, 1982), p. 197.

21. B. Ghiselin, *The Creative Process* (New York: Mentor, 1959), p. 45.

22. Ibid.

23. George Keeler, interview with author, April 2011.

24. "Dopamine Apparently Enhances Anticipation of Pleasure in Humans," *Health Jockey*, November 13, 2009, http://www.health jockey.com/2009/11/13/dopamine-apparently-enhances-anticipation -of-pleasure-in-humans/ (accessed November 22, 2010).

25. Ibid.

26. Tali Sharot et al., "Dopamine Enhances Expectation of Pleasure in Humans," *Current Biology* 19 (December 29, 2009): 2077–80.

27. Ibid.

28. Shelley Carson, *Your Creative Brain: Seven Steps to Maximize Imagination, Productivity, and Innovation in Your Life* (New York: Jossey-Bass, 2010).

29. Shelley Carson, "The Unleashed Mind," *Scientific American Mind*, May/June 2011, p. 26.

30. Ibid., 28.

CHAPTER 4: MENTAL HYPERLINKS

1. Tim Berners-Lee with Mark Fischetti, *Weaving the Web: The Original Design and Ultimate Destiny of the World Wide Web by Its Inventor* (New York: HarperCollins/HarperSanFrancisco, 1999), p. 1.

2. Ibid., p. 4.

3. Ibid., p. 16.

4. Ibid., pp. 1–23.

5. Ibid., p. 2.

6. Ibid., p. 3.

7. Ibid., p. 6.

8. Ibid., p. 12.

9. Joe Z. Tsien, "The Memory Code," *Scientific American*, July 2007, pp. 52–59.

10. Kriston Leutwyler, "Making Smart Mice," *Scientific American*, September 7, 1999, http://scientificamerican.com/article.cfm?id=making -smart-mice (accessed November 5, 2010).

11. Tsien, "Memory Code," p. 57.

12. Victoria F. Holst and Kathy Pezdek, "Scripts for Typical Crimes and Their Effects on Memory for Eyewitness Testimony," *Applied Cognitive Psychology* 6 (1992): 573–87.

13. E. Loftus and H. G. Hoffman, "Misinformation and Memory: The Creation of New Memories," *Journal of Experimental Psychology* 118 (1989): 100–104.

14. Elizabeth Loftus, "Our Changeable Memories: Legal and Practical Implications," *Nature Reviews: Neuroscience* 4 (Fall 2003): 231–34.

15. R. Keith Sawyer, *Explaining Creativity: The Science of Human Innovation* (Oxford: Oxford University Press, 2006), p. 298.

16. Daniel Durstewitz et al., "Abrupt Transitions between Prefrontal Neural Ensemble States Accompany Behavioral Transitions during Rule Learning," *Neuron* 66, no. 3 (2010): 438–48.

17. Cell Press, "Eureka! Neural Evidence for Sudden Insight," *Science Daily*, May 14, 2010, http://www.sciencedaily.com/releases/2010/ 05/100512125226.htm (accessed November 17, 2010).

18. Chesley Sullenberger, *Highest Duty: My Search for What Really Matters* (New York: William Morrow, 2009).

19. Bill Newcott, "Wisdom of the Elders," *AARP Magazine*, May–June 2009, p. 52.

20. Sullenberger, *Highest Duty*.

CHAPTER 5: THE BRAIN'S BIG BANG

1. *How William Shatner Changed the World*, directed by Julian Jones, aired on Discovery Network, November 13, 2005, Allumination, 2007.

2. Maggie Shiels, "A Chat with the Man Behind Mobiles," BBC News, April 21, 2003, http://news.bbc.co.uk/2/hi/uk_news/2963619 .stm (accessed November 2, 2011).

3. Ibid.

4. Jerome Swartz et al., "Toward a Quantitative Framework for Sudden-Insight Problem Solving and the Feeling of Aha!" presented at Dynamical Neuroscience XVI symposium, Washington, DC, November, 2008.

5. Bhavin S. Sheth, Simone Sandkuhler, and Joydeep Bhattacharya, "Posterior Beta and Anterior Gamma Oscillations Predict Cognitive Insight," *Journal of Cognitive Neuroscience* 21, no. 7 (2008): 1269–79.

6. S. Wehling and J. Bhattacharya, "Deconstructing Insight: EEG Correlates of Insightful Problem Solving," *PLoS ONE* 3, no. 1 (2008): 1459–71.

7. John Kounios and Mark Jung-Beeman, "The Aha! Moment: The Cognitive Neuroscience of Insight," *Current Directions in Psychological Science* 18, no. 4 (2009): 210–16.

8. WebMD Health News, "Scientists Explain Aha! Moments," WebMD, April 3, 2004, http://men.webmd.com/news/20040413/scientists-explain-aha-moments (accessed November 5, 2010).

9. Jonah Lehrer, "The Eureka Hunt," *New Yorker*, July 28, 2008, 40–45.

10. Kary Mullis, Nobel lecture, December 8, 1993.

11. Ibid.

12. Ibid.

13. Ibid.

14. Ibid.

15. Ibid.

16. Ibid.

17. Kary Mullis, *Dancing Naked in the Mind Field* (New York: Pantheon, 1998), p. 7.

18. Ibid.

19. Ibid., p. 10.

20. William Speed Weed, "Noble Dude," Salon, March 29, 2000, http://www.salon.com/health/feature/2000/03/29/mullis (accessed April 20, 2011).

21. John Geirland, "Go with the Flow," *Wired*, September 1996, http://www.wired.com/wired/archive/4.09/czik.html (accessed September 18, 2010).

22. S. Ramsland, "The Experience of Flow: A Qualitative Analysis" (unpublished dissertation, Rutgers University, New Brunswick, NJ, 1988), p. 28.

23. Katherine Ramsland, *Dean Koontz: A Biography* (New York: HarperCollins, 1996), pp. 318–20.

24. Mihaly Csikszentmihalyi, *Beyond Freedom and Boredom* (San Francisco: Jossey-Bass, 1976), p. 36.

25. Mihaly Csikszentmihalyi, "Happiness in Everyday Life: The Uses of Experience Sampling," *Journal of Happiness Studies* 4 (2003): 197.

26. Lan N. Nguyen, "Joy Mangano Invents Her Way to Success, January 1, 2010, http://www.walletpop.com/2010/01/01/joy-mangano -invents-her-way-to-success/ (accessed May 2, 2010).

27. Nicole Brewer, "The dzdock Story," CBS3, http://www.dzdock .com/aboutus.php (accessed April 24, 2011).

28. Mihaly Csikszentmihalyi, *Flow: The Psychology of Optimal Experience* (New York: Harper & Row, 1990), p. 4.

29. Ivars Peterson, *Newton's Clock: Chaos in the Solar System* (New York: W. H. Freeman, 1993), pp. 143–70.

30. Henri Poincaré, "Mathematical Creation," in *Mathematics in the Modern World*, ed. James Newman (San Francisco: W. H. Newman, 1948), p. 14.

31. Ibid., p. 16.

32. Ibid., p. 14.

33. Ibid., p. 16.

34. Ibid.

35. Ibid., p. 17.

36. Ibid.

37. Ibid.

38. Ibid., p. 16.

39. Ibid., p. 17.

CHAPTER 6: PERCEPTUAL SETS

1. Charles Panati, *Panati's Extraordinary Origins of Everyday Things* (New York: HarperCollins, 1989).

2. Ibid.

3. E. C. Tolman, "Cognitive Maps in Rats and Men," *Psychological Review* 55, no. 4 (1948): 189–208.

4. James J. Knierim, "The Matrix in Your Head," *Scientific American Mind* 18, no. 3 (June–July 2007): 42–47.

5. Eric Kandel, *In Search of Memory: The Emergence of a New Science of the Mind* (New York: W. W. Norton, 2006), p. 306.

6. Carl Gustave Jung, *Modern Man in Search of a Soul*, 1933, (New York: Harcourt, Brace & World, 1961), p. 170.

7. E. Maguire et al., "Navigational Related Structural Change in the Hippocampi of Taxi Drivers," *Proceedings of the National Academy of Sciences* 97 (2000): 4398–403.

8. Bruce Bower, "Body in Mind," *Science News*, October 25, 2008, p. 25.

9. Matthew Moore, "Eureka! Moment Most Likely to Strike at 10:04 PM," *Telegraph* (London), October 20, 2008.

10. Silvia Costa and Peter Shaw, "'Open Minded' Cells: How Cells Can Change Fate," *Trends in Cell Biology* 17, no. 3 (2006): 101–106.

11. Candace Pert, *Molecules of Emotion: The Science behind Mind-Body Medicine* (New York: Simon & Schuster, 1999).

12. Gordon Logan and Mathew Crump, "Cognitive Illusions of Authorship Reveal Hierarchical Error Detection in Skilled Typists," *Science* 330, no. 6004 (2010): 683–86.

13. William Barrett, *Irrational Man: A Study in Existential Philosophy* (New York: Doubleday, 1958), pp. 177–205.

14. Friedrich Nietzsche, "Composition of Thus Spake Zarathustra," in *Ecco Homo*, reprinted in *The Creative Process*, ed. Brewster Ghiselin (Los Angeles: University of California Press, 1952), p. 209.

15. Ibid.

16. Ibid., p. 210

17. Emily Sherwood, "Artist Chuck Close Triumphs over Learning Disabilities," *Education Update Online*, June 2007, http://www.educationupdate.com/archives/2007/JUN/html/speced-artistchuck.html (accessed March 20, 2011).

18. Raghuvir Viswanatha, "Aha! Tufts Professor Measures New Learning Phenomenon," *Tufts Daily*, April 1, 2002, http://www.tufts

daily.com/2.5541/aha-tufts-professor-measures-new-learning
-phenomenon-1.605931 (accessed October 18, 2010).

19. Michael J. A. Howe, *Genius Explained* (Cambridge: Cambridge University Press, 1999), pp. 130–56.

20. Ibid.

21. Jacques Hadamard, *The Psychology of Invention in the Mathematical Field* (Princeton, NJ: Princeton University Press, 1954).

22. Ibid.

23. "Control the Flow," *Pet Product News*, January 10, 2011.

24. Tim Marks, personal interview with author, April 2011.

25. Hugh Moore Collection, Princeton University Library, http://diglib.princeton.edu/ead/getEad?eadid=MC153&kw= (accessed April 12, 2011).

26. Colin Beavan, *Fingerprints: The Origins of Crime Detection and the Murder Case that Launched Forensic Science* (New York: Hyperion, 2001), p. 46.

CHAPTER 7: READING BETWEEN THE MINDS

1. "Sir Alec Jeffreys on DNA Profiling and Minisatellites," ScienceWatch, 2008, http://archive.sciencewatch.com/interviews/sir_alec_jeffreys.htm (accessed October 29, 2011).

2. A. J. Jeffreys, V. Wilson, and S. L. Thein, "Individual-Specific 'Fingerprints' of Human DNA," *Nature* 37 (1985): 67–75.

3. Joseph Wambaugh, *The Blooding: The True Story of the Narborough Village Murders* (New York: William Morrow, 1989).

4. Jeffreys et al., "Individual-Specific 'Fingerprints' of Human DNA."

5. Harlan Levy, *And the Blood Cried Out: A Prosecutor's Spellbinding Account of the Power of DNA* (New York: Basic Books, 1996).

6. Nancy Andreasen, *The Creating Brain: The Neuroscience of Genius* (New York: Dana Press, 2005), p. 21.

7. Ibid., p. 22.

8. Ibid., p. 31.

9. R. Newmarch, *Life and Letters of Peter Ilyich Tchaikovsky* (London: John Lane, 1906), pp. 274–75.

10. Andreasen, *Creating Brain*, p. 63.

11. Ibid., p. 73.

12. Ibid.

13. Joel Katz, interview with author, March 22, 2011.

14. Howard Gruber, *Darwin on Man*, 2nd ed. (Chicago: University of Chicago Press, 1981).

15. Andreasen, *Creating Brain*, p. 77.

16. Ibid., p. 78.

17. Rick Beyer, *The Greatest Science Stories Never Told* (New York: HarperCollins, 2000), p. 20.

18. Jacques Futrelle, "The Problem of Cell 13," in *The Thinking Machine* (New York: Modern Library, 2003), pp. 15–48.

19. Richard Platt, *Eureka! Great Inventions and How They Happened* (Boston: Kingfisher, 2003), pp. 48–49.

20. Lou Beach, "Specialis Revelio! It's Not Magic, It's Neuroscience," *Science News*, April 25, 2009, p. 24.

21. Ibid.

22. Stephen Macknik, Susana Martinez-Conde, and Sandra Blakeslee, *Sleights of Mind: What the Neuroscience of Magic Reveals about Our Everyday Deceptions* (New York: Henry Holt, 2010), p. 5.

23. Ibid., p. 64.

24. Ibid., p. 16.

25. Beach, "Specialis Revelio!" pp. 22–25.

26. Ibid., p. 20.

27. Jonah Lehrer, "Magic and the Brain: Teller Reveals the Neuroscience of Illusion," *Wired*, April 20, 2009, http://www.wired.com/science/discoveries/magazine/17-05/ff_neuroscienceofmagic (accessed October 29, 2011).

28. Ibid.

29. U. Neisser and R. Becklen, "Selective Looking: Attending to Visually Specified Events," *Cognitive Psychology* 7, no. 4 (1975): 480–94.

30. A. Mack and I. Rock, *Inattentional Blindness* (Cambridge: MIT Press, 1998).

31. Daniel Simons and Christopher Chabris, "Gorillas in Our Midst: Sustained Inattentional Blindness for Dynamic Events," *Perception* 28 (1999): 1059–74.

32. Beyer, *Greatest Science Stories*, p. 52.

33. Jonah Lehrer, "Think Better: Tips from a Savant," *Scientific American Mind*, 2009, p. 61.

34. Ibid.

35. Ibid., p. 63.

36. Michael Jackson, *Moonwalk* (New York: Crown, 2009), p. 39.

37. Randy Taraborrelli, *Michael Jackson: The Magic, The Madness, The Whole Story, 1958–2009* (Terra Alta, WV: Grand Central Publishing, 2009).

38. Royston M. Roberts, *Serendipity: Accidental Discoveries in Science* (New York: John Wiley & Sons, 1989), pp. 75–81.

39. R. W. Gerard, "The Biological Basis of Imagination," *Scientific Monthly*, June 1946, pp. 477–99.

40. "How Rooms and Architecture Affect Mood and Creativity," http://www.interior-decorating-diva.com/roomsandarchitectureaffect moodandcreativity.html (accessed April 20, 2011).

41. "Inventions that Didn't Work the First Time," http://www .bkfk.com/inventor/accident.asp (accessed April 23, 2011).

42. Alice Flaherty, *The Midnight Disease* (New York: Houghton Mifflin, 2004), p. 30.

43. Rudyard Kipling, *Something of Myself* (Garden City, NY: Doubleday, 1937).

44. Steve Turner, *A Hard Day's Write: The Stories behind Every Beatles Song*, 3rd ed. (New York: Harper, 2005), p. 83.

45. Beyer, *Greatest Science Stories*, p. 114.

46. Flaherty, *Midnight Disease*, p. 226.

47. Marcus Chown, "Physics with a Human Touch," *New Scientist*, March 10, 1988, p. 72.

48. Lewis Smith, "Eureka Moment Solves 140-Year-Old Puzzle," *Times*, March 4, 2008.

49. J. K. Rowling, "Biography," JKRowling.com, http://www.jk rowling.com/textonly/en/biography.cfm (accessed April 20, 2011).

CHAPTER 8: THE TAO OF DATA MINING

1. Jeff Hecht, "Gordon Gould Recalls His Creative Moment," AIP, 1983, http://www.aip.org/history/exhibits/laser/interviews/gould_creativemoment_interview.html (accessed April 23, 2011).

2. François Eugène Vidocq, *Memoirs of Vidocq: Master of Crime* (Philadelphia: T. B. Peterson, 1859, translated).

3. E. A. Hodgetts, *Vidocq: A Master of Crime* (London: Selwyn & Blount, 1928).

4. Samuel Edwards, *The Vidocq Dossier: The Story of the World's First Detective* (Boston: Houghton Mifflin, 1977).

5. Nancy Koehn, *Brand New: How Entrepreneurs Earned Consumer Trust from Wedgwood to Dell* (Cambridge: Harvard Business Press, 2001).

6. Andrew Carnegie, *James Watt* (New York: Doubleday, Page, 1905), p. 55.

7. Michael Polanyi, *The Tacit Dimension* (Gloucester, MA: Peter Smith, 1983).

8. Alice Flaherty, *The Midnight Disease* (New York: Houghton Mifflin, 2004), p. 225.

9. Ronald Finke, Thomas Ward, and Steven Smith, *Creative Cognition: Theory, Research, and Applications* (Cambridge: MIT Press, 1992), pp. 178–79.

10. Ibid., pp. 241–42.

11. Scott Barry Kaufmann, "Conversations on Creativity with Allan Snyder," *Psychology Today*, January 13, 2010, http://www.psychologytoday.com/blog/beautiful-minds/201001/conversations-creativity-allan-snyder (accessed November 2, 2010).

12. Ibid.

13. Irving Wallace, *The Fabulous Originals* (New York: Alfred A. Knopf, 1955), pp. 22–46.

14. Ely Liebow, *Dr. Joe Bell* (Bowling Green, OH: Bowling Green University Press, 1982), p. 116.

15. Ibid., p. 177.

16. Ibid., p. 132.

CHAPTER 9: PSYCHO-ENTANGLEMENT

1. Quotes in this section are from Rick Arlow, personal interview with author, May 2011.

2. Albert Einstein, "How I Created the Theory of Relativity," trans. A. Ono Yoshima, *Physics Today* 35, no. 8 (1998): 45.

3. Ibid., p. 46.

4. Ibid., p. 47.

5. Søren Kierkegaard, *Concluding Unscientific Postscript*, trans. David F. Swenson and Walter Lowrie (Princeton: Princeton University Press, 1968), p. 26.

6. Tom Siegfried, "Clash of the Quantum Titans," *Sciences News*, November 20, 2010, p. 16.

7. Gerald Holton, *Victory and Vexation in Science: Einstein, Bohr, Heisenberg, and Others* (Cambridge: Harvard University Press, 2005), p. 39.

8. Vera John-Steiner, *Creative Collaborations* (Oxford: Oxford University Press, 2000), p. 47.

9. Irwin D. Mandel, "Carl Koller: Mankind's Greatest Benefactor? The Story of Local Anesthesia," *Journal of Dental Research* 77, no. 4 (1998): 535–38.

10. *Nova*, "Solving Fermat: Andrew Wiles," 2000, http://www.pbs.org/wgbh/nova/physics/andrew-wiles-fermat.html (accessed November 2, 2010).

11. Ibid.

12. Ibid.

13. Maddalena Fabbri-Destro and Giacomo Rizzolatti, "Mirror Neurons and Mirror Systems in Monkeys and Humans," *Physiology* 23 (2008): 171–79.

14. Vittorio Gallese, "Embodied Simulation: From Neurons to Phenomenal Experience," *Phenomenology and the Cognitive Sciences* 10, no. 4 (2005): 23–48.

15. Joel Katz, interview with author, March 22, 2011.

16. Howard Gardner, *Five Minds for the Future* (Cambridge, MA: Harvard Business School Press, 2007).

17. Herbert A. Simon, *Models of My Life* (New York: Basic, 1991), p. 367.

18. Corrine May Botz, *The Nutshell Studies of Unexplained Deaths* (New York: Monacelli Press, 2004), p. 34.

19. Laura Miller, "Frances Glessner Lee: Brief Life of a Forensic Miniaturist," *Harvard Magazine*, September/October 2005, http://harvardmagazine.com/2005/09/frances-glessner-lee-html (accessed June 18, 2006).

20. Ibid.

CHAPTER 10: RISK AND INCENTIVE

1. Thomas Blass, *The Man Who Shocked the World* (New York: Basic Books, 2004), p. 21.

2. Stanley Milgram, *Obedience to Authority* (New York: Harper Perennial, 1983), p. 1.

3. Stanley Milgram, *The Individual in a Social World*, 2nd ed., ed. J. Sabini and M. Silver (New York: McGraw-Hill, 1992), p. xxxi.

4. Blass, *Man Who Shocked*, p. 291.

5. C. Tavris, "The Frozen World of the Familiar Stranger," *Psychology Today*, June 1974.

6. Tom Carhart, personal correspondence with author, April 23, 2011.

7. Tom Carhart, *Lost Triumph* (New York: Putnam, 2005), pp. 233–36.

8. William Brooke-Rawle, *The Right Flank at Gettysburg* (Philadelphia: Allen, Lane & Scott, 1878), p. 482.

9. John J. Pullen, *The Twentieth Maine, A Volunteer Regiment in the Civil War* (Dayton, OH: Morningside House, 1991), p. 119.

CHAPTER 11: SNAPS ON DEMAND

1. Richard Platt, *Eureka! Great Inventions and How They Happened* (Boston: Kingfisher, 2003), pp. 34–35.

2. Evan Schwartz, *Juice: The Creative Fuel that Drives Today's World-Class Inventors* (Boston: Harvard Business Press, 2004), pp. 118–19.

3. "Cemetery Guide to Le Pere Lachaise," n.d., acquired in Paris, 1997.

4. Isaac Asimov, "The Eureka Phenomenon," *Magazine of Science Fiction and Fantasy*, 1971.

5. Janet Rae-Dupree, "Reassessing the Aha! Moment," *New York Times*, http://www.nytimes.com/2008/02/01/business/world business/01iht-UNBOX.1.9684125.html (accessed January 15, 2010).

6. Sindya N. Bhanoo, "How Meditation May Change the Brain," *New York Times*, January 28, 2011.

7. Nancy Andreasen, *The Creating Brain: The Neuroscience of Genius* (New York: Dana Press, 2005).

8. Benedict Carey, "Tracing the Spark of Creative Problem Solving," *New York Times*, December 6, 2010, http://www.nytimes.com/2010/12/07/science/07brain.html?_r=1 (accessed October 31, 2011).

9. Joshua Hyatt, "The Eureka Moment: What Sets Legendary Entrepreneurs Apart Isn't What They Do but How They Do It," CNN Money, October 1, 2002, http://money.cnn.com/magazines/fsb/fsb_archive/2002/10/01/330570/index.htm (accessed March 15, 2009).

10. Nancy Koehn, *Brand New: How Entrepreneurs Earned Consumers' Trust, from Wedgewood to Dell* (Boston: Harvard Business Press, 2001).

11. John Knific, interview with author, April 2011.

12. Shelley Carson, *Your Creative Brain: Seven Steps to Maximize Imagination, Productivity, and Innovation in Your Life* (New York: Jossey-Bass, 2010).

13. "Inspirational Stories of Successful Women Entrepreneurs Online," IncomeInsiders.com, April 13, 2010, http://www.incomeinsiders.com/inspirational-stories-of-successful-women-entrepreneurs-online-1216/ (accessed April 15, 2011).

14. Chris Kanaracus, "Software Flushes Out the Eureka! Moments," *CIO*, January 29, 2009, http://www.cio.com/article/478426 (accessed March 15, 2009).

15. Lisa Getzler-Linn, interview with author, April 2011.

16. Tim Berners-Lee, *Weaving the Web: The Original Design and Ultimate Destiny of the World Wide Web* (New York: HarperCollins, 1999), p. 12.

INDEX